Rescued by Europe?

Rescued by Europe?

Social and Labour Market Reforms in Italy
from Maastricht to Berlusconi

Maurizio Ferrera & Elisabetta Gualmini

AMSTERDAM UNIVERSITY PRESS

To Giulia and Sofia

Cover illustration: Civica Raccolta delle Stampe 'Achille Bertarelli', Milano.
All rights reserved.

Cover design: Jaak Crasborn BNO, Valkenburg a/d Geul
Lay-out: Adriaan de Jonge, Amsterdam

ISBN 90 5356 651 1
NUR 754 / 759

Contents

List of Tables and Figures

Introduction

For much of the post-war period, Italy was regarded as the sick man of Europe. The Italian disease had both political and economic components: harsh ideological divisions, chronic executive instability, an inefficient bureaucracy, uneven socio-economic development, organised crime and unbalanced public finances, just to mention the most emblematic symptoms.

In the course of the 1990s, some encouraging signs of a healing process have, however, appeared on the scene. The most visible and relevant indicator of this is certainly Italy's entry into the Economic and Monetary Union (EMU) by the established deadline of 1998, at the same time as the other 'core' European countries. At the beginning of the decade, this event seemed almost unimaginable to any observer gifted with some realism. Meeting the Maastricht criteria would in fact have required a massive effort of macro-economic adjustment, which in turn would have needed both a stable politics and coherent policies: two items which had always been in very scarce supply south of the Alps.

But the entry into the EMU was only the tip of the iceberg. In addition to macro-economic adjustment, the 1990s witnessed a multitude of other reforms – some quite big, some small, but nevertheless significant – which have slowly redesigned the country's institutional fabric, enhancing its political and policy capabilities. The budgetary process has been incisively changed, allowing a more effective management of public finances. A new framework has been put in place for industrial relations and 'social concertation' between the government and the social partners. The national executive has been re-organised and strengthened. Innovation has been particularly important in the sphere of the welfare state (broadly conceived): important changes have been introduced in the pension and health care systems, while the highly rigid regulatory framework of the labour market has finally started a much-needed process of defrosting. Change has affected not only benefit formulas and service standards, but also organisational designs and decision-making procedures.

Internationalisation – but especially the dynamics of European integration – has played a major role in fostering these positive developments. In the specialised literature, internationalisation is often portrayed as a threat to domestic welfare state and employment regimes. Equally often, what is suggested is that these regimes can be preserved (or successfully adjusted) by mobilising existing state capabilities in order to neutralise or attenuate exogenous challenges and shocks.

With respect to this line of debate, the Italian experience seems to go exactly in the opposite direction. First, the Italian disease (including structural unemployment and an unbalanced welfare system) was there long before the winds of globalisation started to blow. Second, the new dynamics of economic internationalisation, which started to unfold themselves in the 1980s, did not produce in Italy those harmful effects on employment and income distribution that made their sinister appearance elsewhere in the OECD. Quite to the contrary, what seems to emerge from the available empirical literature on the issue is that neither the foreign penetration of domestic markets nor the internationalisation of Italian firms have demonstrably resulted in significant job losses: as a matter of fact, the latter process has probably generated an additional domestic demand for labour. Third, the pressures and constraints connected with internationalisation and supranational integration have stimulated a real 'quantum leap' in terms of institutional capabilities: in other words, they triggered a sequence of changes which are correcting many traditional weaknesses of the Italian state, gradually enabling it to act on a par with its political allies and economic competitors in the inter-state arenas (including, obviously, the EU).

The transformation initiated in the 1990s is not complete. And there are worries that Italy's vulnerability to exogenous challenges may dramatically increase in the new phase that the international economy is now facing, characterised by further steps in trade liberalisation at the global level and by a new competitive environment at the regional level, in the wake of the Eastern enlargement of the EU. But the recently acquired institutional capabilities may help Italy to respond to the new challenges – provided that such capabilities are further consolidated and aptly mobilised. This proviso is not a small one. As we shall see at the end of our analysis, the further consolidation and apt mobilisation of the new institutional capabilities cannot be taken for granted. But we believe that the path to an effective and virtuous 'statehood' is still visible and open ahead of Italy's key political and social actors. The sick man can get well if the right treatment is continued.

This book is aimed at exploring how the new path was embarked upon in the course of the 1990s, against the background of politico-institutional and economic developments in the 1970s and 1980s. The first chapter will set out the general argument and analytical framework. The second chapter will illustrate the start-up constellation in terms of problems, policies and actors and will discuss the endogenous and original contradictions of 'welfare capitalism Italian-style' as they manifested themselves in the 1970s. The third chapter will consider the consequences, opportunities and limits of internationalisation, with particular reference to the European integration process. The fourth chapter will reconstruct the winding process of adjustment from its early (and largely unsuccessful) steps in the 1980s to the turning points of the 1990s. The fifth chapter will discuss the internal features of the Italian economic and political system which have at first hampered but then encouraged the process of adjustment. We will interpret this adjustment essentially in terms of an institutional learning process. The final chapter will discuss the general orientation and first policy moves of the new Berlusconi government, voted into office in May 2001, highlighting the unsolved questions and remaining challenges of Italy's economic and political transition.

This book is the end result of a research project on the politics of Italy's adjustment during the 1990s that we started in 1998, in the framework of a wider comparative project on 'The adjustment of national employment and social policy regimes to economic internationalization', directed by Fritz Scharpf and Vivien Schmidt at the Max Planck Institute of Cologne. Our participation in the Max Planck project has originated two main products: the chapter on Italy in the book *Welfare Work in the Open Economies*, edited by Fritz Sharpf and Vivien Schmidt (Oxford, Oxford University Press, 2000) and a short book in Italian, *Salvati dall'Europa? Welfare e lavoro in Italia fra gli anni '70 e gli anni '90* (Bologna, Il Mulino, 1999). The present volume constitutes a further elaboration, expansion and update of the latter book. A number of institutions have provided us with organisational and financial support: the Department of Political and Social Studies of the University of Pavia, the Department of Organisation and Political System and the Centre for Public Policy Analysis of the University of Bologna – and their director Giorgio Freddi – the Centre for Comparative Political Research 'Poleis' of Bocconi University, the Italian CNR. We thank all these institutions for the kind support received. Many friends and colleagues have helped us throughout the years, giving us precious suggestions, for which we are very grateful. Jelle Visser and Anton Hemerijck have given us detailed comments on the first draft of this book, helping us to improve it. Without their encouragement we would have never brought our enterprise to an end.

We are finally thankful to Alberta Santini and Ilaria Madama for their effective assistance in data collection and editorial packaging of the final text. We remain obviously solely responsible for mistakes, shortcomings and imprecision.

The text that follows is the fruit of a joint effort. Elisabetta Gualmini has written par. 2 of Ch. II; Ch. III except for par. 6; par. 1,2,4 and 5 of Ch. IV; par. 1, 2 and 5 of Ch. V; par. 2 of Ch. VI. The remaining parts have been written by Maurizio Ferrera.

I   Adjusting to Europe: a Learning Perspective

1   Deviant Italy chooses to adjust: the puzzle

The experience of the 1990s has shown that welfare reforms are daunting balancing acts, especially from a political point of view. Observing the way in which the various European governments have coped with this challenge, one is tempted to quote the lapidary comment that Samuel Johnson once made about a dog walking on its hind legs: 'it was not a good walk, but what is surprising is that it managed to do it somehow'. This comment sounds especially appropriate for the Italian case. Italy's adjustment and this country's entry into the EMU were definitely not a good walk. The pace was unsteady, often veering in style and direction. At the most critical moment – the second half of 1997 – a risky 'confidence trick' had to be played *vis-à-vis* the other EU partners and, especially, the international financial markets in order to meet the 3 per cent deficit target (Chiorazzo and Spaventa 1999). On paper, the reform record of the 1990s looks very impressive, especially in the field of pensions: three major reforms were passed in 1992, 1995 and 1997 (cf. Table 1.1)[1]. As we shall see, several criticisms can be raised against the content, modalities and effectiveness of such reforms. But for an unstable political economy such as the Italian one having achieved EMU membership is what matters most at the systemic level: the dog has reached a safe destination. Hence the puzzle: how has fragile Italy managed to 'limp' its way into the exclusive EMU club? What factors made the sequence of social reforms passed between 1992 and 1998 possible? And, more prospectively: how stable is the new institutional configuration put in place by those reforms? These are the central questions that this book sets out to explore.

Italy's heavy limp in the early 1990s can hardly be questioned. The data listed in Table 1.2 clearly signal the poor performance of this country compared to its EU partners in terms of macro-economic and employment indicators.

Table 1.1 Major social reforms during the 1990s

1992	Amato reform of pensions
	"Reform of the reform" in health care
1992/93	Abolition of automatic wage indexation and reform of collective bargaining
1995	Dini reform of pensions
1997	Treu reform of labour market regulations
	Prodi reform of pensions
1998	Reform of means-tested benefits
1999	Health care reform
	New rules on part-time and temporary employment
2000	Reform of social assistance

Table 1.2 Macro-economic and employment indicators, Italy and main EU partners

Indicators		Countries	1992	1995	1998	2001
Macro-economy and public finances	Inflation (%)	Italy	5.0	5.4	2.0	2.3
		Germany	5.1	1.8	0.6	2.4
		France	2.4	1.8	0.7	1.8
		UK	4.7	2.8	2.7	2.1
		EU average	4.0	2.8	1.3	2.3
	Deficit (%)	Italy	10.7	7.6	2.8	2.2
		Germany	2.5	3.3	2.2	2.8
		France	4.2	5.5	2.7	1.4
		UK	6.5	5.7	-0.2	-0.8
		EU average	4.9	4.9	1.6	0.8
	Debt (%)	Italy	107.7	123.2	116.3	109.8
		Germany	42.9	57.0	60.9	59.5
		France	39.6	54.6	59.5	57.3
		UK	39.2	51.8	47.7	39.1
		EU average	63.6	70.6	68.7	63.1
	Long-term Interest Rate (%)	Italy	13.3	12.2	4.9	5.2
		Germany	7.9	6.9	4.6	4.8
		France	8.6	7.5	4.6	4.9
		UK	9.1	8.2	5.5	4.9
		EU average	9.7	8.7	5.1	5.0
Unemployment rates	Total	Italy	9.4	11.5	11.7	9.4
		Germany	6.3[1]	8.0	9.1	7.7
		France	10.2	11.3	11.4	8.5
		UK	9.7	8.5	6.2	5.0
		EU average	9.2[2]	10.1	9.4	7.4

Long-term		Italy	5.4	7.3	6.9	5.8
		Germany	2.3	4.0	4.9	4.0[3]
		France	23.7	4.8	4.9	3.1
		UK	3.5	3.7	1.9	1.3
		EU average	4.9[4]	4.9	4.5	3.1
Youth		Italy	27.2	33.7	33.8	30.7[3]
		Germany	6.0[1]	8.8	9.8	9.1[3]
		France	23.7	27.6	26.3	20.0[3]
		UK	16.9	15.9	13.6	12.7[3]
		EU average	17.7[2]	21.5	19.5	16.2[3]
Employ-ment rates	Total	Italy	48.8	50.9	52.0	54.9
		Germany	66.4	64.6	63.9	65.4[3]
		France	59.9	59.6	60.2	62.8
		UK	68.2	68.6	70.6	71.8
		EU average	55.4[2]	60.1	61.4	64.1
	Female	Italy	34.5	35.4	37.3	41.1
		Germany	55.9	55.3	55.8	57.9[3]
		France	51.4	52.2	53.1	56.0
		UK	61.2	61.8	63.6	65.1
		EU average	44.0[2]	49.7	51.6	55.0

1 It refers to B.R.D.
2 It refers to Eur 12.
3 (2000)
4 (1994)
Debt: General government consolidated gross debt as a percentage of GDP.
Deficit: Net borrowing/lending of consolidated general government sector as a percentage of GDP
Long-term interest rates: 10 year benchmark government bond yields.
Sources: Eurostat, Structural Indicators, various years; long-term interest rates: OECD, Financial Indicators, various years.

The welfare state displayed in its turn very pronounced disequilibria – an oversized pension system on the one hand; modest or no spending for many other delicate functions on the other hand – and was plagued by internal inefficiencies and clientelistic manipulations. Political instability was at its highest. The 1980s had witnessed a relatively long (by Italian standards) season of executive continuity under the aegis of Bettino Craxi, the leader of the socialist party (PSI). The xth legislature (1987-1992), however, witnessed a rapid return to cabinet instability (cf. Table 1.3). Moreover, at the beginning of the decade, the *Mani Pulite* (Clean Hands) investigation launched by a pool of Milan's attorneys disclosed a system of massive and widespread corruption (private kickbacks in return for political favours) involving top businessmen and party leaders, ministers in office and high civil

Table 1.3 Italian executives, 1978-2001

Government	Parties in government	In office from
Andreotti IV	DC	Mar 1978
Andreotti V	DC, PSDI, PRI	Jan 1979
Cossiga I	DC, PSDI, PLI	Aug 1979
Cossiga II	DC, PSI, PRI	Mar 1980
Forlani	DC, PSI, PSDI, PRI	Sept 1980
Spadolini I	DC, PSI, PSDI, PRI, PLI;	Jul 1981
Spadolini II	DC, PSI, PSDI, PRI, PLI;	Aug 1982
Fanfani V	DC, PSI, PSDI, PLI;	Dec 1982
Craxi I	DC, PSI, PSDI, PRI, PLI;	Aug 1983
Craxi II	DC, PSI, PSDI, PRI, PLI;	Aug 1986
Fanfani VI	DC	Apr 1987
Goria	DC, PRI, PSI, PSDI, PLI;	Jul 1987
De Mita	DC, PSI, PSDI, PRI, PLI;	Apr 1988
Andreotti VI	DC, PSI, PSDI, PRI, PLI;	Aug 1989
Andreotti VII	DC, PSI, PSDI, PLI;	Apr 1991
Amato I	PSI, DC, PSDI, PLI;	Jun 1992
Ciampi	(technical executive) DC, PLI, PSDI, PSI, PDS	Apr 1993
Berlusconi I	FI, AN, Lega Nord;	May 1994
Dini	(technical executive) PDS, PPI, Lega Nord;	Jan 1995
Prodi	PPI, PDS, Dini, Verdi;	Jun 1996
D'Alema	PDS, PPI, Verdi, SDI, PDCI, UDR, Ri	Nov 1998
Amato II	(technical executive) PDCI, Democratici, UDEUR, PPI, Verdi, RI, SDI;	May 2000
Berlusconi II	FI, AN, Lega Nord, CCD-CDU-Bianco Fiore	Jun 2001

Abbreviations: AN (Alleanza Nazionale), CCD (Centro Cristiano-Democratico), CDU (Cristiano-Democratici Uniti), DC (Democrazia Cristiana), Dini (Lista Dini), FI (Forza Italia), PDS (Partito Democratico della Sinistra), PLI (Partito Liberale Italiano), PPI (Partito Popolare Italiano), PDCI (Partito dei Comunisti Italiani), PRI (Partito Repubblicano Italiano), PSDI (Partito Social-Democratico Italiano), PSI (Partito Socialista Italiano), SDI (Social-Democratici Italiani), UDEUR (Unione dei Democratici per l'Europa), RI (Rinnovamento Italiano).
Source: Presidenza del Consiglio dei Ministri, Roma.

servants. The whole national establishment saw its credibility and legitimacy crumble in the space of a few months. This serious economic and political crisis peaked in the summer of 1992 when – under the attack of financial markets – the lira suffered a heavy devaluation and had to exit from the European monetary system, while many ordinary savers were crowding banks in order to sell their *Buoni del Tesoro* (state bonds), for fear of a public debt default.

Behind this critical conjuncture lay a complex structural syndrome, with roots well entrenched into the country's historical path of modernization.

For the purposes of our analysis, the most salient trait of this syndrome was the marked weakness of the state. If we take the classical dimensions of 'stateness' highlighted by the literature on political development (Tilly 1975), Italy definitely scored poorly on all of them. The *formal autonomy* of the Italian state (i.e. its legal capacity to act) was *de facto* constrained – almost paradoxically – by the excesses of formalism and legalism and by a Constitution tuned in a hyper-consensualist vein, more preoccupied to veto than to uphold state powers. The lack of centralised and homogeneous standards and methods for training and recruiting top civil servants (as is the case in France for instance thanks to the *Ecole Nationale d'Administration*) substantially reduced the power of the bureaucratic élites, making them strongly dependent on the one hand on the turnovers of the political system, on the other on clientelistic ties with pressure groups. The *differentiation* of the state apparatus from non-governmental organisations had always remained incomplete, especially in respect of political parties: as highlighted by an articulated debate of the 1980s, Italy was internationally considered as an almost emblematic example of a 'party-state' (Bufacchi and Burgess 1988; Vassallo 1994), with a public apparatus easily permeable by partisan interests, if not virtually colonised by them. In terms of *centralisation*, despite its Napoleonic blueprint the Italian state displayed a highly fragmented centre (including a huge 'para-state' sector of semi-autonomous parallel administrations or *enti pubblici*), with a disparate and incoherent reach in the peripheries (Cassese 1984; Dente 1989). Last but certainly not least, the *internal co-ordination* (both vertical and horizontal) of the various state organs was very poor, especially when trying to reach substantive (as opposed to formal) objectives: the excess of legalism, the proliferation of veto points, the fragmentation of agencies and offices made problem-solving interactions very difficult and left Italian Prime Ministers under the almost constant blackmail of a multitude of disparate vetoes, originating from political parties, bureaucratic élites or interest groups (La Palombara 1964; Di Palma 1977; Hine 1993). The metaphor of 'an archipelago crossed by centrifugal currents' suggested by Giuliano Amato (1990) during his first experience as Treasury Minister in 1987-89 captures well the acentric and soft nature of the Italian state *circa* 1990, at the nadir of the so-called First Republic (i.e. the political regime in place between 1948 and 1992)[2].

Why did a limping dog choose to venture in such a risky walk as the one leading from Maastricht to the EMU? Here we must call into play the peculiar relationship between Italy and the EU and the role historically played by 'Europe' as both carrot and stick in the national arena. Ever since the establishment of the EC by a treaty signed in Rome, a number of influential domestic élite groups 'bet' on European integration as a wedge for stabilising and modernising Italy's political and economic system. Contrary to all the other member states, Italy's acceptance of and compliance with the rules of Western-style liberal democracy and market capitalism could not be taken for granted as irrevocable pledges, rooted in normative and cognitive beliefs at both the mass and élite levels. Certainly until the 1970s and still significantly until the fall of the Berlin wall, Italy remained a polarised polity, ideologically divided, witnessing the presence of two explicitly 'anti-system' poles within the political spectrum: the communist pole, which expressed the largest Communist party of the West (the PCI), and the extreme right pole, represented by a neo-Fascist party (the NHS) mustering between 2 and 8.7 per cent of the vote (Table 1.4). The extreme right and the communist bloc were 'anti-system' formations in that they explicitly questioned and challenged not only the policies pursued by the government but also the fundamental traits of the regime (such as, precisely, market principles, liberaldemocratic procedures, membership in the Western bloc, etc.). By anchoring the country's destiny to that of other, more pacified and stable market democracies, the political bet of the 'integrationist' élite was that of keeping polarization under control and of actually reducing it overtime. The EC anchor could serve a double function: it could offer incentives for a virtuous re-orientation of economic (and thus social and even political) attitudes and behaviours 'from below', in the wake of the gradually unfolding four freedoms (workers, goods, capital and services); it could offer the integrationist élite (not only state officials and party leaders but also representatives of the most influential economic and social institutions) precious resources 'from above' in order to legitimise (or at least justify) difficult policy measures. In both cases, the EC would work at times as a carrot, promising or actually delivering desirable goods (e.g. subsidies, greater opportunities – including migration – for both workers and firms, higher growth, the inclusion in a prestigious club, etc.) and at times as a stick (e.g. sanctions of inefficient practices through the penalties of the market, or forcing the Italian government to introduce unpopular policies of liberalisation).

Between the 1950s and the 1970s, the integrationist élite did not form a cohesive and distinct bloc. They can rather be depicted as a relatively loose 'advocacy coalition' (Sabatier and Jenkins-Smith 1993), transversally distributed across the various 'pro-system' parties and associations – including of course the *Democrazia Cristiana* (DC, Christian Democracy). This was the largest party controlling the government, forming alliances with other smaller parties such as the Liberals (PLI), the Republicans (PRI), the Social Democrats (PSDI) and, since the early 1960s, the Socialists (PSI). Despite

Table 1.4 'First Republic' elections: parties and votes (percentage values)

Parties	DC	PCI	PSI	MSI	PRI, PSDI PLI	Others
1948	48.5	31.0[1]		2.0	2.5	16.0
1953	40.1	22.6	12.7	5.8	9.1	9.7
1958	42.4	22.7	14.2	4.8	9.5	6.4
1963	38.3	25.3	13.8	5.11	4.5	3.0
1968	39.1	26.9	14.5[2]	4.4	8.1	7.0
1972	38.7	27.2	9.6	8.71	1.9	3.9
1976	38.7	34.4	9.6	6.1	7.8	3.4
1979	38.3	30.4	9.8	5.3	8.7	7.5
1983	32.9	29.9	11.4	6.8	12.1	6.9
1987	34.3	26.6	14.3	5.9	8.8	9.1
1992	29.7	21.7[3]	13.6	5.4	10.0	19.6

1 In the 1948 elections, the PCI and the PSI presented themselves jointly in the FDP (Fronte Democratico Popolare), which gained 31% of the votes.
2 PSI+PSDI
3 21.7% results from the summing up of the votes of Rifondazione Comunista and those of PDS (Partito Democratico della Sinistra).
Abbreviations: DC (Democrazia Cristiana), PCI (Partito Comunista Italiano), PSI (Partito Socialista), MSI (Movimento Sociale Italiano), PRI (Partito Repubblicano Italiano), PLI (Parito Liberale Italiano), PSDI (Partito Social-Democratico Italiano)
Sources: Istituto Nazionale di Statistica, ISTAT, various years.

their political misdemeanours (unveiled by the *Mani Pulite* investigations in the early 1990s, but systematically practised throughout the whole First Republic period), the DC-led coalitions were indeed inspired by the integrationist agenda and essentially pursued the European anchoring strategy mentioned above, for purposes of domestic regime stabilisation. Italian governments were of course interested in the specific contents of EC policies: since the very establishment of the European Communities – to the extent that executive instability and administrative weaknesses allowed it – they tried to obtain all the possible benefits from the EC budget and regulations. But the primary interest was in the anchor as such, for the systemic and virtuous implications that the link with Europe could bring to an unstable and internally challenged regime. This domestic constellation helps to explain the peculiar style of Italy's EC membership during the First Republic, i.e. a seemingly paradoxical combination of federalist enthusiasm in EC arenas and a constant failure to comply with EC norms at home. Although too weak to take the lead, Italy always backed even the most ambitious initiatives to strengthen the EC in a federal direction. On the other hand, up until the late 1980s, Italian governments were systematically the worst offenders in terms of domestic transposition of EC law (Giuliani 1996, 2000; Giuliani and Piattoni 2001). Support for federal integration was in line with the interests of the integrationist élite and was also a politically promising strategy for the pro-system parties as it made the stabilising anchor stronger. Internal transposition was, however, difficult, owing to low stateness and high ideological polarisation.

This paradoxical syndrome reached its apex in the 1970s. As we shall see in Chapter 2, this was a very turbulent decade for Italy. Politically, the alliance between the DC and the PSI entered a period of severe strain, the PCI was growing increasingly stronger, ideological radicalisation started to spiral, and the country came to be plagued by terrorism. Economically, the oil crisis precipitated an acute crisis (both monetary and real), rooted in a series of endogenous unsolved questions. Italian governments kept their grip on the EC anchor and warmly supported all the initiatives made in that decade to consolidate the EC architecture (from the Werner Plan to the direct elections of the European Parliament in 1979). But domestic developments were increasingly deviant from European standards. In 1977 the DC inaugurated a new alliance with the PCI – which under Berlinguer's leadership had started a process of ideological and political moderation. In principle, the PCI and the trade unions were not against European integration, but were strongly opposed to embarking upon the new ambitious initiative of the late 1970s, i.e. the European Monetary System (EMS). Although it had secured regime stability in a very critical political and economic conjuncture, the 'historical compromise' between the DC and the PCI was thus seen as a liability for the integrationist project – also due to the suspicions that the PCI's participation in government raised in other European capitals.

In December 1978 the Andreotti government decided to join the EMS, breaking the historical compromise with the PCI and inaugurating a new political phase known as *Penta-partito* (five party coalition: DC-PSI-PSDI-PRI-PLI). We will discuss in more detail how and why this decision was taken in Chapter V. Suffice to say here that, at least in hindsight, this decision played a crucial role in redefining Italy's link to and membership of the EC. Participating to a hard currency regime had a number of significant policy implications that could not be ignored or somehow 'fixed' via the traditional tactics of delayed and/or incomplete implementation. Thus, upgrading domestic policy performance – especially in the fiscal and social policy sphere – became an increasingly pressing imperative. Regime stabilisation through the European anchor remained an important goal. But in the early 1980s conditions had changed: the regime had indeed become more stable, largely thanks to Europe's sticks and carrots; but the *vincolo esterno* (i.e. the actual constraints posed by EC membership) had become more serious, more demanding and more stringent in terms of policy performance. A thoroughgoing structural adjustment was now in order.

The new pressure to adjust raised two delicate questions: a 'what' question and a 'how' question. What changes (in what areas, through what instruments) were necessary to comply with the new monetary regime and to align domestic policy performance with European standards? How could such changes be introduced politically, given the features of Italy's institutional system? These were the two big issues that confronted the integrationist élite at the beginning of the 1980s. Italy had to learn how to become more European: and this raised both intellectual dilemmas, for which expertise and knowledge had to be mobilised, and practical challenges, linked to consensus-building and muddling through the decision-making system of a weak state. The 1980s witnessed some progress in terms of adjustment: or at least improvement in putting in place some pre-conditions for adjustment. However, the traditional blocks to structural reform remained operative, and the new decade began with the performance crisis signalled by the indicators in Table 1.2. It was only after 1991 that both the substantial and political dilemmas of adjustment were seriously and effectively tackled. Though still partly 'limping', the country had to meet the Maastricht criteria and be admitted into the EMU. Since 1992, joining the EMU was considered as the coronation of the political bet and the modernization project of the integrationist camp. Policy-makers also clearly perceived that failing this deadline would have jeopardized many of the hard-won achievements of such a project. Thus, crossing the EMU finishing line by the end of 1998 became a 'must', even if it meant walking on two legs...

The next chapters of this book will reconstruct the story of this relatively successful journey. Before starting, however, we need to briefly present the analytical perspective that will be used to frame our factual reconstruction.

2   Learning how to adjust: the analytical framework

The adjustment of national economies to internationalisation and European integration may be considered as a highly complex process of institutional change. It involves various elements and aspects of the political system: the specific instruments and mechanisms that regulate different policy sectors (for example, the discount rate, the contributory rates or the pension formula); the wider rules of the game that discipline the policy-making process and specify the prerogatives of various actors and their modes of interaction (for example, the relationship between different levels of government, between executives and parliaments, between governments and social partners, and so on); and finally the ideas, the interpretative frames, the 'philosophies and paradigms' that inspire public action in general (for example, the idea of a new welfare state that 'promotes opportunities' instead of 'compensating for losses').

How does institutional change occur? This is, of course, one of the core questions of many social sciences and of political science in particular. In this book, we will adopt a 'learning' perspective, which looks at institutional change as a delicate process whereby policy makers come to adjust the existing institutional status quo in the light of the consequences of past policy and of new information[3]. Learning processes are particularly difficult, since they involve the restructuring of the norms and practices that were successful in the past and that have thus generated widespread trust and loyalty. Such restructuring brings disorder and uncertainty where order and stability reigned. This is why decision makers tend to resist change, by sticking to the extant policy systems and political arrangements where their identity and values can be easily legitimised and re-enforced. The more these 'old' arrangements are institutionalised, the more they detach themselves from the original goals and the more they are taken for granted by the actors, whose strategies and routines end up by preserving exactly those arrangements[4].

What is needed to break the cycle and bring about innovation? Obviously, much depends on the 'failures' originated by the status quo and on the pressure exerted by the specific problems that need to be dealt with. Failure (especially repeated failure) is a potent trigger of policy learning dynamics: it leaves actors without solutions to the problems they face and thus originates problem-induced searches aimed at restoring satisfactory policy efficacy (Visser and Hemerijck 2001). As already highlighted by Heclo's pioneering work, the type of learning typically occurring in policy change can be assimilated to 'operational conditioning' (Heclo 1974)[5]. In processes of operational conditioning, subjects finds spontaneously the possible answers to environmental stimuli, selecting options based on the positive or negative reinforcements obtained by their trials and errors. The logic of operational conditioning is consequentialist, i.e. linked to the effects of behaviours and choices. Within this logic, negative reinforcements (i.e. the penalties associated with ineffective behaviours or 'failures') are perhaps more important than positive reinforcements, owing to the negativity bias that characterizes social actors (i.e. their greater sensitivity to losses, rather than to gains) (Kahneman and Tversky 1979; 1984). Of course, both success and failure are to some extent relative concepts, subject to variable definitions (March and Olsen 1989). But even allowing for some degree of relativism, there are situations in which policy failures and environmental sanctions are virtually self-evident. The Italian events of the summer of 1992 mentioned above are a clear illustration of this: despite their increasing financial size, *ad hoc* and conjunctural budgetary measures – the routine response to adjustment pressures in the 1980s – proved to be incapable of arresting the speculative attacks against the lira coming from external sources, while currency devaluation and expulsion from the EMS were explicit signs that Italy had failed an important test and was incapable of keeping up with her European partners.

A critical role in the learning process is played by the orientations and qualities of the relevant actors: for the process to start, the actors must be receptive to new information and be relatively open to modifying their beliefs in order to perceive and correct failures. Ideological dogmatism is inimical to experiential learning, as it freezes the 'paradigm' or 'deep core' of values and cognitions regarding particular states of the world (Surel 2000). But, again, the perception of failure and the willingness to search for new ways of solving problems (including the adoption of a new paradigm) can be greatly stimulated and enhanced by exogenous developments: for example, the appearance of a focusing event such as a sudden crisis or a deadline, which serves as a catalyst of public attention and forces upon actors a feeling of responsibility and urgency. The Maastricht process offers an emblematic example in this respect. Not only did this process specify quantitative values to determine success or failure (in terms of inflation, exchange and interest rates, deficits and debts), but it also attached to these values a temporal dimension: member states had to be 'successful' by a fixed date. Both the quantitative values and the temporal deadline had been solemnly included in a Treaty signed by national governments after extenuating negotiations and ratified by national Parliaments. Thus, the Maastricht criteria and schedules had to be treated as 'givens' by domestic policy players, even when their full and unpleasant implications became clear. It is possible that the option of a re-negotiation continued to loom for some time in the back of some actors' minds. For example, a few months after his election, in May 1996, the Prodi government approached its Spanish counterpart to probe its readiness to coalesce with Italy for a loosening of the convergence criteria and/or timing. But the lack of readiness of the Aznar government ruled out that option completely and prompted Prodi to embark on the only possible path, i.e. an extraordinary effort of financial adjustment.

The Maastricht process also induced learning-based policy change by altering the significance and cost of 'failure'. Especially for the weaker economies, as the 1999 deadline approached it became in fact clear that being denied entry into the new EMU club would originate high penalties on the side of international financial markets. Thus, the real alternative was no longer between adjusting for EMU or maintaining the status quo: it was an alternative between adjusting or losing ground. Actors had to choose between a potentially positive sum outcome (adjustment and entry) and a negative sum outcome (no or insufficient adjustment, non-entry and therefore high losses for virtually all actors). Choosing in favour of the first scenario was facilitated by the fact the losses started to hit immediately: between 1995 and 1997 the exchange and interest rates of EMU candidate countries (especially the weaker ones) were closely linked to the probabilities of admission assigned by international rating institutions. As we shall see, the Italian events of the winter of 1995 offer a clear illustration of this choice configuration: the low (and actually declining) probabilities of EMU admission due to the political crisis and the stalling negotiations on pension reform resulted in high penalties on both the exchange and interest rates. Actors (especially the unions) thus learnt that failure to reform could no longer mean maintaining the distributive status quo, but implied instead suffering unexpected and unavoidable new losses. As the *vincolo esterno* was no longer negotiable, the only option for avoiding such new losses was to go ahead with some credible reform.

Failure-induced searches for new policy solutions require specific capabilities of analysis, diagnosis, programme-based elaboration on behalf of actors (both at the individual and collective level). Such capabilities are not always available when failure occurs – especially if failure is originated by or associated with exogenous shocks. But they can be developed during the search itself. In many member states, the Maastricht process triggered off not only substantive policy reforms, but also organizational and procedural reforms aimed at upgrading the diagnostic and programmatic skills of policy actors (including non-governmental actors). Though with a lesser urgency, the processes of 'recommended convergence' towards common objectives based on the new open method of co-ordination (OMC) are producing a similar impact on many national policy systems. This is especially the case with the European employment strategy, whose effects on Italy's weak capabilities in terms of labour market governance will be discussed in Chapter IV.

A final important factor for policy learning processes that we would like to highlight is the style and mode of interaction among policy-makers. The manner in which exchanges between actors take place – consensual and co-operative vs. adversarial and antagonist – significantly influences the type of decision-making outputs. In general, as is suggested by both game theory and social psychology, co-operative and consensual modes of relationships tend to produce superior results in terms of welfare: they stimulate communication, the exchange of information, the pooling of resources for searching out innovative solutions (Scharpf 1997; Visser and Hemerijk 2001). It must also be remembered, however, that in certain cases hyper-consensual styles of policy-making (and certain types of corporatist settings) may lead to stalemate and 'immobilism' (Crouch and Traxler 1995).

Centred as they are on problems and solutions, on knowledge and reasoning, learning perspectives on policy innovation tend to highlight the substantive dimension of change, the 'what to do' questions. But changing a policy is always a political exercise too: it raises not only substantive dilemmas, but also dilemmas related to consensus building. To evoke Heclo's famous distinctions, 'puzzling' (i.e. raising questions about policy problems) and 'powering' (orchestrating the political consensus for changing the status quo) must proceed together (Heclo 1974). And while it is true that the two processes are inspired by different forms of logic, they are also intertwined and display significant similarities and overlaps.

A first simple point to make on this issue is that politicians (i.e. elected officials or would-be officials) are themselves learning actors *qua* politicians: they puzzle about consensus strategies and adjust these strategies according to the (political) consequences of past policies and past strategies and in the light of experience (e.g. on electoral gains and losses). Thus, besides problem-centred, *substantive* learning, when analysing policy change we must also consider the distinct form of *political* learning, centred on consensus and interaction issues. Many of the dynamics discussed above (and, more generally, in the learning literature) apply to political learning too. In this sense, puzzling should not be regarded as a separate and parallel activity in respect of powering (Heclo's approach), but as a transversal one: puzzling occurs also *within powering*, i.e. when actors set about building consensus around their preferred policy solutions. The reverse is also true: powering tends to crosscut and at time even to encompass puzzling. The play of ideas is constantly disturbed by the contest of power (Visser and Hemerijck 2001). In the first place, the latter often defines *ex ante* the boundaries of feasible programmatic solutions. As stated in the previous paragraph, in an ideologically polarised political system certain policy solutions are simply not an option, even if carefully designed from a substantive viewpoint: the rules of the power game in such a system make certain policies unfeasible and even unthinkable – if the rules are deeply internalised by actors. In the second place, often both the play of ideas and the contest for power take place in the same arenas (e.g. mass media debates): substantive arguments are thus likely to be inherently disturbed by political considerations – when they are not from the start attempts at manipulative persuasion.

The recent literature on policy discourse (e.g. Schmidt 2000; 2001a; 2001b), argumentative persuasion (e.g. Checkel 2001) and 'pacting' (Culpepper 2002) has suggested promising insights on how puzzling and powering, the play of ideas and the contest for power, the substantive and political dimensions of policy change can interact and combine with each other. Policy discourses are arguments about the rationale that justifies change, given a failure of the status quo. These arguments contain both cognitive and normative propositions and typically result from serious and genuine substantive puzzling. As discourse can affect actors' preferences, it may be a precious instrument in the contest for power. Not only does discourse serve an interactive, communicative function (Schmidt 2000) *vis-à-vis* the interests affected by policy change, thus facilitating negotiation or passive acquiescence, but under certain circumstances it can altogether alter the beliefs and the behaviours of relevant actors, persuading them to actively accept and support change and thus exerting a direct causal impact on the latter. In many continental and south European welfare states, during the 1990s policy-makers elaborated a distinct 'vice-into-virtue' discourse (Levy 1999), targeting the inequities of past arrangements (e.g. over-generous disability pensions or tax evasion) as first priority of the adjustment agenda. Such discourse has been very effective in changing the cognitive and normative perspective of social groups – including in some cases those affected by the reforms.

Argumentative persuasion is most likely to alter preferences, create consensus and thus 'cause' a policy change when the persuadees face novel challenges in uncertain environments, have no dogmatic cognitive or normative priors, when the persuaders command in their turn authoritative reputation and 'act out principles of serious deliberative argument' and finally when the interaction takes place in relatively unpoliticised settings (Checkel 2001). In the specific field that interests us, i.e. welfare state reform, another important factor is the ideological proximity between the trade unions and the governing coalition. Especially in consensual democracies, where policy change is typically accompanied by tripartite negotiations, argumentative persuasion is easier for pragmatic, centre-left coalitions, whose motives and promises encounter higher sympathy and trust with trade unions (Ross 1998). The scope conditions for argumentative persuasion are not very likely to prevail simultaneously, especially in the most delicate policy areas. But the presence of only a subset of these conditions is sufficient for opening significant margins of manoeuvre for this type of mechanism and for the learning dynamics associated with it.

If discourse and argumentative persuasion can sometimes 'power' a reform into being, bypassing the traditional mechanisms of exchange-based consensus building, the latter can in turn produce goods that may be very important for solving both substantive and political puzzles in reform processes. If equipped with appropriate organisational capabilities, interest groups (and especially trade unions) can for example provide governmental policy-makers not only with original problem diagnoses and possible technical solutions, but also with delicate 'local and relational' information (Culpepper 2002). The latter is related to the preferences of the members of the associations and with the distribution of costs and benefits of various reform proposals. This type of information is crucial for politicians puzzling on how to identify a technically sound, but also politically feasible solution to a given policy problem – especially if there is a past experience of political failure. The Italian pension reform of 1995 illustrates this point very well. After the political failure of the first Berlusconi government (1994) and under the pressure of financial markets, the Dini government had a desperate need to find a solution to the pension crisis, which could be accepted by the unions. The unions knew what the alternative was (as explained above) and in the end supplied the government with the precious local and relational information they needed. They also mobilised all their dialogic capacity (i.e. actions aimed at encouraging problem-solving discussions among members; cf. Culpepper 2002) to secure grass-root acceptance of the reform package negotiated with the government. As we shall see, the aggregative and deliberative procedures of the Italian unions played a very important role in the reform process (Baccaro 2002).

Emphasising the role of discourse, argumentative persuasion, relational information, dialogic capacities and, more generally, problem-induced learning dynamics does not exclude that policy change may also rest on various forms of political exchange, i.e. *quid pro quo* interactions in which actors confront their diverging goals by mobilising support and try to reach agreements based on mutual concessions, without necessarily modifying their original and 'true' preferences. Learning perspectives are not incompatible with exchange perspectives: they suggest however that actors' preferences are malleable and may change in the wake of extraordinary events and/or during the course of interaction. They also suggest that knowledge and information may not only facilitate political exchanges, but can also be an object of such exchanges. Between pure argumentative persuasion in which change occurs merely as a consequence of discourse-induced preference change and pure power confrontations in which change is the result of juxtaposed 'brute' interests, backed by mobilized social supports, a wide grey area exists of mixed forms of interaction and change dynamics. As we shall see, the logic of exchange must be called into question for an accurate and full account of Italy's adjustment in some crucial moments. But the learning perspective illustrated so far will be the main frame of reference for our factual reconstruction. This choice is justified by two considerations. First, as we have tried to argue, the Maastricht process put in place a number of conditions that have widened the scope for problem-induced learning leading to policy change. Second, this form of change has received much less attention than it deserves in the analysis of Italy's policy developments – despite the fact that it was precisely in this country that the Maastricht process exerted its greatest impact, given the huge 'lack of fit' with the convergence criteria (Sbragia 2001). An interpretation of the 1992-1998 reforms from this angle will also allow us to contrast that phase of Italy's adjustment with the post-1998 phase (and especially the new Berlusconi era) in which the *vincolo esterno* and the Maastricht conditions have been gradually weakening, leading to a resurrection of more traditional dynamics of interest based games driven by rather rigid preferences – with worrying signs of such games degenerating again into brute power confrontations. But let us now offer a more detailed look at how we model the dynamic of Italy's reform process from Maastricht to Berlusconi – the title of our book.

3   Rescued by Europe? The argument in brief

The sequence of reforms listed in Table 1.1 will be our main object of analysis in the following chapters. We see these reforms as the result of a complex learning process, prompted by a sudden change of the actor constellation in the early 1990s, in the wake of both internal and external developments. This learning process unfolded itself along two dimensions: the substantial problem-solving dimension and the interactive consensus-building dimensions (cf. Figure 1.1).

The starting point of the process was the 'old' actor constellation prevailing in the First Republic (1948-1992), whose basic features, genetic roots and problem load will be presented in Chapter 11. As mentioned above, the European anchor already played a significant role in such constellation, especially after the lira's entry into the EMS in 1978. And in the 1980s some

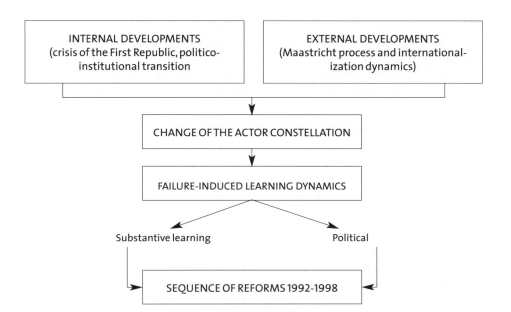

```
┌─────────────────────────────┐    ┌─────────────────────────────┐
│   INTERNAL DEVELOPMENTS      │    │   EXTERNAL DEVELOPMENTS      │
│ (crisis of the First Republic,│   │ (Maastricht process and      │
│   politico-institutional     │    │   international-              │
│      transition              │    │   ization dynamics)          │
└─────────────────────────────┘    └─────────────────────────────┘
```

CHANGE OF THE ACTOR CONSTELLATION

FAILURE-INDUCED LEARNING DYNAMICS

Substantive learning   Political

SEQUENCE OF REFORMS 1992-1998

Figure 1.1   Italy's reform sequence in the 1990s: the explanatory model

promising signs of learning-based policy change started to appear, prompted by the new winds of globalisation and the hardening of the *vincolo esterno*: these signs will be illustrated and discussed in Chapter III. But the political logic of the First Republic was still holding Italy's policy making system
under its grip, and the first generation of fiscal, social and labour market
policy reforms stopped short of correcting the original sins of Keynesian
welfare Italian-style.

The early 1990s marked a critical watershed: the actor constellation suddenly changed. This change had two main sources. One was external, primarily stemming from the new Maastricht process, internationalisation
and the link between the two. Such external developments altered in very
significant ways the costs and benefits of domestic policy options and their
distributive implications for policy actors. The second source of change was
internal, primarily linked to the crumbling of the First Republic and the
transition to the Second via the introduction of institutional reforms. This
internal politico-institutional transition had two main effects: it changed
many of the actors on the scene (the disappearance of old parties, the birth
of new ones, the formation of 'technical' cabinets, etc.), and it altered the
rules of both political competition and of policy-making.

This new constellation offered fertile grounds for the rapid unfolding of learning dynamics, along the lines illustrated in the previous paragraph. Under the increasingly stronger spurs produced by the Maastricht process and the constraints/opportunities of the new domestic rules of the game, actors developed new orientations, new capabilities and new modes of interaction. The shift from a centre-right government in 1994 (the first Berlusconi government) to a technical executive and then to a centre-left government led by Prodi eased the reformist process: as was argued above, it enhanced the effectiveness of discursive factors and of dialogic persuasion both between the government and the trade unions and between the leadership and membership of the unions themselves.

In 1998 however the actor constellation started to change again. The acquisition of EMU membership altered the significance and nature of the *vincolo esterno*, basically softening its pressure on domestic choices. Prodi (an academic turned politician, embodying the fusion of technical and electoral legitimation) was replaced by D'Alema, leader of a more 'political' executive and – after the brief parenthesis of the Amato cabinet – by Berlusconi, the leader of a centre-right coalition. Substantial puzzling about a broad project of national interest (achieving EMU membership) has been gradually replaced by interest-driven power confrontations in which analysis, arguments, empirically grounded debates have become less salient. Referring back to our initial metaphor: the dog has reached a safe destination. But its walking posture is still far from being firm and steady.

II   The Scene in the 1970s: Light, Shadow and Thunder

For Italy's political economy the 1970s were a complex decade, charac-terised by at least three intertwined dynamics: 1) the institutional comple-tion of the Keynesian welfare state (in its widest sense), in many respects ac-complishing what had been prescribed by the 1948 Constitution; 2) the gradual appearance of endogenous strains, largely connected with some pe-culiar characteristics of those accomplishments; 3) the sudden break of an exogenous crisis, linked with the well-known turbulences of the world econ-omy. The first dynamic culminated in 1978 with a sweeping social reform establishing the National Health Service. The second dynamic became overtly visible in 1974, when the huge debts accumulated by the social secu-rity funds had to be repaid. Prompted by the first oil shock, the third dynam-ic emitted in its turn a dramatic bang in 1976, when the official quotation of the lira had to be officially suspended for excessive devaluation.

1   The light: the rise of Keynesian welfare

In the first two and one half decades after World War II, the Italian economy underwent a process of remarkable growth – one of the highest in Europe – which enabled the country to gain quite a respectable position among the top industrialised powers. Average per capita income grew some 2.5 times between 1950 and 1970. The domestic product boomed especially in 1955-1969, mainly as a result of international trade and the successful penetra-tion of foreign markets. Export-led growth forced the large private indus-tries of Northern Italy to rapidly modernise technologically and financially, aligning themselves with international competitors.

The public industrial sector witnessed, in turn, a marked expansion (more marked than elsewhere in Europe), in the context of a Keynesian economic policy oriented towards industrial planning and moderate nationalisation. A third sector of small and medium-sized enterprises, increasingly success-ful in foreign markets, started to flourish in various niches of production,

31

taking roots also outside the traditional industrial triangle of Piedmont, Lombardy and Liguria.

This long 'economic miracle' was accompanied by a gradual consolidation and articulation of the state apparatus, putting in place and fine tuning the fairly complex institutional framework designed by the 1948 Constitution. Perhaps the major accomplishment on this front was the creation of the regions, which was completed in 1970.

The national executive remained firmly in the hands of the Christian Democrats (*Democrazia cristiana* – DC), but during the 1960s this party struck a new alliance with the Socialists (the so-called Center Left, formed in 1962) which was to last for the subsequent thirty years. The opposition remained monopolised by a Communist Party with strong Marxist-Leninist orientations. Though highly combative in the electoral arena, the PCI was *de facto* involved in the making of the most important domestic policies, especially in the economic and social field. Its involvement took place both formally in parliament and informally, through élite concertation.

The economic miracle and the coming together of the DC and the PSI offered a fertile background for the expansion of the welfare state. The institutional framework inherited by the new Republican regime born in 1948 divided social protection into three separate parts: social insurance (*previdenza*), health and sanitation (*sanità*) and social assistance (*assistenza*). Social insurance included six major schemes (for pensions, unemployment, tuberculosis, family allowances, sickness and maternity, occupational injuries and diseases), administered by a number of separate agencies and funds for selected occupational categories, often with diverse eligibility and benefit regulations. Insurance coverage was limited to employees, thus excluding the self-employed; most benefits were flat rate or related to previous contributions. The provision of health services relied heavily on the private sector. Hospitals were subject to state supervision, but with large administrative and financial autonomy (many of them were under control of the Catholic church). Finally, a plethora of public and semi-public agencies provided social assistance for the needy at a national and local level, paralleled by private and church charities.

This institutional setting witnessed only a few alterations during the 1950s. Yet, at the turn of the decade, things started to change. The economic miracle had brought about greater national well-being, which in turn had produced a growing 'fiscal dividend' in the public budget. In a new cultural and political climate, social problems and policies received increasing visibility and attention. Sociologists and economists started to denounce the distortions connected to the Italian 'model of development', urging a new, serious wave of reforms. Indeed, the centre-left coalition was based on the premise of a new wave of reforms and was committed to a radical modernisation of the country (Centorrino 1976). The formation of the new coalition was followed by several articulated reports on social reforms (Comitato di Studio per la Sicurezza Sociale 1965; Delogu 1967; Manin Carabba 1977).

However, the list of the reforms actually implemented, at least up to the end of the decade, remained quite limited. In 1963 the National Council of Economy and Labour (CNEL) proposed a general reform of the social insurance system (CNEL 1963). With respect to pensions, the CNEL suggested a radical transformation of the existing system, through the introduction of a universal flat-rate 'social' pension, supplemented by occupational schemes (thus creating a proper system of 'social security' against the risk of old age, in line with the Anglo-Scandinavian model). With respect to health care, the CNEL suggested a vigorous rationalisation of the overly complex insurance system, originally based on a plethora of occupational funds, and the extension of hospital care to the whole population, as a first step towards the establishment of a National Health Service. This proposal was mainly based on previous suggestions made by some political parties (in particular the PSI, the socialist party) and the trade unions. The proposal gave rise to a wide and articulated debate, which turned sometimes into harsh political confrontations.

The CNEL plan found only an extremely limited application through the legislative process. In 1965 a law, pompously called 'Launch of the pension reform', established a Social Fund administered by the National Institute of Social Security (INPS), with the aim of providing, in the future, the universal 'social' pension mentioned before. Yet the Fund was used simply to finance a fixed share (called, in fact, 'social component') of pensions, which nevertheless continued to be linked to the previous occupational and contributory status. All in all, the idea of a 'social' pension (as conceived by the CNEL) was soon abandoned. The idea of an extension *erga omnes* of hospital care was aborted too (at least up to the subsequent decade). Perhaps the only significant innovation was the 1962 reform of education, establishing a single comprehensive curriculum for the 11-14 age groups (cf. Table 2.1).

From 1968 onwards, however, the institutional profile of the Italian welfare state started to change rapidly, in the wake of new and heated social conflicts and under popular and union pressures. Hospital care was thoroughly revised in its administrative and financial status. Until then hospitals, called IPAB (Institutes of Public Assistance and Charity), were partially or totally in private hands. The reform transformed the hospitals into public institutions owned and transparently administered by the state,

Table 2.1 Social policy reforms, 1952-1978

Social Insurance

1952	Pension reform: improvement of pension formula and establishment of pension minima
1955	Family allowances reform
1958-1967	Pension insurance extended to farmers, artisans and traders
1968	Unemployment insurance improved
1969	Pension reform: introduction of earnings-related and social pensions, cost of living indexation
1974	Reform of invalidity pensions
1975	Wage indexation of pensions

Health care

1968	Reform of administrative and financial regulations for hospitals
1974	Hospital care transferred to regions
1978	Establishment of the National Health Service

Education

1962	School living age raised to 14; introduction of unified post-elementary curriculum
1969	Access to higher education greatly expanded
1974	Creation of parent/student representative boards

Social Assistance

1972	Jurisdiction over social assistance and services transferred to the regions
1977	Social assistance 'categorical' funds abolished; jurisdiction transferred to local authorities

changed the health care financing system, and introduced new co-ordinating and planning institutions within the Ministry of Health Care. The pension reforms of 1968 and 1969 introduced a very generous 'earnings-related' formula, guaranteeing to employees a replacement rate of up to 80 per cent after 40 years of career at the age of 60 (55 for women). This reform also introduced for employees the possibility of retiring after 35 years of insurance membership, regardless of age, with a replacement rate of 70 per cent (this type of pension, linked to a minimum number of insurance years, was called 'seniority pension', as opposed to the usual old age pension, linked only to the age)[1]. Unemployment insurance was strengthened, especially as regards the *Cassa Integrazione Straordinaria* scheme, which gave a generous wage compensation (70-80 per cent of previous earnings) to workers laid off because of industrial restructuring or reorganisation.

This reformist zeal continued and indeed deepened throughout the 1970s. This decade completed the new edifice built in the 1960s and in many respects reshaped the organisation of welfare. Following constitutional provisions, regions and local authorities were transformed into the main *loci* of welfare policy, gradually suppressing the health insurance and assistance funds run from the centre. Social assistance, health care, housing and vocational training, thus became the competence of sub-national governments. New social and personal services were organised, new housing and transport programmes launched and some first active labour market policies inaugurated. Client participation and control were fostered, especially in education. In 1978 a sweeping reform led to the establishment of the National Health Service, replacing all pre-existing separate professional insurance funds.

Thus in the second half of the 1970s, the Italian welfare state emerged as a relatively distinct and coherent institutional configuration. Though largely centred on the Bismarckian principles of social insurance typical of all Continental, conservative-corporatist welfare regimes (Esping-Andersen 1990; 1996), in the field of health care this configuration included a 'Beveridgean' element – or at least a Beveridgean aspiration to universal and uniform coverage (an aspiration which was already present in the 1948 Constitution). The Bismarckian transfer schemes provided relatively generous benefits, most of which were earnings-related and fully indexed. The formerly dispersed health care and social services had been replaced by a relatively unitary – though highly decentralised – national and universal service, based on citizenship; education had been reformed and greatly expanded, and housing broadly decentralised. A process of incisive secularisation, moreover, had accompanied these transformations, greatly reducing the role of the Catholic church in social policy and clearly disconnecting the notion of 'welfare' from that of 'Christian charity'.

The institutional growth of the welfare state was paralleled by a rapid and substantial quantitative expansion. In the mid-1950s, total social expenditure (including income maintenance, health care and social assistance) absorbed around 10 per cent of GDP – a relatively low level by international standards. In 1970 this percentage had risen to 17.4 per cent, reaching 22.6 per cent in 1975 – a level in line with that of France or Belgium and higher than that of Britain (Flora 1983; Flora 1986/87; Ferrera 1984).

2   A 'guaranteed' labour market

The long economic miracle caused profound modifications of the employment structure. At the beginning of the 1950s, Italy was to a large extent still an agrarian country: more than 40 per cent of the labour force was occupied in the primary sector, with a large number of independent farmers and sharecroppers. By 1970 this proportion had fallen below 20 per cent, with the secondary and tertiary sectors at about 40 per cent each. Although definitively more modern, in the early 1970s the profile of Italy's labour force continued to display some typical traits of the Italian labour market tradition, such as the high incidence of the self-employed (about 20 per cent) and a very low female participation rate (at about 30 per cent).

In the 1970s a generous system of *ammortizzatori sociali* (social shock absorbers) was brought to completion in the field of unemployment. These were entirely based on passive policies (i.e. cash transfers) and mainly addressed to the regular adult workers who constituted the core of the employment structure. Three different but intertwined phenomena contributed to improve social protection against the risk of unemployment: the extension and improvement of cash benefits; the overall institutionalisation of labour relations through the Workers' Statute; and the rise in union power.

After the war, state regulation of the labour market rested on three main pillars: a) a general unemployment insurance scheme; b) a scheme for short-term earnings replacement in case of temporary redundancies (*Cassa integrazione guadagni ordinaria*); and c) centralised employment services. We will analyse each of these three provisions in turn.

The ordinary unemployment insurance scheme had been introduced in 1919 by the Nitti government, which was moved by sincere reformist intentions, in contrast with previous liberal governments. The 1919 law established a compulsory insurance scheme addressed to private sector workers remaining without job, with at least two years of contributions. The allowance was very low and based on a flat daily rate (180 liras for each day of unemployment).

A new *Cassa Integrazione* scheme was introduced between 1945 and 1947 following a private agreement between trade unions and employers' associations initially applying to the northern regions, and then extended to the whole country. The allowance still required a minimum period of contribution, but was related to previous earnings (60-65 per cent) and was aimed at protecting those workers who had been temporarily hit by working time reductions and whose re-entry into the firm was thought to be certain. The allowance compensated the employers for the prohibition of dismissals imposed on them just after the declaration of the armistice (1943) up to August 1947.

Finally, in 1949 the state monopoly on the employment services was established by Law no. 264 (the so-called 'Fanfani law'). In theory, the design of the new employment service system seemed highly coherent and articulated: general competencies were given to the central administration, placement procedures (and thus outcomes) had to be unbiased, in order to avoid any discrimination. The Ministry of Labour had to implement its exclusive competence through a network of provincial offices. The procedures were typically bureaucratic: the unemployed had to register on compulsory lists, their position depending on the one hand on predefined criteria such as the professional sector, the productive category, the qualification and the specialisation, and, on the other hand, on need-related criteria such as family dependants, the period of enrolment in the lists and family income. The unemployed had to periodically confirm their availability for work. Finally, the principle of automatic assignment, which the whole system was based on, guaranteed the procedure against any discrimination. In fact, the employers were not allowed to choose any worker they preferred, but they had to notify the placement office of the characteristics of the worker they needed to hire and the worker was automatically assigned to the firm, depending on the position on the list and the qualifications required.

From the 1950s to the 1970s, these three pillars operated in mutual reinforcement to the disadvantage of the outsiders of the labour market. The amount of the ordinary unemployment insurance benefit was adjusted several times (in 1960, 1966 and 1974), but continued to be based on a daily rate without any connection (until 1988[2]) to wages: between 1949 and 1974 the ratio of this sum to the average industrial wage fell from 17 per cent to less than 9 per cent (Ferrera 1986/87). Besides monetary erosion, the ordinary unemployment scheme became less effective over time in terms of coverage: many groups of irregular workers, first job seekers and, obviously, the increasing number of workers in the underground economy had no access to unemployment benefits.

On the contrary, the *Cassa Integrazione* scheme literally boomed and started to function as a substitute for the former scheme. The requirement of 'transitory' reductions of working time was *de facto* abandoned, and the replacement rate was increased from 60 per cent to 70 per cent. But the most remarkable innovation was the introduction of a new social shock absorber through Law no. 1115/1968: special short-term earnings replacement benefits (*Cassa integrazione guadagni straordinaria*). Based on the same logic of the regular *Cassa Integrazione* scheme, the new programme was introduced to guarantee workers in cases of large-scale industrial restructuring, reorganisation or conversion. In this way, the new benefit had not only transitory conjunctural aims, but also broad economic and political aims: it enabled massive dismissals and social conflicts due to workforce expulsions to be avoided. The benefits, which were financed through employers, and workers' contributions, amounted to 80 per cent of the pay (up to a ceiling). In 1975 after a social agreement between the trade unions and Confindustria[3], which was then incorporated in Law no. 164, the replacement rates of both the regular and the special *Cassa Integrazione* were unified at the level of 80 per cent, a record high in the European scenario. In addition, the duration of the benefits was extended to a maximum period of two years – a limit often surpassed in practice through discretionary *ad hoc* measures. Throughout the 1970s the *Cassa Integrazione* was extended from the industrial sector to artisan firms of the construction sector, mining firms, the agricultural sector and finally to state employees.

As for employment services, their functioning did not evolve in the desired direction. They became increasingly bureaucratised over time and the whole placement system, that was supposed to assure impartiality and fairness of treatment among the workers, ended up by encouraging a parallel, underground, labour market.

The social protection schemes against unemployment were integrated by the introduction of a new legislation on workers' rights. In 1970 the Workers' Statute (*Statuto dei Lavoratori*) marked the beginning of a new era of industrial relations. The Statute, which was the result of a heated political debate, strongly limited the employers' power by imposing constraints and sanctions in case of union activity repression. Individual and collective workers' rights in the factories were acknowledged and widened. The law was to be applied in enterprises with more than 15 employees. It included rules for the protection of the dignity and freedom of the worker, for the defence of union political activities and for the exercise of a rich set of social rights connected to the work life. The new rules on firing are particularly worth mentioning. The old legislation on individual dismissals (dating back to 1966) had replaced the freedom to fire foreseen by the 1942 civil code with a new regime that allowed firings in firms with more than 35 employees only in the case of a 'justified' (i.e. demonstrable) reason or 'right' (i.e. demonstrable) cause. If a dismissal was declared illegal, the employer could choose whether to employ the worker again within three days or pay a substitutive allowance corresponding to 5-12 months' wages. The Workers' Statute instituted the rule of compulsory re-hiring in the case of no 'justified reason' or 'right cause' in all enterprises with more than 15 employees, thus abolishing the option of paying the penalty instead.

In addition, the Workers' Statute reinforced the presence of trade unions in the workplace. This was also the result of the changed political and social climate at the end of the 1960s. Thanks to their increased political and or-

Table 2.2   Labour policies, 1945-1978: a summary

1919	General unemployment insurance
1945-47	Regular short-term earnings replacement benefits (*Cassa integrazione guadagni ordinaria*)
1945	Wage indexation (*scala mobile*)
1949	Public employment services
1955	Apprenticeship regulated
1966	Law on individual dismissals
1968	Special short-term earnings replacement benefits (*Cassa Integrazione straordinaria*)
1970	Workers' Statute
1975	Improvement of wage indexation and unification of the regular and special *Cassa Integrazione* scheme to 80 per cent of the previous earnings
1977	Law on youth employment
1977	Law on industrial mobility and restructuring
1978	Law on vocational training

ganisational power, trade unions were able to emancipate from their traditional subjection to political parties, gaining a more active role in policy making[4]. In 1969 the rule of the incompatibility between party and union positions was officially established. The explosion of conflicts and strikes during the 'hot autumn' of 1969 allowed the unions to take on a primary role in the battle for reforms (for pensions, housing, taxes) and higher wages. Union demands were unanimous: higher control on income policies, active participation in the firm management, and 'egalitarianism' (i.e. the reduction of wage differentials among genders, categories and qualifications) (Cella and Treu 1989; 1998). The 1969 agreement for the metal workers can be considered as the symbol of this new epoch. The agreement included a basic wage increase, full wage continuation for sick workers, strong limitations to overtime work and the introduction of decentralised bargaining. In the same year the so-called 'wage cages' (i.e. the possibility of differentiating wages on the basis of different earning categories corresponding to various geographical areas) were abolished. These 'cages' had been introduced in 1961 within a joint unions' and employer's agreement whose aim was to reduce earnings dispersion. Italian provinces, from the richest to the poorest, had been divided into seven categories according to the levels of the cost of living. If a worker belonging to the area 'zero' (Milan, Turin, Genoa and Rome) earned 100, an equally qualified worker working in a province included in the area 'one' (Florence, Como, Sondrio) earned 97 and a worker of the area 'six' (Southern Italy) gained 80. Mobility from one category to another (as the metaphor of the 'cage' suggested) was discouraged. Before the 1961 agreement wage dispersion was significantly higher (more than 30 per cent) (Turone 1988).

The rise in power of national trade unions was reflected in a parallel rise of union membership. Between 1968 and 1975 the members of the CISL, the Catholic-oriented union, rose from one million to two and a half million, while those of the CGIL, the communist-oriented union, grew from two and a half million to four and a half million (Ricciardi 1986). From 1970 to 1980 the overall Italian union membership rate rose from 33.4 per cent to 44.1 per cent, exceeding the Dutch rate (33.8 per cent), the German rate (34.3 per cent) and the EC average rate (38.1 per cent) (Carrieri 1995: 149).

3   The shadow: an internally flawed constellation

The socio-economic and institutional dynamics illustrated thus far gave a great and unquestionable contribution to the overall modernisation of Italy. However, they left a number of unresolved structural questions on the floor. Moreover, they planted some new, dangerous seeds for the emergence of additional problems: as stated at the beginning, the 1970s witnessed the appearance of an endogenous crisis, the most visible symptoms of which concentrated in the sector of welfare state financing.

The unresolved questions were basically related to the persistence of the country's historical divisions: the socio-economic division between a rapidly industrialising north and a deeply backward south; the ideological and political division between a moderate, largely Catholic, 'white' sub-culture and a radical, largely communist, 'red' sub-culture.

Despite the huge flows of resources channelled into the *Mezzogiorno* by the central government, the southern economy was still lagging far behind at the beginning of the 1970s. North-south differentials were still particularly dramatic in occupational terms. In 1970 the unemployment rate was 4.9 per cent in the south as against 2.3 per cent in the centre-north. By 1979, these figures had risen to 10.9 per cent and 6.2 per cent, respectively (Gualmini 1998). In the early 1970s the first statistics on the black economy brought to light almost three million underground workers, mainly concentrated in the southern regions (CENSIS 1976). The state-assisted industrialisation of the *Mezzogiorno*, which was the privileged economic and political strategy of the 1950s, had not had a positive impact on employment. On the one hand, the massive creation of state-participated firms, particularly in the manufacturing, petrochemical and steel industries (whose financing was also made possible by draining the surplus produced in the richer regions of the country) originated an irreversible exodus from the countryside to the cities and from small to large firms, obstructing the possibility to develop a web of small and family-led enterprises, as was happening in many regions of the north. On the other hand, the continuous rise in public employment (which was considered particularly attractive by the younger generations) inhibited opportunities for mobility but multiplied occasions for clientelism (Graziano 1984; Trigilia 1992).

The north-south dualism was only one of the deep and persisting domestic tensions of the hot 1970s. That decade witnessed also a dramatic intensification of the traditional political divisions of the country. The most visible symptoms were the growing competition between the Communist Party and the governing coalitions, the widespread and heated social conflicts and the rise of terrorism. In 1975, in the second regional elections after the establishment of the regions, the Communist Party extended its control from the traditionally 'red' regions (Emilia-Romagna, Tuscany, Umbria) to three other regions (Piedmont, Liguria and Lazio), becoming the official and legitimate competitor of the highly institutionalised 'white' block. Many activists of the Communist Party were also members of the CGIL, which in that period turned to more radical positions on economic and social reforms. The waves of strikes and social conflicts that had exploded in the hot autumn of 1969 kept their momentum. The students' protest movements intertwined with those of the blue-collar workers. Some of the largest and well-known universities were occupied (Trento, Torino, Milan, Pisa). Terrorist attacks made their sinister appearance, culminating in the tragic kidnapping and murder of the leader of the Christian Democratic Party, Aldo Moro, in 1978.

The persistence (and in some respects even the aggravation) of the old questions was not the only shadow on stage during the 1970s. New problems were in fact opening up in the wake of the social policy and labour market regimes built in the previous decades. Using summary formulas, we can say that those two regimes had posed the basis of five 'original sins' of welfare capitalism Italian-style, which have been (and still largely are) the object of articulated debates and policy actions in the 1980s and 1990s.

4   Five 'original sins' of welfare capitalism Italian-style

The first two sins can be characterised as 'distortions'. The social insurance reforms listed in Table 2.1 caused, firstly, an *allocative* distortion, clearly favouring certain risks/functions of social policy (most notably, old age and survival) at the expense of certain others (most notably, family benefits and services, total lack of employment/income and the relief of poverty). As mentioned, the 1969 pension reform introduced what probably was, at the time, the most generous earnings-related formula of the Western world (70 per cent of previous wages after 35 years' work with no age threshold or 80 per cent at the age of 60 for men and 55 for women). On the other hand, the schemes aimed at catering for the needs of large and poor families remained underdeveloped and underfunded. At the beginning of the 1950s, pensions and family benefits absorbed a roughly equal share of the GDP (Ferrera 1984). By 1980, pension expenditure was almost seven times higher than that for family benefits: the highest ratio in the EC except for Greece (EC 1993). The 1969 reform set the country on the road to becoming a 'pension state' rather than a modern, fully-fledged welfare state responding to a variety of needs with a variety of instruments. And even the new social activism of the regions could do little to contrast the expansive momentum of public pension growth, which started to crowd out – financially and institutionally – most other types of benefits and services.

The second distortion is of a *distributive* nature. Centred as they are on occupational status, all Bismarckian systems give rise to some disparity of treatment across sectors and categories. The fragmented development of Italy's social insurance, however, resulted in a true 'labyrinth' of categorical privileges which has very few comparative counterparts (Ferrera 1996). The main cleavage (which had already become easily visible in the 1970s) opposed workers located in the core sectors of the (industrial) labour market to those located in the more peripheral sectors (semi-regular and unemployed). As this strong dualism still remains one of the most important features of the Italian employment regime, it may be useful to discuss it in some detail.

The dualism finds its roots in two distinct phenomena: the institutional design of unemployment schemes and the dynamics of wage policies. The system of social shock absorbers illustrated above was mainly centred on insurance mechanisms. The eligible workers were those who had paid contributions for at least two years of regular work. In other terms, the main beneficiaries were industrial workers belonging to the primary labour market (the so-called insiders). The two major instruments of labour policy, the unemployment insurance and the *Cassa Integrazione* schemes, had adopted this kind of logic. By the same token, the procedures for placement were based on two different trajectories, one for the formerly employed (recipients of insurance benefits) and the other one for the other categories of job seekers. The former could move from one firm to another without respecting the rule of the 'call by lot' (i.e. the numerical order of the list), but simply responding to the employers' 'nominative call' (i.e. a job offer *ad personam*); the latter were, instead, subjected to the rule of the 'call by lot' – which meant no freedom of choice for the employers and automatic placement for workers. The most immediate effect was the propensity of employers to hire the formerly employed (the insiders) to the full disadvantage of the other job seekers (the outsiders) (Ichino 1982).

This strong orientation of the social protection towards the insiders of the labour market would not have been so peculiar (and perverse) if a system of active or targeted labour policies had been established for the outsiders (as for instance in Sweden). But this was not the case. The young unemployed in search of first jobs or the long-term unemployed with no benefits were not offered such programmes. Nor did they have the chance to obtain a minimum guaranteed income. Only at the end of the 1970s did the government start to encourage active policies, such as training and mobility (cf. Table 2.2), but with scarce results.

Such a distortion in the distribution of the benefits was also reinforced by union strategies on wage policy. The social conflicts of the 1970s resulted in significant improvements of real wages and of the indexation regime. Unions insisted that earnings should become 'independent variables' (no longer dependent on inflation and the economy in general), and the immediate beneficiaries of this kind of policy, which has become notorious as 're-versed incomes policy' (Rossi 1998), were, of course, the members of the unions, once again the insiders[5]. During the hot autumn, union wage claims pursued numerous goals: to extend union control over wage dynamics (i.e. to bring inside the area of collective bargaining the highest number of wage items and the greatest number of workers); to increase the wage scale; to reduce differentials among the various categories of workers; to fill the gap between the less protected workers and the more protected ones; to abolish most of the productivity- and performance-related wage components (Somaini 1989). An impetuous rise in earnings was in fact achieved during that period[6].

Of particular importance was the reduction of wage differentials, resulting from the elimination of the so-called 'wage cages' in 1969. This system, as already stated, was based on a list of geographic areas characterised by different wage minima. The strikes for the dismantling of the 'cages', which were thought to be a tangible sign of the undemocratic backwardness of the past, began in 1968 both in the public and in the private sector. The opposition of employers, who on the contrary considered the 'cages' as instruments of flexibility, was strong. The first to surrender were the employers of public firms, followed by the associations of the small- and medium-sized firms and finally the Confindustria. The suppression of fixed wage categories paved the way for the strengthening of national centralised collective bargaining, which – though representing a step forward in the institutionalisation of industrial relations – inevitably introduced some degrees of rigidity in the regulation of the labour market, distorting incentives for both territorial demand and supply of labour.

In 1975, the national trade unions and Confindustria signed an agreement which established a new system of wage indexation for industrial workers[7]. For each percentage point of increase in consumer prices, all wages were to grow by a single flat rate amount (the so-called *punto unico di contingenza*). This meant that lower wages were more strongly protected than higher wages, leading to a gradual 'egalitarian' ironing out of the earnings pyramid. The agreement was soon extended by the government to all employees in the state and private sector. But the new *scala mobile* concealed many counter effects: it was at the same time a powerful barrier against the inflationary erosion of (lower) wages and a powerful incentive for the spiral wages-prices-wages (and thus inflation)[8].

The third original sin that characterised the start-up, 'Keynesian' constellation has to do with the financing of public, and in particular social, expenditure. In 1950-1964 Italy's public finances witnessed a phase of relatively balanced growth, in which the expansion of outlays was matched by a parallel expansion of revenues. The subsequent decade was marked, however, by a new pattern of unbalanced growth, in which outlays continued to rise while revenues stagnated around a figure of 30 per cent of GDP[9]. This 'flat decade' on the revenue side created a hole in Italy's public finances which made things much worse when the exogenous shocks hit in the mid-1970s (Gerelli and Majocchi 1984). In Italian debate, this hole is often referred to as the 'original hole' because it marked the beginning of the public debt spiral of the subsequent decades. We count it among the 'sins' because it was caused by the choice of not raising taxes and delaying the modernisation of the tax apparatus.

The shift from balanced to unbalanced growth was the product of a more or less deliberate choice by policy-makers of the centre-left coalition. This choice followed a long debate on the correct interpretation of Article 81 of the Italian Constitution, which states that any law involving the disbursement of public money must indicate the source of the necessary financial coverage in advance. The debate consisted of two conflicting interpretations on this point: an 'orthodox' one, which interpreted the prescription as an obligation to balance expenditure with real revenues (i.e. with no resort to borrowing) and a 'Keynesian' one, which accepted the notion of deficit spending in cases where this would stimulate unexploited productive resources, especially through the growth of public investments. The latter interpretation prevailed, and after 1965 deficit spending became the current practice.

The development during the subsequent decade did not, however, correspond to the intentions and expectations of the Keynesian school. It was not public investment that grew, but current expenditure (transfers and subsidies in particular), leading to a rapid erosion of public savings. General government net lending rose from 0.8 per cent of GDP in 1964 (the last virtuous year) to 7.0 per cent in 1974 and 11.4 per cent in 1975 – the peak of the first oil shock slump. And public deficits largely served to finance the growth of the welfare state. Starting from the mid-1960s, the aggregate balance between statutory contributions and benefits began to be negative for many pension and most sickness funds: contribution rates were in fact kept artificially low, in the hope of stimulating job creation but also to please social categories which were crucial for political stability. Despite repeated *ad hoc* financial aids from the Treasury, the budgetary situation of the social security sector continued to deteriorate, and in 1974-75 the government had to launch an extraordinary operation to repay the enormous debts accumulated by the funds, amounting to 5.2 per cent of GDP (another deep dig in the hole).

The remaining two original sins had to do with legality and efficiency. Although highly articulated from a legislative and organisational viewpoint, the social policy configuration built between the 1950s and the 1970s was characterised by high institutional 'softness'. Especially in some sectors and areas, the degree of compliance with the rules disciplining the access to benefits and the payment of contributions remained very low, not only on the side of the various clienteles of social programmes, but also on the side of public authorities. This syndrome assumed inordinate proportions in the sector of disability pensions, which became the privileged currency of an extended clientelistic market: between 1960 and 1980 the total number of disability pensions rose almost five times, and in 1974 (following an expansive reform) it came to surpass the total number of old age pensions: an unparalleled record in the OECD area (Ferrera 1984; 1986/87; 1996).

As to the efficiency of public services (in virtually all fields of public intervention), the situation of the 1970s fell short of all expectations of the Keynesian modernisers of the 1960s. The lack of a pragmatic culture, the partisan colonisation of the administrative apparatus, the opportunistic use of public employment by the patronage system, the failure to design rational systems of incentives: these and other factors gave rise to an oversized bu-reaucracy with very low levels of performance (Cassese 1974). Within the welfare state, the problem was particularly acute in the case of health care and employment services. The 1978 reform establishing the NHS introduced many perverse incentives from a financial and organisational point of view: as a matter of fact, the institutional design of the 1978 reform was largely responsible for the chaotic developments and growing financial strains wit-nessed by this sector throughout the 1980s. At the end of the 1970s, the ma-jor part of the expenditure for the employment services was absorbed by personnel wages instead of being used for employment creation initiatives and the percentage of workers successfully employed through public place-ment offices amounted to only 10 per cent of the total labour force (Ichino 1996). In addition, the tripartite Ministerial commissions, that were related to the placement offices and were formed by representatives of the Ministry, members of the unions and representatives of the employers, were often are-nas for patronage operations. The efficiency and legality deficits were thus partly intertwined with each other.

5   Polarized pluralism: the political roots of poor policy performance

The five original sins of 'welfare capitalism Italian-style' were partly the re-sult of specific policy choices (or non-choices) made in the formative decades of 1950-1970: choices that in their turn reflected quite closely the overall 'political logic' of what is currently called Italy's First Republic (1947-1992). This is especially true for the aforementioned distortions: the devel-opment of a pension-heavy welfare state, financially unsound and inclined towards particularistic-clientelistic manipulations, was highly congruent for example with the competitive dynamics of Italy's unstable political sys-tem and, more particularly, with the interests of the three major parties (DC, PCI and PSI). The emphasis on pensions as 'deferred wages' and the neglect of family policy mirrored in fact the social doctrines of both Marxism and Catholicism. More crucially, the expansion of a highly fragmented social in-surance system offered ample opportunities for distributing differentiated entitlements to selected party clienteles. It must not be forgotten, however, that to some extent the distinctive elements of the welfare *all'italiana* (to use a well-known metaphor of the national debate, cf. Ascoli 1984) find their roots in a number of broader historical features of Italian society, such as the traditional 'uncivicness' of political culture[10], the above mentioned histori-cal divisions of economic and ideological nature, the failure to create a We-berian administration.

The imprint left by the political logic of the First Republic on the welfare state can be illustrated in relation to the pension policies of the 1960s. As mentioned above, that decade witnessed an articulated debate and two important reforms, whose legacy is still largely reflected in today's spending patterns and interest constellations. Italy's post-war party system has been characterised as a form of 'polarised pluralism' (Sartori 1976; 1982), displaying not only high fragmentation (many parties), but also a wide ideological distance between left and right. The centre of the political spectrum was occupied by the Christian Democratic party (DC), which presented itself as a watchdog of Western-style liberal democracy and market capitalism. The left wing was occupied by the largest communist party in the Western world (PCI), while the right wing was occupied by a fairly strong neo-Fascist party (MSI). Both the PCI and the MSI were anti-system parties, i.e. they explicitly aimed at altering in fundamental ways the country's political and economic regime. In this setting, electoral competition followed a distinct tri-polar and centrifugal logic. All three poles had an interest in playing on the pro-system vs. anti-system dimension. Sitting in the middle, the DC had an interest in expanding its votes both towards the left and towards the right, trying to capture all potentially pro-system voters. The other two poles had in their turn an interest in capturing all anti-system voters located around the extremes (lest splinter parties emerge), by means of various strategies of issue radicalisation and social mobilization. Squeezed between the DC and the PCI, the socialist party (PSI) oscillated between pro-system and anti-system stances during the 1950s, but opted for the former at the beginning of the 1960s, negotiating an organic alliance with the DC and forming the first Centro-sinistra (Centre-left) government in 1962. By accessing the shrine of state power and thus exerting a direct influence on policy choices, the socialists hoped to expand their support at the expense of the Communists – an experiment that had succeeded in the previous decade in other European countries.

The Centro-sinistra started with grand programmatic ambitions of reform and modernization. As we have seen above, in the field of pensions the idea was that of introducing a universal first pillar scheme, supplemented by occupational benefits. This plan could be presented as a true 'structural reform', progressive yet Western style, i.e. capable of satisfying both the redistributive expectations of the workers' movement and at the same time reassuring the capitalist establishment. The universalistic option would not have harmed the already covered groups (their entitlements would remain unaltered with the interplay of first and second pillar schemes), while it would have benefited a large and politically crucial constituency of uncovered categories, ranging from the self-employed to the unemployed, house-wives, marginal workers, small businessmen, the poor elderly, etc. The pension reform could serve two purposes: strengthening the pro-system attitudes of such categories in general and linking them to the DC and to the PSI in particular. Although matured in a different context, a similar reform in the Netherlands in 1956 had achieved precisely these outcomes (Ferrera 1993; Van Kersbergen 1995). Of course, the PCI could not be entirely excluded from the reform game: this party had huge 'blackmail' power *vis-à-vis* the government and could prompt vast mass mobilizations against policies that it disliked. But in 1964 a softer line was emerging within the PCI, led by Giorgio Amendola: a line sincerely interested in institutional modernization and open to negotiation with the new government coalition. Thus, for a moment a window of opportunity seemed really available for a sweeping pension reform along universalistic lines: and a first move was made in 1965, with the approval of a law bearing the title of 'Launch of the pension reform' (cf. *supra*).

The window of opportunity closed too soon, however, for putting all the pieces together. Despite the compromising and centripetal attitudes of individual leaders such as Moro (DC), Nenni (PSI) and Amendola (PCI), the logic of inter-party competition continued to operate in a centrifugal direction during the 1960s. As a matter of fact, the formation of the Centro-sinistra worked to exacerbate the syndrome of polarized pluralism. After a harsh campaign entirely centred on the political significance and programmatic goals of the new coalition formula, the 1963 elections marked significant losses for both the DC and the PSI, to the advantage of the liberals (PLI) and neo-Fascists (MSI) on the right and of the PCI on the left (cf. Table 2.3). The PSI paid a high price for its entry into the cabinet: in January 1964 a group of internal dissidents left the party and founded the 'Socialist Party of Proletarian Union' (PSIUP). With its highly maximalist stance, this new party conditioned the PCI from the left: the XI party congress held in 1966 defeated the Amendola line and pushed the PCI back towards anti-system intransigence. In the same year the formation of a new Marxist-Leninist splinter party (*Partito marxista-leninista italiano*) unleashed a syndrome of extremist pulverisation to the left of both the PCI and the PSIup. The 1968 elections poured in their turn a chilly shower on the DC-PSI *entente*: not so much for the DC (which came out stronger), but for the PSI and the smaller social democrats (PSDI). These two parties had experimented with a pre-election merger, which was highly penalised by the voters. Participation in government was not delivering its promises in terms of electoral support: in fact it was revealing itself as a dead end.

Table 2.3   Italian elections: parties and share of vote, 1958-1976

Parties	Votes (%)						
	1958	1963	1968	1970	1972	1975	1976
PCI	22.7	25.3	26.9	27.9	27.2	33.4	34.4
PSIUP				4.4	3.2	1.9	
PSI	14.2	13.8	14.5*	10.4	9.6	12.0	9.6
PSDI	4.5	6.1		7.0	5.1	5.6	3.4
PRI	1.4	1.4	2.0	2.9	2.9	3.2	3.1
DC	42.4	38.3	39.1	37.9	38.8	35.3	38.7
PLI	3.5	7.0	5.8	4.7	3.9	2.5	1.3
PDIUM	4.8	1.8	1.3				
MSI	4.8	5.1	4.5	5.2	8.7	6.4	6.1
Others	1.7	1.2	1.5	0.8	1.9	1.6	3.9

Notes: 1970 and 1975 = Regional elections
* In 1968 the Socialist party (PSI) and the Social-democratic party (PSDI) presented together at the polls.
Abbreviations: cf. above, Table 1.3. PDIUM = Partito di Unità Monarchica.
Source: Ferrera (1993:266)

These competitive dynamics worked heavily against the universalistic option in pension reform, especially owing to the strains and divisions inside the left. The gains of the PCI and the losses of the PSI at the 1963 elections alerted the latter party against communist competition, which was particularly acute within working class voters in the industrial north: a growing electoral constituency, increasingly unionised and very sensitive to the destiny of its pension contributions. After the PSIUP split, PSI leaders in government lost touch with the stronger union, the CGIL: most of this union's cadres belonging to the socialist area adhered in fact to the PSIUP and this party did not support pension universalism, pressing instead for a rigorously 'workerist' design of social insurance aimed at defending blue collar interests. The 1966 congress pushed the PCI in the same direction, advocating closer links between the party and workers in the defence of their current and deferred wages. Rather than a universalistic, two-pillar pension system, the PCI started to voice for the strengthening of the existing system, with substantial ameliorations for employees. In such a climate, in the second half of the 1960s, no actor on the left of Italy's political spectrum (not even the leftist currents of the DC) had any political interest in pursuing a universalistic reform design. The government was not prepared, however, to accommodate the financially very demanding requests of the PCI and the

CGIL. In 1968 a partial deal was struck with the other two unions, CISL and UIL. But the disappointing results of the 1968 elections (partly centred, precisely, on the pension issue) re-opened the games. A big package deal was negotiated, 'universalist' only in the sense that all participants got some spoil. The real winners were the PCI and the CGIL, which obtained the introduction for all employees of one of the most generous pension formulas ever introduced in Europe, including the option to retire after 35 years of insurance regardless of age (the infamous – with hindsight – seniority pensions). Politically, the 1969 pension reform inaugurated a new phase of all-inclusive spoils-sharing system, extended to the PCI and to the trade unions (which gained an important role in the actual management of the pension funds, including grass-roots decisions about disability pension applications). Institutionally, the reform created a true 'labyrinth' of different occupational funds, with different regulations, easily permeable to partisan manipulations and mass patronage practices. Financially, it created a spending machine that in the span of two decades brought pension expenditure up from 6.9 per cent of GDP in 1970 to 11.8 per cent in 1990 (1992 = 12.8 per cent)[11]. Whatever their historical origins, and however congruent with the political complexion of post-war Italy, the internal flaws and malfunctioning of the Keynesian-Fordist constellation of the 1970s rendered the country structurally vulnerable to the external shocks that appeared on stage at the beginning of that decade. Hitting on friable grounds, the storm thus produced more serious damage in this country than elsewhere in Europe.

6   Enter the external challenges: from miracles to thunderstorms

Italy's political economy stepped into the 1970s on the wrong foot. In the wake of the wage rises of 1969, the Bank of Italy and the Treasury decided on a monetary squeeze in 1970, which provoked a recession in the following year. This prompted the government to shift back to an expansionist policy in both monetary and budgetary terms. The cycle turned swiftly upwards, but so did inflation, while the balance of payments witnessed increasing strains. With the collapse of the dollar standard (and as a consequence of strong speculative attacks), the lira was devalued in 1973: a move which did not compromise the upward trend of the cycle, but which reinforced the already existing domestic inflationary pressures due to the price increase of imported raw materials. Severe administrative controls were also introduced on the movement of capital, to discourage its alarmingly mounting flight abroad. In 1974 the rate of inflation had risen to 19 per cent, up from

2 per cent in 1968. The first oil crisis produced a dramatic slump in 1975: in that year GDP fell by almost 4 per cent. Inflation also went down. But in 1975 the above-mentioned *scala mobile* agreement created an infernal (with hindsight) stagflation-multiplier whose consequences were to be seriously felt for many years to come. By guaranteeing an immediate adjustment of wages to prices, the new *scala mobile* contributed not only to the spread of inflation throughout all branches of the economy, but fostered an overall climate of self-sustaining inflationary expectations.

At the end of 1975, the government lowered interest rates and created new liquidity in order to exit from the recession and support a severely ailing industrial sector. However, a new massive speculative attack was launched against the lira, and in the winter of 1976 the official quotation of the national currency had to be suspended for forty days. When the exchange rate market re-opened, the lira had suffered a new heavy devaluation. The vicious circle devaluation-inflation-indexation brought the rate of inflation up to 21 per cent by 1980. In the same year, public debt had mounted to 58.1 per cent of GDP (1970 = 38.1 per cent) and public deficit to 8.6 per cent (1970 = 4 per cent) (OECD, Economic Outlook, various editions).

The macro-economic policies pursued by the Treasury and by the Bank of Italy in the 1970s have been severely criticised as inadequate responses to the new international context, and thus for being largely responsible for the ailing conditions of Italy's economy and public finances at the end of the decade. This indictment must be tempered with at least two considerations: the initial conditions were characterised by a peculiarly high degree of vulnerability; the social and political situation posed severe constraints for policy-makers. To some extent, inflation and deficits were the most viable instruments for dispersing the costs of adjustment in a context which allowed very little room for the *ex ante* definition of policy priorities and the imposition of explicit sacrifices (Salvati 1981; 1984).

A deliberate attempt at macro-economic stabilisation was indeed made in the second half of the decade. In 1976, following an outstanding electoral success of the Communists, a 'national solidarity' majority was formed in Parliament, including the PCI. This coalition took significant decisions in many policy domains (e.g. the fight against terrorism). More specifically, it tried to pursue an explicit policy of 'real' macro-economic adjustment.

The point of departure of this attempt was a fully fledged sequence of neo-corporatist agreements, the first ever experienced in Italy, which culminated in the 'EUR' union assembly in February 1978 (taken from the name of the neighbourhood in Rome where it took place) where trade unions and especially the CGIL formally turned to wage restraints. In exchange for that, the government committed itself to protecting the existing employment levels and to finding innovative solutions for combating youth unemployment. A number of fiscal measures followed, with positive effects on labour costs and productivity. More significantly, some innovative industrial and labour policies were introduced (cf. Table 2.2.): the new climate of social co-operation between the unions and the government offered a fertile ground for the development of active labour market policies. In particular, three programmes are worth mentioning: the law for youth employment (n. 285/1977), the law on industrial reorganisation (no. 675/1977) and the general law on vocational training (no. 845/1978).

The main purpose of the law on youth employment was to provide special funds to the regions for organising and implementing vocational training and job creation initiatives for young people in search of jobs. Regional commissions, composed of the representatives of the regions and of the private associations, were established in order to collect and monitor the data and information on territorial employment perspectives and to organise training courses. In addition, the law introduced a set of tax relief measures to encourage the demand of labour. Finally, for the first time the law allowed special contractual conditions for young workers, such as contracts related to training or stages.

Law no. 675/1977 on industrial reorganisation immediately obtained large cross-partisan approval. The big technological transformations made restructuring and innovation particularly urgent, with heavy consequences in terms of massive dismissals in the industrial sector. The law was aimed at reorganising various pre-existing mechanisms of financial support to the industrial sector, the criteria and rules of state intervention, and labour policy provisions targeted at absorbing massive dismissals in a new general integrated design. A new Interministerial Committee for Industrial Policy was set up in order to monitor conjunctural economic trends and to co-ordinate infrastructural interventions. In the field of labour policies, social shock absorbers and active policies were given a new regulatory framework. Special short-term earnings replacement benefits were partially modified through the inclusion of a further case of application: the so-called 'crisis of particularly social relevance'. In addition, a new active policy was introduced: external mobility measures (*procedure di mobilità esterna*) were enacted in order to allow the transfer of redundant workers from one firm to another or from one region to another.

Finally, the law on vocational training (no. 845/1978) provided general guidelines for the regions that starting from 1970 had been assigned vocational training functions. The regions were given responsibility to formulate a detailed discipline on the regulation of training in the different areas of the country. A fund for vocational training was set up, and the appropriate connections with the European Social Fund were established.

In spite of their noble intentions, these three innovative measures were never fully implemented. The regions did nothing but reproduce the old public programmes, and the EC funds were hardly used. External mobility never started since workers seemed to 'prefer' the generous *Cassa Integrazione* benefits; only scattered and fragmented job opportunities for the young unemployed were created, lacking a minimum degree of long-term rationality and co-ordination.

The 'real' adjustment policy of the national solidarity coalition was therefore not very effective. The attempt was short lived (1976-1979) and crumbled due to the continuing political and ideological strains between its main protagonists. It also met with strong institutional obstacles. The effort to reform and innovate the system of financial incentives to industry in 1977 clashed for example against innumerable administrative difficulties and cumbersome decision-making procedures that basically made any change of the status quo impossible (Ferrera 1989). The low institutional capabilities of Italy's governmental machinery remained throughout the decade an additional, significant factor of structural vulnerability *vis-à-vis* old, new, domestic and international challenges.

At the end of the turbulent 1970s, the Italian economy was thus a real mixture of lights and shadows (with hindsight more shadows than lights). As for the lights, after the dramatic effects of the first oil shock, the expansionary macro-economic measures and the strong depreciation of the lira (16 per cent) brought some positive effects, safeguarding the competitiveness of Italian products. Between 1976 and 1979 the trade balance showed a positive trend, thanks to an attentive monetary and exchange rate policy. The volume of export rose by 10 per cent yearly, doubling the EC average. GDP resumed its growth, still higher than the EC average: 5.9 per cent in 1976, 3.4 per cent in 1977, 3.7 per cent in 1978 and 6 per cent in 1979. Investments and consumptions were re-launched.

Based as it was on a sequence of monetary stops and goes, currency devaluations and export-led recoveries, this *reprise* was very shaky. At the end of the 1970s, Italy's 'misery index' was the second highest in Europe, after that of Spain: inflation floated around 15 per cent, and the unemployment rate was particularly high compared to the other EC countries. From 1976 to 1979 it grew from 6.6 per cent to 7.6 per cent, whereas in Germany it floated around 3 per cent and in France and UK around 5 per cent (OECD, Economic Outlook, various editions). This was really a specific feature of the

Italian labour market: the persistence of high unemployment starting already from the 1970s. Only in the United States had the unemployment rate reached such a level, but in the 1980s, unlike Italy, US unemployment was to experience a swift downturn. Three other highlights of the Italian situation were the concentration of unemployment in the southern regions, among women and the young. In 1979 in the *Mezzogiorno* the unemployment rate reached 10.9 per cent whereas in the centre-north it was equal to 6.2 per cent. In the same year male unemployment amounted to 5 per cent, while female unemployment totalled 13.3 per cent. Particularly remarkable was the growth of youth unemployment (15-24 years), which had almost doubled: from 10.2 per cent in 1970 (against a national average of 4.9 per cent) to 25.6 per cent in 1979 (against a national average of 10.3 per cent).

The loss of employment was particularly high in traditional large factories, which in the 1970s underwent a thoroughgoing process of reorganisation. Productive decentralisation became the employers' *motto* in order to pursue economies of scale and to bypass the power of the unions. In fact, decentralisation allowed more flexibility to cope with the adjustments imposed by the market and weakened (or sometimes even zeroed) the power of the unions, since the Workers' Statute and its clauses on behalf of workers' organised activity were applicable only to firms with more than fifteen employees. Flexible, small firms were gradually flourishing, especially in the industrial districts of the north-eastern regions. From 1971 to 1981 the number of firms with less than ten employees rose from 20.2 per cent to 22.8 per cent of total firms, those with less than 20 employees from 8.7 per cent to 12.4 per cent, whereas large firms with more than 200 employees and more than 500 employees declined respectively from 12.8 per cent to 11.1 per cent and from 24 per cent to 19.7 per cent (Brusco and Paba 1997: 270).

The most important (and problematic) features of the Italian 'model' were therefore consolidating at the turn of the decade. But policy-makers seemed unable to interpret and react to these new premonitory signs. The changes in the socio-economic environment were definitely more rapid than those in the politico-institutional system, which indeed remained basically unchanged from the post war-period to the end of the 1970s.

The 1970s closed, however, with a political *coup de reins*, which was to have significant repercussions in the subsequent period: the decision to adhere to the newly born European monetary system (EMS). The issue was quite hot for Italy since it involved the abandonment of the old devaluation-centred monetary policy in favour of a new (and thus more uncertain) monetary regime. In the European arenas, the debate was in fact led by the French and the Germans and actually followed with resignation by the Italians. The decision to abandon the usual devaluation strategies that had traditionally functioned as a mechanism for the safeguarding of Italy's competitiveness involved the change of the entire monetary and economic policy. It was precisely on this issue that the national solidarity government fell, with the PCI joining again the ranks of the opposition.

In December of 1978, the lira finally entered the EMS with a larger fluctuation band (6 per cent instead of 2.25 per cent). The joining of the EMS marked the beginning of a new phase in Italy's EC membership. The participation in a monetary system designed to be 'hard' would decisively condition the development and the management of most policy sectors. We will discuss in Chapter V the complex dynamics which led to such a major policy shift, which planted a first, extremely important 'seed' for the adjustment of the 1990s. Prior to addressing explanatory questions, let us proceed with our reconstruction of politico-economic developments, turning our attention to the 'winding road' of adjustment during the 1980s and 1990s.

III   The Winding Road to Adjustment

1   The new European constraints

At the end of the 1970s, Italy had built up an extended and articulated system of social guarantees, after a prolonged and sustained period of economic growth. The parallel development of particularistic and distributive social policies, on the one hand, and a highly protective labour market regulation to the advantage of the employees, on the other, had resulted in an internally coherent welfare system, with high levels of satisfaction among its beneficiaries. This system appeared closed (if not impermeable) to the external challenges, completely absorbed by the ups and downs of domestic politics, and rather insensitive with respect to the inputs and stimuli towards change that came from outside. It is not surprising, therefore, that the sudden turbulences due to the changing conditions of the international economy and to the process of supranational integration would soon reveal – starting from the early 1980s – the fragility of the Italian welfare state. The strengthening of the European arena (of its institutional identity, competencies and transactions) put the original configuration of the Italian welfare state under the double pressure of a forced financial adjustment on the one side, and of an increasingly rapid process of market integration on the other.

The fact that the European arena can influence the evolution of domestic policy-making, particularly with regard to social policies and labour market regulation, is not a new phenomenon of the 1990s: on the contrary, this influence appeared for the first time at the end of the 1970s, especially after the launching of the EMS, and has continued up to the present day, after the establishment of the EMU. This is the reason why we cannot properly follow the line of development of the Italian welfare system since the 1970s, unless we refer directly to the developments of a major actor such as the European Community (and then Union), which caught the attention of national decision-makers rapidly and decisively.

In this regard, the entry into the EMS represents the first stage of a long process of adjustment to exogenous challenges that came from the international environment and then would deeply influence the functioning of Italy's welfare state. The second stage coincides with the completion of the internal market in the late 1980s, and the third with the convergence towards the Maastricht parameters during the 1990s. The adjustment pressure of the three stages, however, had a different weight, since it was somehow filtered by the domestic dynamics of policy and political change. Still, at all three stages the pressures to make national public policies conform to supranational standards and requirements has acted as a positive stimulus for change in the direction of greater budgetary austerity and institutional modernisation.

Already in the first half of the 1980s some important pre-conditions for an effective adjustment of both the economy and public finances had been posed. But policy makers, disturbed as they were by high political instability, the persisting challenge of terrorism and the inflationary effects of the second oil shock, did not seem to be prepared (or rather were not capable) to undertake incisive reforms and persevered instead with the expansionary and distributive policy strategies of the past. The pressures stemming from integration became more visible starting with the Maastricht Treaty (1992), when the 'restoring to health' (*risanamento*) of public finance and hence of economic and social policies became more a necessity than a virtue. Moreover, in the early 1990s, the international pressures to adjust intertwined with the deep institutional changes following the fall of the 'First Republic'. The rapid transformation of the most familiar rules and ingredients of both the domestic political system and of the international economic environment forced Italian politicians to substantially modify their strategies and to introduce important policy innovations.

In this chapter we will reconstruct and analyse the gradual convergence of national policies to the stimuli and requirements of European integration from two perspectives. On the one hand, from the perspective of the control – and specifically containment – of public finances, a process that had immediate consequences upon all social policies. On the other, from the perspective of the growing openness of markets (that is, the internationalisation process), which has influenced the characteristics of the occupational structure and the overall organisation of the Italian welfare system. This double adjustment to the rigorous discipline of a common economic and monetary area and to the changed configuration of international trade – an often unstable and hesitant process – has slowly created the conditions for a new cycle of more significant and effective reforms in the field of social policy and labour market regulation – a goal that unfolded itself in the course of the 1990s. The next chapter will deal with this new cycle of reforms.

2 The contradictory 1980s: testing adjustment while accumulating a huge public debt

As far as the real economy is concerned, the 1980s were characterised by contradictory trends. On the one hand, the entry into the EMS and the reforms that affected the Central Bank made it possible to pursue a rigorous monetary policy whose main goals were deflation, currency stability and the regaining of national credibility after the gloomy performance of the 1970s. On the other hand, the renewed centre-left coalitions (under the novel name of Penta-party governments) which remained steadily in power for the whole decade (cf. Chapter 1, Table 1.3) were not able to take advantage of the changed economic conditions (a significant GDP recovery starting in 1983 and continuing with the 1986 oil counter-shock, as Figure 3.1 shows) and kept on playing their traditional distributive games based on easy spending. In terms of policy choices too, as will be shown in the next section, the 1980s distinguished themselves for a similarly ambiguous trend.

Participating in the EMS proved to be particularly important for the Italian economy, since it involved a radical transformation of monetary policy. The entry into a fixed band of currency oscillation, though wider than the standard one, caused the abandonment of those traditional devaluation policies that had permitted the safeguarding of Italian competitiveness without embarking in comprehensive strategies of real adjustment. As was to happen again in 1992, Italy accepted the EMS as an external constraint or rather a 'compulsory choice' in order not to be left behind, at the periphery of the European system. The national debate was very lively, with Carli, as

Figure 3.1 Growth rates of real GDP, 1970-2000

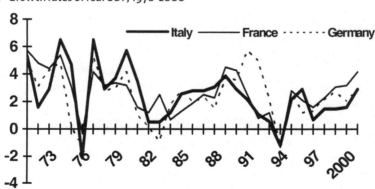

Source: OECD, *Economic Outlook*, various years

the leader of the Confindustria (the biggest business association), Ossola, as Minister for Foreign Trade, and Marcora, as Minister for Agriculture, strongly opposing entry and with the Bank of Italy highly sceptical. In the end, Italy surrendered to the German-French axis and the first pillar of the *risanamento* was posed (Dyson and Featherstone 1999).

Yet entry into the EMS was not the only example of virtuous change initiated by Italy in the late 1970s; just before entry, in August 1978, the national solidarity government had approved a first important reform of budgetary procedures (Law no. 468), aimed at controlling public expenditures more rigorously, after a period of substantial *laissez-faire* in contrast with the already mentioned article 81 of the Italian Constitution.

In fact, this article established the obligation of financial coverage for every legislative act originating additional public expenditures, but left the regulation of relationships between the government – which proposes the budget – and the Parliament – which amends and approves it – to ordinary legislation and parliamentary rules of procedure. As D'Alimonte (1978) clearly explains, the 1978 reform responded to two different pathologies developed during the glorious age of welfare state construction: the proliferation of public agencies and entities with autonomous spending powers, and the accelerating growth of public debt. The reform introduced two new devices: the financial law and the forecasting budget *(bilancio previsionale)*. The financial law was a 'substantive' mechanism (as opposed to the 'formal' nature of the budget law whose task is that of photographing the extant situation) aimed at transposing the allocation of revenues and expenditures into operational objectives, and fixing the budget changes and macro-economic targets (such as the level of public borrowing or the net financial deficit) to be achieved during the next year. The forecasting budget, articulated in a budget based on the existing legislation and a pluri-annual programmatic budget, was aimed at projecting and planning outlays and revenues in the mid-to-long term, up to the next 3-5 years. If the financial law was intended at introducing immediate changes, the forecast budget aimed at inserting such changes in a wider and longer-term policy framework (Verzichelli 1999). All in all, the reform aimed at introducing an explicit programmatic procedure that defined the expenditure targets of the public administration, safeguarding the overall equilibrium of public finances, and thus complying with the requirements of article 81 of the Constitution.

However, actual developments did not correspond, with these noble intentions. The main characteristic of the reform, i.e. its overall programmatic aim, was offset by the improper use of planning procedures made by a sequence of unstable cabinets, more inclined to exploit all opportunities they had to spend, than to stick to the budgetary targets of their predecessors. In this way the financial law soon became an occasion for distributive initiatives on behalf of various particular interests, causing the fast acceleration, rather than the much-needed containment of public expenditure.

Returning to monetary policy, the early 1980s witnessed a new wave of austerity and stability measures stemming from an important reform. Two years after entering the EMS, in 1981, a 'divorce' between the Treasury and the Bank of Italy was passed: under the new regime the latter ceased to be the last-resort buyer of unsold government bonds, and the instruments of monetary and credit policy were modified through the dismantling of direct controls on credit and of administrative obligations, in favour of a more market-oriented regulation (Addis 1987; Epstein and Schor 1987). The most immediate aim after the 'divorce' was to curb inflation through a smaller emission of currency. In addition, the new Governor Ciampi began to call for a substantial reform of the budgetary process and for a new bargaining regime in order to keep wages and productivity under control. Ciampi's repeated calls opened the way for the 1988 reform (cf. below), which introduced new rules and instruments for the planning and control of public accounts (Verzichelli 1999). As for wages and productivity, a wide political agreement among the government, trade unions and employers' associations was signed in 1983.

The restrictive monetary policy carried out by the Central Bank had a series of interrelated effects: inflation began to diminish, but the trade balance progressively deteriorated both for goods and for services, mainly due to the impossibility of using devaluation. The high interest rates, whose aim was to stimulate the inflows of compensatory financial capitals, had a depressive effect on domestic investments, which witnessed a constant decline (from 24.5 per cent of GDP in 1980 to 19.7 per cent in 1987) (OECD, Statistical Compendium 1997). Public debt continued to soar (cf. Figure 3.2), and the resort to foreign borrowing was thus inevitable.

But in the second half of the 1980s, in the wake of the oil counter-crisis, the indicators of the real economy improved significantly. The GDP growth rate surpassed 3 per cent while the inflation rate fell below 6 per cent. The trade balance showed a surplus, investments rose (from 18.8 per cent in 1986 to 20.3 per cent in 1990), and exports boomed.[1] The Single European Act (1986), soon followed by the liberalisation of financial capitals (1988), encouraged further mobility of goods and capitals outside national boundaries. Thus, for example, in the period 1981-1990 Italian foreign direct investments amounted to 28,707 million USD compared to 3,597 million USD in the previous decade (OECD, International Direct Investment Statistics 1996).

Figure 3.2 Gross public debt as a share of GDP, 1970-2000

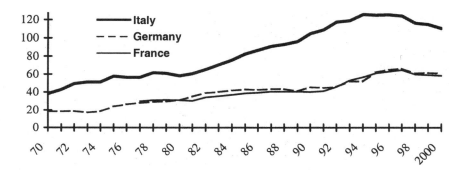

Source: OECD, *Economic Outlook*, various years

These positive economic conditions did not, however, stimulate national policy makers to tackle the problem of public finances, in spite of their declared intentions. The figures relative to public debt do not need much of a commentary. Between 1980 and 1990 public debt rose from 58.1 per cent of GDP to 104.5 per cent, as Figure 3.2 shows, reaching a record high in Europe (except for Belgium). In the same period the debt service increased from 4.7 per cent to 8.2 per cent of GDP and public deficit from 8.6 per cent to 11.1 per cent (cf. Figure 3.3) (OECD, Economic Outlook, various years).

Throughout the decade, public outlays remained higher than public receipts. The dynamics of social expenditure did not help the process, due to a number of ameliorative social reforms and the continuing growth of public employment[2]. Public revenues rose too, but not enough to keep up with total government expenditures.

The worrying growth of public debt was a major factor behind the second reform of the budgetary process, introduced in 1988 by law 362, under the auspices of Ciampi. The law established new rules and new instruments, and in particular obligation to prepare every year, prior to the financial law, a detailed 'economic and financial document' (DPEF, *Documento di programmazione economica e finanziaria),* aimed at identifying broad economic policy objectives, setting financial targets and offering budgetary projections for the medium and long term. The 1988 reform was passed in the wake of two other important changes: 1) the establishment of the so-called 'budgetary sessions' (introduced in 1983 for the lower Chamber and in 1985 for the Senate), i.e. a period starting in October entirely devoted to the approval of the financial law and the budget; and 2) the abolition of the procedure of secret voting with respect to expenditure decisions (1986).

Figure 3.3 Public deficit as a share of GDP, 1970-2000

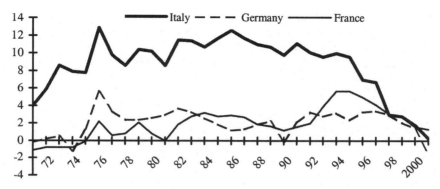

Source: OECD, *Economic Outlook*, various years

With the introduction of the DPEF, expenditure targets started to be planned well in advance, and the issue of planning was given more visibility and attention. The DPEF was presented in May (4 months prior to the actual financial law) and reported on the main macro-economic goals of the executive, linked to an assessment of the state of the national and international economy. Therefore, it represented an important constraint upon the governmental action and, at the same time, a basis for the policy reform to be proposed to (and negotiated with) the social partners. The 1988 reform, moreover, changed the nature of the financial law, moving several public policy issues onto the so-called 'connected provisions' (*provvedimenti collegati*, i.e. separate bills), and concentrating its focus on explicit changes of the legislation in force (Vassallo 2000; Verzichelli 1999).

The sequence unfolding through the DPEF, the budget law, the financial law and its 'connected bills' greatly improved the overall design of Italy's budgetary process (cf. Tables 3.1 and 3.2). However, the original aims of the 1988 reform were partially distorted by frequent delays in the presentation of the DPEF and a tendency to overburden the 'connected provisions'. The genuine implementation of the 1988 reform was also structurally limited by the persisting approval of distributive policies, whose characteristics (diffuse costs and benefits concentrated upon specific groups) well suited the aims of the five parties in government: indeed, for these parties, considering the high instability and the short duration of the political cycle, it was perfectly rational to try to attract voters through selective benefits (Dente 1991). The very short duration of the executives, with the exception of

Table 3.1   Policy reforms of the budgetary process, 1970-1989

Before the reforms   Art. 81 of the Constitution (1948)
- Budget law as the main instrument for outlays planning (general programmatic document with no operational objectives);
- Obligatory financial coverage for special and additional public expenditures;
- Ordinary law (and no constitutional rules) for the regulation of Government/Parliament relationships in the process of resource distribution.
- As a consequence: low co-ordination and no monitoring of public expenditures dynamics.

After the reforms   Law no. 468/1978
- *General aim*: introduction of a more co-ordinated and formalised 'budgetary process'; improvement of the degree of rationality and transparency of the overall budgetary policy.
- *Specific aims*: introduction of two new policy instruments: *a)* the financial law (for substantial and short-term definition of fixed expenditure targets); *b)* the so-called 'forecasting budget' (for mid- and long-term planning of outlays and revenues).

1983
- Introduction of the 'budgetary session' in the Chamber of Deputies.

1985
- Introduction of the 'budgetary session' in the Senate.

1986
- Abolition of the procedure of secret voting with respect to spending decisions.

Law no. 362/1988
- *General aim*: More emphasis on the 'programmatic' moment of the budgetary process; widening and further rationalisation of the decision-making sequences.
- *Specific aims*: Introduction of two new policy instruments: *a)* the Document for economic and financial planning (*Documento di programmazione economica e finanziaria*- DPEF) for the formulation of broad economic policy objectives, the setting of financial targets and projections for the medium- and long-term; *b)* the so-called 'connected provisions' for eventual modification of extant legislation and specific policy problems with no quantitative repercussions.

those led by Craxi, left very limited opportunities for the imposition of sacrifices – a 'competitive blame avoidance' syndrome that blocked any proposal perceived as potentially unpopular.

Table 3.2   The unfolding of the budgetary process after the reforms of the 1980s

March
The State General Accounting Office (*Ragioneria generale dello stato*) prepares outlays and revenues projections for the following year based on existing legislation.

April
Ministers present to the State General Accounting Office their own budget proposals.

May
Official presentation of the Document for Economic and Financial Planning (DPEF) on behalf of the Council of Ministers.

July
The Minister of the Economy is called to 'negotiate' the DPEF with the Inter-ministerial Committee for Economic Planning and the regional governments together with the budget law project.

September
The Committee for Economic Planning approves the DPEF and the main contents of the budget law.
The financial law, the forecasting budget and the connected provisions are defined and submitted by the Council of Ministers to Parliament.

October
The budgetary session opens up in Parliament.

December
Deadline for the budget and financial laws approval.

March
The Minister of the Economy presents the annual Report on the general economic situation of the country.

April
Deadline for extraordinary 'temporary budget' period (in case the December deadline is missed).

May
The Minister of the Economy presents to Parliament and to the Court of Accounts the first Report on current cash management.

June
Parliament receives the Court of Accounts' evaluation of the Report.

July
Parliament can approve further variations of the budget of previous year (summer budget session).

Source: Verzichelli (1999: 112)

In the early 1990s, besides the alarming conditions of public finances, other additional symptoms of crisis made their appearance: a decrease in production, the fast acceleration of labour costs and the declining competitiveness of the tertiary sector[3]. In such a difficult situation the signature in February 1992 of the Maastricht Treaty on the side of Italian government could be seen (and was indeed seen by many national and international commentators) as an act of temerariousness or even folly. And the immediate aftermath seemed to confirm this view.

The Maastricht Treaty, as is well known, established that the third and last stage for the completion of the monetary union – i.e. the creation of the Euro – was to start by 1997 (with at least seven countries joining in) or at the latest by 1999 (with no quorum). The whole process had actually begun in 1988 when at the Hannover council the EC President Delors and the German Premier Köhl prepared a joint document on the EMU's phases. In 1989 the Delors Report envisaged three different stages for the EMU and was signed by all the central banks' governors. The British governor also accepted the agreement notwithstanding the sharp opposition of the then Prime Minister, Mrs. Thatcher. As it is known, the wider 'enabling' condition for the implementation of the EMU was however the fall of the Berlin Wall and the political weakening of France in the wake of the reunification of Germany. At that point, the French government matured an interest in accelerating the process of European convergence in order to counterbalance the increasing German power. The final decisions for the EMU were then frantically taken in different quarters: within the Rome intergovernmental conference in 1990, in three ECOFIN meetings and in several meetings of EU leaders (Dyson and Featherstone 1999).

In order to participate to the common currency, member states were to comply with specific requirements: the national inflation rate was not to exceed the mean of the three countries with the lowest inflation by more than 1.5 per cent; the national long-term interest rate was not to surpass the mean of the three countries with the lowest interest rate by more than 2 per cent; the public deficit was not to exceed 3 per cent of GDP, and the public debt was not to run beyond 60 per cent of GDP, finally, the exchange rate was to be constantly within the range allowed by the EMS. Therefore, in the immediate aftermath of Maastricht, it seemed almost impossible that Italy could comply with all these requirements, although the Italian representatives, led by Prime Minister Andreotti and including Minister of the Treasury Carli and Foreign Minister De Michelis had obtained some amendments to the Treaty which were substantially favourable to Italy (cf. *infra*).

In the summer of 1992, after the negative result of the Danish referendum on EMU and in view of the French referendum to be held in September, a strong speculative attack was launched against the lira. The Central Bank tried to counterattack by wearing out currency reserves and by virtually risking a financial collapse. The risk could be avoided, however, by some interrelated circumstances that, added together, produced a sudden and rather extraordinary turn towards a virtuous adjustment.

The turning point was the appearance of the first 'technical' executive[4], led by Giuliano Amato, on the Italian political scene. The last 'political' executive of the First Republic, led by Giulio Andreotti, had been oscillating between a strategy of 'wait and see' and public announcements of financial austerity, ending up with a financial manoeuvre for 1992 cutting 55,000 billion liras (28,000 million Euros, i.e. 3.8 per cent of GDP) from the public budget. Yet this was not enough to compensate for past disequilibria. But the outbreak of the scandal called 'Tangentopoli', involving several corrupt party leaders, soon swept Andreotti's government away. After the May 1992 elections, the new Prime Minister Amato tackled the financial problems in two steps. Firstly, in July 1992 he passed an additional 'correcting' manoeuvre of 30,000 billion liras (15,000 million Euros, i.e. 2.0 per cent of GDP), and asked the Parliament to delegate to the executive the task of reforming the pension system, the national health service, the civil service and local government finances. Just two months later, in late September 1992, when the speculative attack to the currency reached its apex (the lira had already been devalued by 30 per cent), Amato managed to pass (with the financial law) an impressive financial manoeuvre of 93,000 billion liras (48,000 million Euros, i.e. 6.1 per cent of GDP), which can be considered as the first fundamental step in the direction of correcting the disequilibria of Italy's public finances, after almost fifty years of spending profligacy[5]. In the meanwhile, the executive had started to elaborate the reform plans on the four mentioned points following Law no. 421, which had delegated those matters directly to the executive.

In the academic and public debate, 1992 has come to be considered a sort of *annus fatalis*, mainly referred to as a watershed between the 'maladjustment' and the 'adjustment' era. Some authors have spoken of a 'Copernican revolution' (Salvati 1997), some of a 'big turn' (Bodo and Viesti 1997) or at least of a 'profound change' (Graziani 1998). In fact, it can hardly be denied that 1992 witnessed a successful combination of various positive events; it was the beginning of a rather fortunate chain of 'policy windows' (Kingdom

1984) that offered the conditions for the continuation of financial adjustment and thus for a positive response to international challenges. Indeed, if one considers Italy's economic performance in the rest of the 1990s, this view is clearly confirmed.

The strong devaluation (by 30 per cent) and the subsequent exit of the lira from the EMS, were at the basis of a considerable export increase that allowed Italy to catch up and gain a remarkable position in international trade. The renewal of government bonds was assured by the high levels of private savings[6] and the abolition of wage indexations in 1992 generated a positive cooling of wage dynamics (Quadrio Curzio 1996; Signorini and Visco 1997).

Another crucial factor behind the new virtuous circle was the ability shown by the Italian political and technical negotiators to play two different games. The first game aimed at linking Italy with the first 'coach' of the EMU (i.e. the first group of countries to form the new club), and implied the reduction of the monetary power asymmetry with respect to Germany. The second game aimed at 'exploiting' monetary integration, with particular regard to the third stage, as an external constraint, strict enough to force the Italian government to neutralise and overcome the numerous obstacles to financial adjustment represented by the mutual vetoes posed by political parties (Ferrera 1991; Dyson and Featherstone 1996; 1999; Radaelli 2000). Furthermore, the Amato government was successful in breaking away from the past: its executive was entrusted with important delegated powers by Parliament and thus could negotiate directly with the trade unions, since the Parliament, delegitimised by the scandal of Tangentopoli, stayed on the sidelines[7].

These conditions also continued to facilitate the action of the Ciampi government, another 'technical' executive, which managed to gain new international credibility, freeing itself from the hold of domestic political parties. Ciampi continued the direct relationship with the trade unions, negotiating with them important structural reforms such as the abolition of the automatic system of wage indexation (the notorious *scala mobile*), the privatisation of employment and placement services and the reform of collective bargaining, favoured by the support of the President of the Republic and the former Communist Party – renamed as Democratic Party of the Left (PDS) – in search for legitimacy as potential governing party (Vassallo 2000). The Ciampi government (1993-94), like the preceding Amato government, acted in two steps. Firstly, in May 1993, it approved a 'correcting' manoeuvre of 12,500 billion liras (6,400 million Euros, i.e. 0.8 per cent of GDP); subsequently, in September 1993, it presented the financial law in advance, reducing public expenditures by 28,000 billion liras (14,000 million Euros, i.e. 1.8 per cent of GDP) and introducing a package of measures on civil service reform.

The scenario radically changed with the shift from the technical governments of Amato and Ciampi to the political executive of Berlusconi, the first government elected in 1994 after the reform that introduced the majority principle in the electoral system. The fragmentation of the coalition he was supposed to lead, consisting of three different parties (Alleanza Nazionale, Forza Italia and the Lega Nord), and the choice not to continue that concertation with interest organisations that had been actively pursued by his predecessors disintegrated the alliance. Berlusconi tried to push through a sweeping pension reform, but the trade union opposition and the defection of the Lega Nord on this delicate issue precipitated a government crisis. The 1995 financial law, which envisaged 21,000 billion liras (10,800 million Euros, i.e. 1.3 per cent of GDP) of additional revenue and 29,000 billion liras (14,900 million Euros, i.e. 1.8 per cent of GDP) of expenditure cuts on pensions and health care, underwent an endless series of corrections, negotiations and compromises that weakened much of its efficacy. The lira's re-entry into the EMS again became uncertain.

After Berlusconi, another technical executive, led by Lamberto Dini, a former Director of the Bank of Italy and Minister of the Treasury in the Berlusconi government, managed to pass the pension reform, introduced by Law no. 345 of 1995. The Dini government, in spite of some initial hesitation, went on with the strategy of austerity and financial adjustment: a correcting manoeuvre of almost 20,000 billion liras (10,300 million Euros, i.e. 1.1 per cent of GDP) in the spring of 1995 and the financial law for 1996 introduced a new series of cuts, including in particular the suspension of recruitment in the public sector, another inlay of the mosaic flooring that powered the way into the Euro.

The Dini government was then followed by Romano Prodi, the leader of the Olive Tree coalition, which won the elections of April 1996. Since the electoral campaign, Prodi indicated the entry into the EMU as the main theme of his governing strategy[8]. In the 1996 Document for Financial and Economic Planning, the 3 per cent target for public deficit was already mentioned, even though the drastic adjustment measures needed to reach this target were not fully spelled out. In September 1996, in the Valencia meeting with Aznar, Prodi tried to convince the Spanish Prime Minister to join forces in order to obtain a more flexible interpretation of the convergence rules, but Aznar did not go along (Spaventa and Chiorazzo 2000). The only way to make it into the EMU was to launch yet another extraordinary fiscal manoeuvre.

Table 3.3 The main steps of Italian financial adjustment in the 1990s

Executive	Year	Manoeuvre	% GDP
Andreotti	1991	Financial manoeuvre of 55,000 billion liras of cuts.	3.8%
Amato	1992	Correcting manoeuvre of 30,000 billion liras in the spring.	2.0%
		Financial manoeuvre passed with the financial law of 93,000 billion liras.	6.1%
Ciampi	1993	Structural reforms (privatisation of employment and placement services, reform of collective bargaining and abolition of the automatic wage indexation).	
		Correcting manoeuvre of 12,500 billion liras.	0.8%
		Financial law reducing public expenditures by 28,000 billion liras.	1.8%
Berlusconi	1994	The 1995 financial law envisaged:	
		21,000 billion liras of additional revenues;	1.3%
		29,000 billion liras of cuts in health care and pensions expenditures.	1.8%
Dini	1995	In the spring passed a correcting manoeuvre of 20,000 billion liras; The financial law introduced a series of cuts including the suspension of recruitment in the public sector.	1.1%
Prodi	1996	Financial law of more than 60,000 billion liras based on: a series of cuts, including the pensions reform and fiscal restrictions; a 'tax for Europe' levied on all incomes.	3.2%

In spite of internal contrasts with *Rifondazione Comunista* (RC: an old-style communist party that was necessary in parliament to reach the majority), Prodi managed to pass a financial law of more than 60,000 billion liras (30,900 million Euros, i.e. 3.2 per cent of GDP) based on two different sets of components: a series of cuts (including, as we shall see, a new pension reform) and fiscal restrictions, and a specific 'tax for Europe' levied on all incomes. Heavily criticized by the international press, the latter was a crucial component of the 'confidence trick' that Prodi and Ciampi played *vis-à-vis* the international markets. The trick consisted of: 1) committing to meet the 3 per cent deficit target through a tax accompanied by the promise to pay it back; so as to 2) obtain public recognition (informal and then formal) of EMU admission, which would rapidly bring down Italian interest rates and thus the debt service; and 3) creating room for repaying the tax at a later time. The trick succeeded: the Euro-tax was actually and largely paid back in 1998. But it also succeeded because it could build on the structural reforms already passed in 1996/1995 (Chiorazzo and Spaventa 1999). The RC party led by Bertinotti, with much hesitation and after having obtained the promise of introducing a limit of 35 hours to weekly working time by 2001 on the part of the executive, finally gave its approval to Prodi's financial law, allowing the 'trick' to unleash its virtuous effects.

The Prodi government also introduced a third important reform of the budgetary process through Law no. 94 of 1997, strongly advocated by the Minister of the Treasury Ciampi and the General Director of the Treasury Mario Draghi, another protagonist of the Italian financial adjustment in the 1990s. The 1997 reform deeply simplified the structure of the budget, reducing the budgetary items to be approved by Parliament, and establishing homogeneous budgetary centres under the supervision of single directors responsible for each of them. It also made the ratification procedures of the Parliament easier and more intelligible (cf. Table 3.4)[9].

While launching a phase of wide-ranging reformist activity, the Prodi government witnessed a marked improvement of Italy's macro-economic performance. Between 1992 and 1998 inflation fell from 5.0 per cent to 2.0 per cent, public deficit from 10.7 per cent to 2.8 per cent, and the public debt, after the 1994 peak of 125 per cent of GDP, gradually diminished (1998 = 116.3 per cent). The lira re-entered the EMS. Interest rates started to go down, and hopes for investments were revived. Between 1996 and 1998 the amount of Italian privatisations was the highest in Europe: the most important public enterprises (SME, Enichem, Eni, Telecom, etc.) and the most renowned public banks (Cariplo, Banca di Roma, San Paolo) were sold, thus alleviating the state budget. One year later, in May 1998, under the Prodi government, Italy finally joined the EMU with the first group of countries, in satisfactory compliance with the Maastricht parameters.

Yet the support of *Rifondazione Comunista* to the Prodi government did not last for long, and broke up exactly when Prodi's third financial law (for the year 1999) was in the pipeline. The RC leader, Bertinotti, asked the government repeatedly for a concrete 'signal' of a leftward policy turn, especially in terms of public subsidies for the unemployed of the south. Prodi did not accept Bertinotti's diktat – which would have meant going back to the passive and distributive policies of the past in contrast with the reformist policies of the centre-left coalition and the EU's orientations – and the Olive

Tree government collapsed in October 1998. A new coalition, led by D'Alema (leader of the Democrats of the Left, main heir of the old PCI) with the (unexpected) participation of former President Cossiga and his small centre party (the UDR), took its place.

The D'Alema government, the first executive led by a post-communist leader, managed to approve Prodi's draft financial law almost in its integral version and to pass some of the reforms of the previous government which were still standing by, such as the one concerning the national budget, introduced by Law no. 208 of 1999. The bill's general aim was that of conforming to supranational prescriptions and procedures and in particular to the Growth and Stability Pact's constraints officially stated in the 1997 Amsterdam Treaty. The budget calendar was slightly modified, and the government was given a stronger role in the co-ordination and guidance of the whole process (Vassallo and Verzichelli 2003). But the reform represented also the occasion to change and correct the nature of the financial law and of connected provisions, widening the contents of the former and limiting the boundaries of the latter. Thanks to the new rules, the financial law became a wider container for the modification of all public policies in force while connected provisions were turned into specific policy documents aimed at sectoral policy change, to be approved in the springtime and no longer in the month of November (cf. Table 3.3).

The difficulty in maintaining the coalition united – due to the plurality of parties with different programmatic standpoints –, the difficulty in carrying on the structural reform of the welfare state urged by various international organisations, and finally the weakening of the centre-left coalition in the

---

Table 3.4: Policy reforms of the budgetary process, 1990-2000

Law no. 94/1997
– *General aim*: further simplification and rationalisation of budget formulation and approval.
– *Specific aims*: identification of pre-determined budgetary provisional units (*unità provisionali di base*); widening of Ministries' top civil servants-responsibilities; simplification of parliamentary procedures; strengthening of the government's role in the budgetary process.

Law no. 208/1999
– *General aim*: Adjustment of the budgetary procedure to European constraints (i.e.: the 1997 Growth and Stability Pact); modification of the financial law for the introduction of spending measures.
– *Specific aims*: micro-changes in the budgetary calendar and session; widening of the contents to be regulated by the financial law and turning of connected provisions into sectoral policy change documents.

2000 regional elections posed many obstacles in the way of the Prime Minister who in April 2000 was replaced by the last executive of the 13th legislature (1996-2001) led, again, by Giuliano Amato. This executive was also the last one of the centre-left coalition, bound to lose the elections in May 2001.

However, notwithstanding the uncertainties caused by political instability, the post-1992 virtuous circle has borne fruit. As mentioned above, some pre-conditions for the post-1992 virtuous circle had already been posed in the previous decade; and several shadows still spoil the picture today, as will be shown later. But the fact remains that the 1990s will be remembered as a crucial decade for Italy's firm and irreversible 'anchoring' to the European core: one of the few national unifying grand objectives of the country ever since the 1950s.

4   Italy's international economic profile: the recovery of the 1990s

Italy's remarkable macro-economic adjustment has been accompanied by significant changes in the country's international economic profile, especially as regards exports, alliances and partnerships with foreign companies and direct financial investments. Compared to the previous decade, a strong diversification in the geographic areas of destination, in the subjects and in the instruments of international activities can be noticed. While in the 1980s most of Italy's trade was concentrated in the EC countries, in the 1990s Eastern Europe, the Asian countries and developing countries have become relevant destinations as well.

In addition, large firms, traditionally highly specialised in export activities, have been joined by small- and medium-sized firms. Contrary to what was expected by some analysts, the depreciation of the lira favoured small companies in search of innovative investments (Cossentino, Pyke and Sengenberger 1997; Brusco and Paba 1997). From 1992 to 1996 the openness of the total economy (calculated by adding the export to the production sold in the internal market and exposed to competition from imported goods and services) jumped from 35.5 per cent to 43.3 per cent of GDP (OECD, Statistical Compendium 1997). In 1993 the export of goods and services grew by 12.5 per cent, one of the highest values in the OECD area, compared to only 0.7 per cent in the previous year. In the same year the balance of trade grew from 0.3 per cent to 3.4 per cent of GDP, reaching the peak of 4.1 per cent in 1995 (OECD, Statistical Compendium 1997). It is only after 1996 that the crisis of East-Asian countries started to have a negative impact on Italy's export (European Economy 1999).

Besides the export of goods, other forms of foreign direct participation and financial investments have flourished: collaborative ventures, technological agreements, co-design and co-making (Cominotti and Mariotti 1997). From 1985 to 1995 the stock of Italian FDI grew from 3.8 per cent to 8.7 per cent of GDP (Faini *et al.* 1999).

In 1995 the geographical articulation of FDI (measured on the basis of the number of employees) was as follows: 249,648 in Western Europe, 48,780 in North America and 297,119 in developing countries. In the same year more than six hundred Italian multinationals could be counted, with 1,842 affiliates all over the world, and the total of Italian employment abroad reached 595,547 units, about 12.6 per cent of national industrial employment. More recent estimates calculate that from 1986 to 1998 total employment in affiliates of Italian multinationals in Central and Eastern Europe grew from 2,100 units to 102,503, i.e. 20 per cent of total Italian employment abroad (Barba Navaretti 1999).

If we compare this figure with those of the main investor countries, we notice – as stated previously – that Italian multinational activity in the 1990s was still rather low (the number of French employees in manufacturing foreign affiliates was 1,359,000 in 1990; the German ones amounted to 1,868,000 in 1995 and those of the US to 4,376,600 in the same year) (Faini *et al.* 1999; European Economy 1999).

However, this process of internationalisation has not fully alleviated Italy's historical problems. Exports have indeed increased, but the 'specialised polarisation' of Italian industry has intensified: maximum export in the traditional sectors (shoes, clothes, textiles, ceramics, furnishing) and relatively small in the other sectors (especially high-tech). In addition, Italy has remained poorly attractive for foreign investors, given the scarce reliability of the state bureaucracy, public services and communication systems. R&D expenditure is still among the lowest in the OECD countries. Between 1982 and 1994 R&D expenditure grew from 0.9 per cent to 1.2 per cent of GDP: a small increase if compared to the United States, where it rose from 2.6 per cent to 2.8 per cent of GDP between 1982 and 1992, or France, where R&D expenditure grew from 2.0 per cent to 2.4 per cent between 1982 and 1993 (OECD, Main Science Indicators, various years). More seriously, as we will show in the next section, the social and economic gap between a highly industrialised north and a backward south has continued to persist and even widened.

5   Internationalisation and national employment: a multi-faceted Italy

It is not easy to explore the relationships between internationalisation and the employment/welfare regimes in Italy: empirical investigations of these issues are still scant, and the high diversification of Italy's regional and sectoral realities makes it difficult to elaborate unitary interpretative models.

This is especially true for the internationalisation-employment nexus. The effects of the former on the latter have been different according to the local conditions of both factors and actors. Large and small firms, exposed and sheltered sectors, northern and southern regions have all given their own response to exogenous challenges. The winds of internationalisation have blown upon all regional and sectoral realities of the country, in a differentiated and often subtle way, sometimes stimulating, sometimes disturbing or reshuffling the existing configuration of actors and resources. The overall positive effects of the internationalisation process have intertwined with pre-existing conditions, economic processes and institutions. Where actors were already showing innovative capacities and were surrounded by a dynamic social and political environment, they were also able to take advantage of the new international opportunities, triggering off virtuous circles of development and growth, also in terms of employment: this was especially the story of industrial districts and small/medium enterprises. Where instead actors were already facing great economic difficulties and showed weak innovative capacities, internationalisation has created more problems than opportunities: this has largely been the story of the *Mezzogiorno*. In this latter case, however, the blame must be put less on internationalisation *per se* (a factor that has only worsened an originally complex and fragile situation) than on local conditions and general institutional rigidities embedded in the past.

According to the most recent economic literature, Italian employment has not suffered much from the growing openness of markets[10]. For the Italian case there is no evidence of those trends that are typically associated with internationalisation in other industrial countries, such as increasing unemployment among low-skilled and uneducated workers and/or a shift of wages in favour of skilled employees. Moreover, there appears to be no significant correlation through time between the standard set of trade indicators – such as the trade balance or the degree of import penetration – and labour market conditions. In fact, the data reveal that Italy has so far witnessed a relatively low degree of import penetration from low wage countries (potentially harmful to national employment) and that the growing internationalisation of Italian firms (including the increased number of employees in foreign affiliates of Italian multinationals) bears much less responsibility for the unemployment problems in the manufacturing sector than developments in production technology. To put it in the words of a recent, well-articulated econometric study:

> '... international trade does not seem to have been a primary cause for job losses or increased inequality in Italy. On the contrary, there is a presumption that the overall tendency towards increased international trade in the past two decades may have benefited, on average, Italian workers: increasing trade possibilities have resulted in growing demand for labour intensive manufacturers' (Faini *et al.* 1999: 129).

What explains this relatively low vulnerability of Italy's national employment to economic internationalisation? According to the debate, the answer lies with the peculiar model of Italian specialisation in international trade. This model is primarily based on labour-intensive productions in traditional sectors and in some specialised suppliers industries, potentially very vulnerable to the competition of labour-abundant, low-wage economies. But within these sectors,

> 'Italy is mainly specialised in the top end of the vertically differentiated spectrum of products. Many of these products are characterised by a relatively high level of skill intensity and by a price elasticity which is not high and is decreasing over time' (*ibidem*: 106).

It is this peculiar pattern that has allowed Italy to survive well – in aggregate terms – in the new environment, taking advantage of profitable niches in a growing and opening world trade.

Two recent analyses (Barba Navaretti 1999; Barba Navaretti *et al.* 2002) concerning the impact of internationalisation on firms' employment levels allow us to confirm this interpretation. According to the results of the first one (Barba Navaretti 1999), focused on the textile and clothing sector, the steady growth of imports due to the growing liberalisation of markets contributed modestly to the decline of the domestic demand of labour, since there were at least three other endogenous and institutional factors pushing in that direction: the rigidity of the Italian labour market, technological change and the particular mode of organisation of production. Italy managed to increase its competitive advantages in the export markets between 1990 and 1996, owing not only to the devaluation of the lira in 1992, but also to the widespread presence of small firms and industrial districts endowed with high levels of mobility and flexibility of adjustment (so as to escape some of the heaviest rigidities of the Italian labour market). Moreover, the data collected in this first investigation show that the investments in low wage countries by Italian firms allow them to maintain, instead of reducing, their employment levels in Italy.

The second research project examined in more detail the effects in terms of employment of firms' delocalisation strategies: 876 companies with at least 50 employees were selected. In 1994 – the starting year of the inquiry – 608 companies had never invested abroad, while the other 268 already operated as multinationals. In the subsequent three years, 64 companies in the first group tried to delocalise production outside Italy, while 110 in the second group strengthened their foreign activity. Internationalisation processes gave remarkable results. In the companies where at least one branch had been opened abroad, the average number of employees increased from 110 in 1994 to 127.8 in 1998 and domestic profits from 100 to 142.9. In the firms which in contrast remained tied to domestic markets, employment reached only 117.3 and profits 133.9. The same was true for multinationals; in those that broadened their activity abroad, employment grew by 24.6 per cent and profits by 39.7 per cent against, respectively, 14.6 per cent and 34 per cent for those witnessing no expansion abroad (Barba Navaretti *et al.* 2002).

Yet this favourable match between some niches of the international environment and the characteristics of Italian production may not last forever. In fact, the profitable niches of Italian producers are increasingly at risk in the wake of some forthcoming developments of world trade[11]. Thanks to these niches, however, the Italian economy has been able to withstand, in the 1980s and especially in the 1990s, the de-stabilising winds of globalisation. Italy's unemployment problems thus appear to be primarily connected to domestic rather than exogenous factors.

This relatively optimistic assessment must be qualified, however, by geographical area. The intensification of international trade has in fact thrown new light on Italy's regional and sectoral cleavages. First and foremost it is necessary to distinguish between three different Italies: the industrialised north – and especially the historical industrial triangle of Piedmont, Lombardy and Liguria (first Italy); the 'classical' *Mezzogiorno*, characterised by backwardness and underdevelopment (second Italy); and the so-called 'third Italy', comprising the north-east, Emilia-Romagna, Tuscany, Umbria and the central Adriatic rim (Marche, Abruzzi). The sectoral composition of the three Italies is also divergent. In the north companies are mainly large and specialised in manufacturing and services. The third Italy is mainly based on family-led small firms and on industrial districts specialised in those products which are at the edge of Italy's competitiveness: textiles and apparel, footwear, ceramics, precision mechanics. Southern regions, though it is not fully correct to consider them as an homogeneous territory, are characterised by a mixed productive profile: large (and declining) firms in the chemical, iron and steel industry (the old traditional sectors of the state-assisted industrial development launched in the 1950s); small firms mainly operating in the (backward) constructions and tertiary sector; and large public bureaucracies.

The territorial concentration of firms with different sizes is particularly significant. If we consider for instance the manufacturing sector, we discover that the biggest part of total employment belongs to firms with 1 to 49 employees (more than 60 per cent in the mid-1990s), attesting to the typical polarisation of Italian industry, and that from the 1970s to the 1990s employment in companies with more than 50 employees constantly declined, while in companies with 1 to 50 employees it increased remarkably. The growth of employment in small firms has thus not been negatively affected or slowed down by international competition (Brusco and Paba 1997). Compared to northern and southern firms, the small and medium-sized companies of the 'third Italy' have registered a remarkably positive reaction to international pressures. Their export capacity has grown closer to that of larger firms, as these figures show: in 1992 the exported volume of sales amounted to 18 per cent for firms with 20-49 employees; 22.4 per cent for those with 50-99 employees, 25.6 per cent for firms with 100-199 employees and 23.5 per cent for firms with 200-499 employees. As regards employment, from 1971 to 1991 it rose from 47 per cent to 49.9 per cent whereas, as said before, it declined in big firms from 27.2 per cent to 23.1 per cent (*ibidem*).

There is a kind of a paradox in these data. According to the economic literature of the 1980s, the nexus between small firms and globalisation should be a negative one: compared to big firms, small companies should find it hard to internationalise due not only to size, but also to the lack of human/financial resources and technological instruments and to the fierce competition of multinationals. But in the Italian case these disadvantages have not played a significant role because of the high product specialisation of small firms on the one hand and the outstanding degree of entrepreneurship and innovation that traditionally characterise the 'industrial districts' culture on the other. Small firms seem to have successfully exploited the new opportunities offered by internationalisation, perceived as a stimulus to expansion and change.

Table 3.5 Employment and imports: sectoral trends

1992-1996	Change in employment (%)	Change in import penetration level	Import penetration level (average value)
Mineral & non-mineral products	-3.8	4.2	35.68
Non-metallic mineral products	-2.4	1.2	10.83
Chemical products	-3.7	3.8	35.43
Metal products	-2.1	2.7	8.10
Agricultural & industrial machinery	-0.8	3.4	31.53
Office machinery	-1.5	-0.8	79.33
Electrical apparatus	-0.3	8.4	14.75
Motor vehicles	-3.3	4.2	57.75
Food, beverage and tobacco	-1.7	1.5	17.83
Textile & apparel	-1.1	3.6	19.68
Footwear & leather	-1.3	11.5	31.65
Wood & wood products	-1.9	1.1	11.23
Paper, paper products & painting	-2.0	2.1	11.78
Rubber & plastic products	-0.4	2.2	19.03
Total manufacturing	-1.7	4.2	26.45

Source: Faini et al. (1999:120).

Large firms mainly operating in the north of Italy have given a more variegated response to international challenges. The statement that globalisation has had positive effects on employment holds true in general terms, but must be qualified by time. The available data on employment in manufacturing reveal in fact a different, time-related vulnerability to the openness of the economy with both contractionist and expansionary effects.

Two different periods can be identified: the first from 1985 to 1992 and the second starting after 1992. In the first phase the big rise in imports, which was the main result of the export strategies of the 'early internationalising countries' (US, Japan, Germany, etc.), reduced the increase in the Italian labour demand (from +9 per cent to + 5 per cent). After the devaluation of 1992, however, the trend inverted, and export growth allowed compensation of the losses of the past and had a remarkable impact on labour demand (De Nardis and Paternò 1997). It is in fact starting from 1992 that Italy, which is undoubtedly a 'late internationaliser', begins to catch up, and the nexus between internationalisation and employment performance becomes a very loose one.

This is revealed by Table 3.5 (drawn from the already mentioned analysis by Faini et al. 1999), in which the changes in sectoral import penetration from 1992 to 1996 are connected to employment dynamics. The growth of import penetration, which is particularly remarkable for footwear, leather (11.5 per cent) and electrical apparatus (8.4 per cent), does not produce a correspondent reduction of employment, which is instead weak (-1.3 per cent and -0.3 per cent, respectively) and better than the aggregate one (-1.7 per cent).

International challenges have thus combined with domestic economic dynamics, only indirectly conditioning employment and unemployment performance. Prior to 1992 large Italian firms did not seem to be able to respond to the import boom with expansionary strategies, preferring to stick to domestic markets; only after 1992 did devaluation and economic recovery encourage a fuller exploration of European and world markets. The export boom was so intense as to push employers to enlarge and diversify production with positive repercussions on employment levels.

Still different is the picture of the *Mezzogiorno*, which at first sight may appear as the only loser of globalisation. And in fact the big recession of 1991, the stopping of state-aid legislation in 1992, the reform of EC structural funds and the association agreements between the European Union and East-European countries have all contributed to make the 'old' problems of Southern unemployment and poverty even worse (Cafiero 1997).

But, once again, the problems of the *Mezzogiorno* seem more the product of the economic and industrialisation strategies of the past than of globalisation challenges. In particular, de-industrialisation and the end of state subsidies, which are the result of the national legislation of the 1990s, are at the basis of the employment collapse notable in this area of the country. Between 1991 and 1996, 600,000 jobs were lost (Bodo and Viesti 1997). Such an employment slump has no equivalents in the past. De-industrialisation refers to the dismantling and the abandoning of the big state-assisted industries that had been created in the 1950s. The sectoral specialisation of these firms – iron and steel, petrol-chemical, metallurgy – did not keep up with the times: these firms were not able to undertake processes of reconversion (in this respect, many authors speak of a 'lost industrialisation', that is of a sudden jump from old traditional industries to tertiarisation).

But the decline of employment has been particularly dramatic in the sectors which were more strictly dependent on state financial aid: agriculture (-24 per cent between 1992 and 1996), construction (-19 per cent in the same period) and trade (-9 per cent in the same period). In 1996 less than 38 out of 100 southern Italians of working age were employed (52 in the centre-north) (Bodo and Viesti 1997:73). Marked by such a low employment rate and by a high concentration of long-term unemployment, the *Mezzogiorno* stands out as one of the most backward regions of the EU. In these ailing eco-

Figure 3.4 Total, centre-northern and southern unemployment rates, 1980-2000

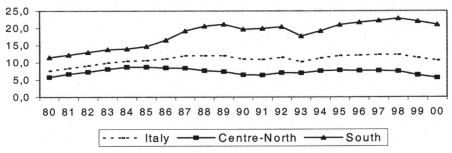

Source: Istat, *Forze di Lavoro*, various years

Figure 3.5 Youth unemployment rates in Italy compared to the OECD average, 1980-2000

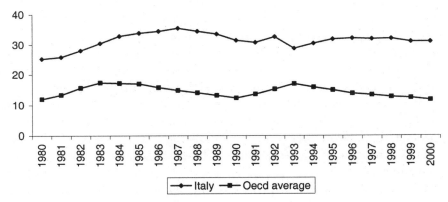

Source: Istat, *Forze di Lavoro*, various years; OECD, *Labor Force Statistics*, various years

nomic conditions, the establishment of the EMU is very likely to aggravate problems (at least in the short run): the disappearance of the exchange rate as a mechanism of adjustment requires higher factor mobility and higher price and wage flexibility – elements which remain quite foreign to the *Mezzogiorno*'s political and economic tradition.

If we now look at unemployment, as mentioned several times, this is particularly concentrated in the south and in some specific categories of the labour force (women and the young). From 1980 to 1998 unemployment in the centre-north increased from 5.8 per cent to 7.5 per cent, only returning to 5.6 per cent in 2000. In the *Mezzogiorno*, from 1980 to 2000, it rose from 11.5 per cent to 21 per cent (cf. Figure 3.4). In the same period, female unemployment increased from 13.2 per cent to 14.3 per cent, while male unemployment increased from 4.8 per cent to 9 per cent (Istat, Forze di lavoro, various years). The 1980s were characterised by a rapid increase of female participation in the labour market (also due to the 'baby boom' of the 1960s), but the demand of labour was not sufficient to absorb the increased supply. As for youth unemployment, Italy holds a record (cf. Figure 3.5): it soared from 25.2 per cent in 1980 to 35.5 per cent in 1987 and remained steadily above 30 per cent throughout the entire 1990s (31.5 per cent in 1990, 32.2 per cent in 1996, 31.1 per cent in 2000, while the OECD average in 2000 amounted to 11.8 per cent), surpassing the alarming level of 60 per cent in Calabria, Campania and Sicily (*ibidem*).

Besides mass unemployment (10 per cent in 2000), a high diffusion of the black economy should be noted: 26 per cent of GDP in 1998, which means 40 per cent of the labour force in the south and 16 per cent in the centre-north. The black economy is mainly concentrated in the service sector (76 per cent) while in the agricultural and industrial ones its incidence is more limited (respectively 12 per cent and 6 per cent) (Tartaglione 2001).

Finally, Italy is internationally notorious for the lowest diffusion of part-time workers compared to the other European countries (5.1 per cent in 1980 and 8.4 per cent in 2000) (Istat, Forze di lavoro various years).

As will be shown in the next section, the opening of international markets and the related higher mobility of citizens and workers has shaken rigid and protected labour markets, like the Italian one, at their roots. And the adjustment of the Italian labour market and labour legislation has been slow, partial and in some parts ineffective, missing a big opportunity of change in order to relieve Italy of old problems and institutional rigidities through a healthy injection of flexibility.

6   Internationalisation and social policy

The impact of internationalisation on social policy has been more straightforward – at least in institutional terms. The *vincolo esterno* (i.e. the constraints posed directly or indirectly by international regimes and especially by the EU) has in fact become an increasingly powerful stimulus for pushing through measures of welfare retrenchment and rationalisation on the side of the national executive.

In order to meet the parameters set by the Maastricht Treaty, Italy had to seriously tackle the problems of public debt and public deficit. The pressing need to reduce both, with a view to joining EMU with the first group of countries, fostered a climate of permanent financial emergency. The margin of

Figure 3.6 Total tax revenue and total expenditure in Italy and total tax revenue in the OECD, 1970-2000

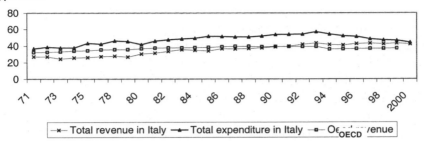

Source: OECD, Revenue Statistics, various years

Figure 3.7 Old-age & survivors expenditure and other social protection expenditure as a share of GDP in 1999

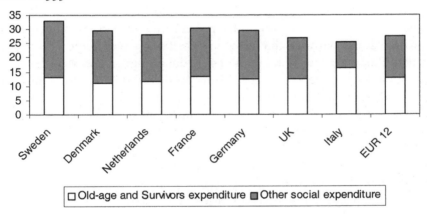

Source: Eurostat, Social Protection in Europe (2002)

manoeuvre for tax increases was extremely narrow. Public revenues had been growing very rapidly since the early 1980s, turning Italy into a relatively big tax country by international standards. In the early 1990s the high level of taxation, which is clearly shown in Figure 3.6, and its uneven distribution (due to widespread tax evasion by some categories) started to provoke clear symptoms of a tax revolt, especially among northern (self-employed) taxpayers. In such an environment, expenditure cutbacks were the only viable strategy for containing public deficits and debt: and social benefits immediately became the prime target of the new policy of *risanamento*.

It is true that in a comparative perspective the size of the Italian welfare system was (and still is) not out of proportion with respect to other countries. Current social expenditures amounted to 25.8 per cent of GDP in 1993: this percentage was the sixth lowest in the EU (which had an average of 27.7 per cent), while in the same year Italy's GDP per head was the fourth highest (EC 1995). Six years later, in 1999, social expenditure remained almost unchanged (25.3 per cent of GDP) and below the European average (27.5 per cent)[12]. Thus Italy could hardly be considered to be a big spender, as shown in Figure 3.7. Yet in domestic public debates around the mid-1990s, welfare programmes were commonly indicted as the main culprit for the country's severe financial problems and, more generally, for its serious politico-institutional predicament.

Why this paradox – in the absence of a 'New Right' majority? There were in the early 1990s a number of reasons that can explain this. First, despite its relatively modest aggregate size, social expenditure was still (and by far) the largest item of total government outlay. Second, both the pension and the health system were in rather shaky financial and (in the case of health) organisational conditions. Demographic projections showed alarming scenarios for the future: with no change of legislation, pension expenditure was expected to increase from ca.14 per cent to ca. 23 per cent of GDP between the early 1990s and the year 2040 (Ministero del Tesoro 1998). Third, the deficits of legality and efficiency mentioned in the second chapter had fostered a mounting 'negativism' against the *stato assistenziale* (a rather pejorative term) in public debates, offering a potential source of legitimisation to retrenchment measures. The combination of peculiarly intense fiscal constraints – disciplined by the EU – and the 'bad quality' of Italy's social spending opened in other words opportunities for a strategy of welfare reform in the name of three (largely apolitical) objectives, i.e. the *risanamento finanziario*, social equity and efficiency recuperation. However faulty and incomplete it may be, this strategy has significantly changed the overall profile of Italian welfare during the 1990s.

The strategy of *risanamento* clashed with the resistance opposed by all affected interests, and particularly by trade unions. This resistance has been partially overcome not only thanks to an open and consensual bargaining style (as will be shown in Chapter V), but also through a patient persuasive action about the long-term advantages connected with financial adjustment and the entry into the Monetary Union, particularly in terms of lower interests on debt. This latter point had a crucial impact on the reform process: the financial adjustment was presented as a 'fight against financial rent', leading to tangible advantages for all workers. In fact in the early 1990s, a relatively modest bank deposit amounting to 260 million liras (135,000 Euros), fully invested in state bonds with an interest rate of 9.5 per cent, could produce a financial rent equivalent to the average yearly wage of a metalworker (Pennacchi 1998). The 'bet' proposed by the government to the social partners (and repeatedly supported by Amato, Ciampi, Dini and Prodi both publicly and privately) was to accept sacrifices (in particular, cuts of social benefits and wage restraint) in order to reduce the enormous and unproductive interests on public debt, divert the resources thus recovered to other objectives, and give birth to a virtuous circle of growth, new public investments and more balanced redistribution (Ciampi 1998).

In retrospect, it can be said that for the most part this 'bet' was won: between 1992 and 1998 interest on public debt declined from 10.2 per cent to 6.4 per cent of GDP, in line with a downward trend that will probably last for a long time, due to the convergence of Italian interest rates with those of Germany, and the gradual restructuring of the debt stock (i.e. a positive consequence of the EMU on Italian public finances). The reduction in interest rates has also produced other advantages, beyond the domain of public finances: for example, the business sector has obtained relevant savings on its commercial loans, and ordinary citizens have got savings on mortgage loans. Which have been, in more detail, the timing, modalities and contents of the 'structural' reforms of the 1990s in the wake of internationalisation and the European integration process? Have these reforms been effective? We will now turn to these questions.

IV   The Cycle of Reform

1   A difficult path

The internationalisation process and European integration have spurred a decisive wave of reforms not only with respect to the overall management of public finances (illustrated in the preceding chapter), but also in welfare and labour market matters. In order to correct the financial disequilibria, several old schemes and programmes had to be revised and restructured, also in order to respond to new challenges: chronic structural unemployment and the need to extend social protection to marginal groups while at the same time keeping costs under control.

As elsewhere in Europe, the 1990s have brought about fundamental structural social policy changes in Italy. During the 1980s some important seeds of change had already been planted, but the contextual conditions were not ripe for the maturation of broad reforms. The increasing international integration acted as a positive incentive to tackle the issue of unemployment, by experimenting with new policy strategies already adopted abroad, mainly centred on the deregulation of labour legislation and on the introduction of active measures. However, these new efforts represented only a drop in a sea of passive policies and subsidy-oriented programmes, increasingly expensive for the public budget. In the welfare arena too, the attempts at introducing structural reforms were repeatedly frustrated by the mass of resistance of past policies and acquired entitlements. The policies inherited from the 1970s revealed a deeply institutionalised nature and hence high hostility to change and innovation.

Only in the 1990s did the new wave of reforms start to produce substantial results. Some reforms planned in the 1980s were effectively legislated, and new measures and programmes were introduced in order to modernise the labour market and restructure the welfare state in a more rational way. The institutional changes that marked the transition from the First to the Second Republic, the new co-operative and consensual style of interest intermediation adopted by the executive and the social partners and, more fundamentally, the perspective of the European monetary integration, have been the main components of a new scenario of structural change: the end of public monopoly on placement offices, the decentralisation of employment services, new active policies and new styles of decision-making (as a response to the prescriptions of the European employment strategy) in the sphere of labour market regulation; the pension and health care reforms in the sphere of social protection.

2   The 1980s: the uncertain deregulation of the labour market

The evolution of labour policies in the 1980s can be broken down into two distinct phases, during which different policy goals were pursued: 1981-1983 and 1984-1989. In the first years of the new decade, the government responded to the second oil crisis-based recession and to the loss of employment in large firms in a defensive way, by expanding already existing income support programmes and by introducing a new onerous passive policy, such as pre-retirement benefits. In the second half of the decade, in a more favourable economic environment, employability and active labour market policies were promoted. In a new consensual social climate both the government and organised interests agreed on the introduction of atypical labour contracts, job sharing and a reform of employment services. The implementation of these measures did not, however, fulfil the original expectations (Del Boca 1996). The policy of deregulation and flexibility still appeared too uncertain to structurally affect the steady growth of unemployment. We now turn specifically to the characteristics of labour market policy in the 1980s.

The decade opened with a severe crisis within large firms and a consequent haemorrhaging of jobs. The case of Fiat is particularly emblematic in this respect: in 1980 a 'state of firm crisis' was officially declared by the government, and more than 20,000 workers were put into the *Cassa Integrazione Straordinaria* scheme at zero hours (that is, they were suspended from the productive process without being formally dismissed, and with earnings replacement benefits). The internal divisions of trade unions and the hostility of white-collar workers towards the aggressive strategy and claims of blue-collar workers made the situation of the labour movement very difficult, precipitating a serious crisis. In those years the *Cassa Integrazione* scheme reached its apex: only in manufacturing, from 1977 to 1984 the paid hours jumped from 170 to 674 million (Pugliese and Rebeggiani 1997)[1]. The slump of large companies and the parallel proliferation of small firms, embedded in the post-Fordist productive paradigm of flexible specialisation, also meant the slump of national trade unions that had consolidated their presence and counted most of their members in exactly those companies.

Like the French, the German and the Spanish governments, the Italian Penta-party governments (Christian Democrats, Socialists, Social Democrats, Republicans and Liberals) tried to face the consequences of increasing unemployment in large companies by encouraging a subsidised exodus from work through pre-retirement benefits. Law no. 155/1981 established the possibility of accessing to pensions, for workers over 55 (male) and over 50 (female) fired by industrial firms outside the building sector, thereby derogating from the existing rules. This derogation was to apply only in 1981, but it was prolonged up to 1987 and then again throughout the 1990s[2]. But while in Germany and France pre-retirement schemes were established for encouraging generational turnover, in Italy (as in Spain) they soon turned into an instrument for avoiding socially risky dismissals, with no effects on workers' mobility and employment. In other words, pre-retirement schemes were used as a purely passive policy device.

In the context of alarming unemployment, also linked with the rapid rise of female participation in the labour market connected to the baby boom in the 1960s and higher levels of education, it was no longer possible to rely purely on medium term interventions and on income support subsidies. Especially in the *Mezzogiorno* it was necessary to radically change the strategy of labour policy for expanding the productive capacity of firms and fostering job creation. In order to pursue such an ambitious goal, the idea of a new social agreement with economic interest groups was launched, which was aimed at restraining wage costs and thus inflation and at introducing new active labour policy provisions. In this way, the world 'deregulation' officially entered the political discourse. In 1983 the national trade unions, the national employers' associations and the Minister of Labour signed an important social pact. As already mentioned in Chapter III, this was the second example of corporatist agreement after the (deceiving) ones that had taken place in the period 1977-1978 during the governments of national solidarity when trade unions decided to commit themselves to wage restraint in exchange for direct participation into the economic policy making (Turone 1988). The negotiation was in fact a complex political exchange involving incomes policies, fiscal policies and incentives policies. Fiscal policy had to tackle the effects of inflation, incomes policy had to slow down the dynamic of labour costs and tax relief (especially on social security contributions) to assure the approval of the employers, who traditionally were not favourably inclined towards social agreements. The outcome was a cut (by 15 per cent) of the *scala mobile* allowance (i.e. of the part of the wage which varies on the basis of the growth of the cost of living), which meant a substantial reduction of increases in future salaries. As regards the collective bargaining system, the agreement established a general hierarchical structure and posed strict limits upon firm-level bargaining, which could no longer decide on issues agreed upon at higher levels of agreement. As far as labour policies are concerned, the agreement introduced a set of new policy instruments favouring higher flexibility in the labour market (Law no. 863/1984).

The concerted action of 1983 was followed only one year later by a second social agreement between the government, the employers and the unions, whose main object was a further restrictive reform of the wage indexation mechanism – the inflationary engine of the *scala mobile* illustrated above. The agreement failed because of the increasing conflicts between the Communist Party (supported by the CGIL union) on the one side and the Socialist Party led by Craxi with the other two trade unions on the other side. Given the great reluctance of the Communist Party to reach a consensual solution, Prime Minister Craxi decided to cut wage indexations by decree in February 1984. Against these cuts a referendum was called, supported by the Communist Party; however, the referendum failed, and the cuts were maintained (Accornero 1992).

Law no. 863 of 1984 introduced three new instruments, all belonging to the family of deregulative policies: a) work-sharing agreements (the so-called solidarity contracts); b) work and training contracts; and c) part-time work. The aim was to stimulate the creation of employment opportunities for the outsiders of the labour market: women and the young unemployed.

Solidarity contracts were a form of working time reduction and sharing. The Catholic-oriented union, CISL, drawing a lesson from the French example, was one of the strongest promoters, viewing these contracts as a solidaristic instrument aimed at facing the problem of youth unemployment in a period of rapid technological transformation. Workers were to accept a reduced number of working hours to avoid dismissals or to encourage new recruitment. In the first case solidarity contracts were called 'internal' or 'defensive' contracts; in the second case they were defined as 'external'. Both of them required a preliminary agreement between the firm and the unions and allowed for a reduction of working time starting from 20 per cent. For defensive contracts, the government provided the workers with an earnings compensation of 50 per cent and the employers with some contributory relief. If the reduction of working time was over 20 per cent, employers got a relief of 25 per cent of the total contributions (30 per cent in the southern regions); if the reduction was over 30 per cent, the relief amounted to 40 per cent of contributions. As regards the 'external' contracts, the employers got, for each new employment contract, a contribution of 15 per cent of the gross wage from the state for the first year, 10 per cent for the second, and 5 per cent for the third. Social contributions were lowered at the level of the employment contract of apprentices.

The second instrument, work and training contracts, allowed the hiring of young workers aged between 15 and 29 for a maximum duration of two years with a variable wage, in firms and public administrations which were not in a situation of restructuring or crisis. The work experience had to be combined with professional training through the help of the regions. The actual timing and modalities of work and training activities were specified by projects presented to and approved by regional committees for employment. Regions could establish specific agreements with the involved firms and agencies, in line with EC regulations. As in the case of solidarity contracts, the employers' social contributions were fixed at the level of the employment contract of apprentices. Moreover, after one year work and training contracts could be converted from fixed-term to permanent contracts.

Finally, the new regulation of part-time work aimed at responding to women's increased participation in the labour market. It allowed the reduction of working time with respect to the standard fixed by the collective bargaining system and introduced a special list of part-time workers to be used by public placement offices. The law recognised two different kinds of contract: horizontal part-time, where the reduction of working time was based on a daily scale, and vertical part-time, where the reduction of working time was spread over the entire year. Both contracts had to specify the worker's duties and the organisation of working time.

The implementation of the three measures was highly differentiated. Work and training contracts immediately achieved remarkable success: they rapidly spread throughout the country, mainly because of their generous (for the employers) incentive structure. Solidarity contracts, on the contrary, were very scarcely taken advantage of. Employers were not so keen on changing regular working time and production regimes. The few contracts that were activated in practice had only defensive goals. Part-time working was also not a success. For the first time Law no. 863 officially promoted an instrument that had previously been left to free negotiations between workers and employers, and now could become a major answer to the increased participation of women into the labour market. Yet it continued to be rarely used – in comparison with other European countries – mainly because of its high non-wage costs (cf. Table 4.1).

Table 4.1 Incidence of part-time employment* in selected countries, 1985-2000

	Italy	Germany	United Kingdom	France	Netherlands
1985	7.5	11.0	19.7	11.2	19.5
1987	8.1	11.0	20.8	12.3	26.4
1989	8.8	11.6	20.2	12.2	27.7
1991	8.8	11.8	20.7	12.0	28.6
1993	10.0	12.8	22.1	13.3	27.7
1995	10.5	14.2	22.3	14.2	29.0
1996	10.5	14.9	22.9	14.3	29.3
1997	11.3	15.8	22.9	14.9	29.1
1998	11.2	16.6	23.0	14.8	30.0
1999	11.8	17.1	23.0	14.7	30.4
2000	12.2	17.6	23.0	14.2	32.1

Source: OECD, Employment Outlook, various years.
* Part-time jobs refer to people who usually work less than 30 hours per week.

Some other active policies were introduced in the second half of the decade. In 1986, Law no. 44 established a set of financial incentives for young employers, aged between 18 and 29, creating new firms and co-operatives. Beneficiaries had to reside in the southern regions. In 1987, Law no. 56 reorganised the structure of the Ministry of Labour, established new regional agencies for promoting active employment and modified the procedures for placement. This reform represents the first step of the employment services reform eventually passed in the subsequent decade[3]. The new provisions were generally aimed at enhancing active labour policies and services and at creating a new balance between the state and the regions, enhancing the role of the latter.

As to the ministerial structures, an Observatory of the labour market was established at a central level in order to monitor occupational trends in all economic sectors and produce data and analysis. The General Directorate for Workforce Placement was transformed into the General Directorate for Employment, with new responsibilities in the field of active policies. At the local level, social committees for employment were established in order to co-ordinate and implement active policies for mobility. The regional agencies for employment became technical and advisory bodies of regional committees. The general philosophy on which the new reform was based was to convert the traditional placement offices, originally conceived as instruments of bureaucratic certification and intermediation between labour demand and supply, into structures apt for planning and implementing active labour policies. The main task of these agencies was to stimulate the matching of labour demand and supply through specific initiatives aimed at increasing the level of employment and inclusion of weak categories in the labour market.

Finally, Law no. 56 of 1987 allowed placement offices to derogate from the automatic system of numerical call for new recruitment, particularly where there were specific sectoral agreements with firms or business associations.

In conclusion, the 1980s represented an ambiguous decade for labour policies. New active measures were introduced, and higher flexibility was fostered. But the innovative policy choices did not seem to be enough to affect the structural factors of unemployment. Certainly, the existing system of *ammortizzatori sociali* (and especially the *Cassa Integrazione Straordinaria*) played a primary role in helping (large) Italian firms to reorganise, reconvert and restructure in response to the intensifying challenges of internationalisation. But the situation of the weak segments of the labour force continued to deteriorate over the decade. The new active instruments were institutionally timid, poorly implemented and not systematically funded. This notwithstanding, the expenditure related to active policies rose, and a more balanced ratio between active and passive policies financings was noted: from 1985 to 1989 active policies expenditure increased from 0.45 per cent to 0.77 per cent of GDP, whereas passive policies diminished from 1.33 per cent to 0.9 per cent (OECD, Employment Outlook 1996). But these new resources were unable to significantly alter the logic of public intervention in this policy sector.

3   The chaotic restructuring of the welfare state

Despite their unremitting lip service to the exigencies of financial adjustment, the various penta-party governments that held office during the decade did not accomplish much in terms of welfare modernization. Since the beginning of the decade, proposals for a new pension reform were discussed in Parliament and included in the agenda of the different cabinets. All these proposals went in the same austerity direction: rationalising the system, raising the age of retirement and trimming benefit formulas in order to restore financial balances in the medium and long term.

The financial and organisational problems raised by the newly established *Servizio Sanitario Nazionale* – SSN (1978) – in turn prompted an articulated debate on how to 'reform the reform'. The proposals in this field included changes in the overall chain of command from central government down to the regions and to the local health units; the limitation of the power and competencies of partisan organs at the local level; the exclusion from coverage of higher-income categories; the enactment of stricter controls over providers and (later in the course of the decade) the introduction of quasi-market relationships between public purchasers and providers. Neither the pension reform nor the 'reform of the health reform' made much progress until the early 1990s. The 1980s did however witness some first cuts in both sectors: relatively peripheral and not very effective cuts in the case of pensions, more substantial ones in the case of health.

In the pension field, starting in 1983, a number of measures were taken that were aimed at subordinating some entitlements to the actual income conditions of recipients and at controlling abuses. Income ceilings were established for maintaining the right to minimum pensions and to multiple benefits (e.g. an old age and a survivor pension). The rules concerning invalidity pensions were in their turn completely revised in 1984, tightening medical criteria and introducing periodical reviews of the physical conditions of the beneficiaries.

Though important in symbolic terms, these steps in the direction of a greater 'targeting' of Italy's social insurance were only modestly effective in financial terms. Not only were they programmatically limited to the margins, so to speak, of the system, but they also activated some counter-developments that largely neutralised their positive impact on costs. The ascertainment of the income requisites for minimum pensions and multiple benefits was entrusted to the INPS, the social insurance institute. But this institute lacked both the technical instruments and the formal powers to implement accurate controls: thus, the introduction of income testing[4] produced enormous organisational chaos, many injustices (unwarranted withdrawals and, much more often, unwarranted confirmations of benefits based on false income declarations on the part of beneficiaries) and a massive increase of litigations between recipients and the social security administration, which had to be cleared with a general amnesty at the end of the decade. The most absurd epilogue of the 1983 targeting provisions came in 1993/94, when the Constitutional Court ruled that they were partly illegal and forced the government to repay arrears for several trillion liras.

In the field of invalidity, the cuts were also largely circumvented, in this case not through legal action but through the mobilisation of a lateral channel. The new discipline introduced in 1984 only regarded, in fact, the invalidity benefits paid by the INPS on the basis of contributions, but did not affect the non-contributory benefits paid by the Ministry of the Interior. The second half of the 1980s witnessed a huge increase in precisely these latter benefits, which almost completely offset the restrictive impact of the new INPS regulations (Ferrera 1996). Thanks to this articulated organisational restructuring and institutional 'relocation', the traditional particularistic-clientelistic circuits were kept in full operation throughout the decade, possibly widening the aforementioned deficit of legality.

The 1984 reform forced this 'clientelistic market' to change its currency (from the contributory to the non-contributory invalidity benefit), the arena for its transactions (from the INPS to the Ministry of the Interior), the place and modalities of the 'benefit-hunting' (from the regional committees and the INPS medical committees to the prefectural committees for public aid, in connection with the administrative boards and medical committees of the local health units or USLs on the one hand, and the public health care agencies on the other). But the actors of the clientelistic exchange continued to be the same: parties, trade unions and patronage institutions. Moreover, the amount of financial resources channelled through the clientelistic circuit remained the same. In fact, between 1984 and 1990 INPS invalidity pensions decreased of 712,000 units. But for the most part this decline was offset by an increase of 510,000 units of the invalidity allowances paid by the Ministry of the Interior, with an evident syndrome of substitution.

Cutbacks were more substantial and more effective in the field of health-care. Alarmed by post-reform expenditure increases and aware that a new 'reform of the reform' would take its time, the penta-party government inaugurated a policy of 'financial management' of the health system aimed at curbing the demand for services by imposing expenditure ceilings to the regions and by making users pay in part for services. The annual budget bill became the instrument *par excellence* to run the health-care system from the centre. Allocations were set on the basis of available public funds, to be shared out among the regions. The savings deemed necessary to remain in line with the ceiling were produced through co-payments and other cuts (reduction of facilities, staff, investments, etc.).

Co-payments or "tickets", as they are known by the Italian public, were (and still are) without doubt the most visible and the most unpopular instrument of government action in the health-care sector throughout the 1980s. As in the field of pensions, the turning point was 1983. Alarmed at the worrying increase in health-care costs (especially for prescription drugs) in the previous two years, the government decided to change the co-payment from a modest fixed fee to a percentage, making consumers pay 15 per cent of the cost of the drugs. This percentage was then raised on several occasions in later years, reaching 30 per cent in 1989. The ticket was also extended from drugs to diagnostic tests and referrals (i.e. consultations with specialised physicians prescribed by family doctors). Although heavily criticised, the co-payment policy generally achieved its aims, which were primarily financial. Besides bringing revenues to state coffers, co-payments did stabilise health-care consumption, especially as regards pharmaceuticals.

As noted for the pension sector, health care 'targeting' through user charges did produce a number of perverse counter-developments. To mitigate the social impact of such charges, detailed legislation on exemptions was passed during the decade, combining different criteria (income, type of illness, family and work status, age, etc.). But Italian patients soon learned how to exploit the loopholes of this legislation. Exactly like INPS, the National Health System bureaucracy lacked moreover the organisational capacity to administer the norms in force. The result was a rapid increase, through time, of the number of exempted consumers, which reached the impressive figure of 25 per cent in 1989, accounting for 75 per cent of total pharmaceutical expenditure. Only part of this increase can be attributed to the gradual relaxation of co-payment norms. To a large extent, it must be attributed to a growth of frauds and abuses, in the form of unfaithful declarations (of income status by users or of health conditions by physicians, or both) and free riding on exemption cards by non-exempt users.

If on the expenditure side the 1980s were definitely an ambiguous decade (continuing expansion, accompanied by various chaotic attempts at retrenchment), on the revenue side the dominant trend was much clearer: increases on all fronts. Contributory rates were repeatedly raised, especially for self-employed categories. In aggregate real terms, the revenue from contributions paid by both employers and the insured rose by 48 per cent between 1980 and 1990, increasing from 16.2 per cent to 17.4 per cent of GDP; the real size of contributions from the self-employed almost doubled in the same period. The total tax take of general government also grew extremely rapidly during the past decade, rising from 30.2 per cent to 40 per cent of GDP between 1980 and 1990. According to EU calculations, Italy's actual average tax rate on the incomes of employees rose by 11.4 percentage points (from 31.8 per cent to 43.2 per cent) in the period 1980-1993, as against an average EU increase of 6.2 percentage points. The actual average rate on the incomes from self-employment rose in its turn by as much as 18.8 percentage points in the same period (from 21.7 per cent to 40.5 per cent), as against an average decline of 6.4 percentage point in the EU[5].

Through this rapid and intense increase of taxation, Italy fully completed during the 1980s its catching-up march with respect to the revenue levels of her European partners, filling the distance created by the 'flat decade' of

1965-1975, during which revenues remained stagnant despite soaring public spending (cf. *supra*, Chapter III). But this remarkable tax adjustment did not suffice to cure the structural imbalance of national accounts. As previously mentioned, the deterioration was due to a large extent to the self-sustaining dynamic of the 'debt spiral' in an unfavourable international conjuncture. But the internal imbalances of the welfare system (especially pensions) did play a relevant part in the story[6].

4   The 1990s: the 'new deal' of the labour market

The 1990s marked a turning point in the history of Italian employment policy. On the one hand, the alarming state of the labour market, especially during the first half of the decade, called for extensive reform of the institutional framework of both the demand and supply of labour. On the other, there were certain compelling external challenges (firstly in the form of the urgent need to remedy the country's financial position to gain entry into the EMU, and then in the form of the European employment strategy), which combined to speed up the modernisation process.

Labour market indicators point to a split between the first and the second half of the 1990s. The negative trend following the 1992-93 recession was balanced by more positive developments during the second half of the decade, and in the 1998-2000 period in particular, in the wake of economic recovery and outstanding American growth.

From 1993[7] to 1995, the employment rate fell from 53.1 per cent to 50.6 per cent following twenty years of positive growth; this contraction was more marked in the case of male workers (employment fell from 68.2 per cent to 65.9 per cent) – the majority of whom were employed in large industrial companies – than it was for women (from 35.8 per cent down to 35.4 per cent). From 1995 onwards, a slight recovery was seen (from 50.6 per cent to 53.5 per cent in 2000), in particular during the 1998-2000 period (+1.8 per cent) and especially among female workers (+ 4.2 per cent). The increase in the employment rate encouraged people to look for a job, lifting the overall participation rate by 2.2 per cent (from 51.1 per cent to 53.3 per cent) during the period from 1995 to 2000.

The unemployment rate rose continuously over the decade up until 1999 (from 10.1 per cent in 1993 to 11.8 per cent), before dropping to 10.6 per cent in 2000 and then to 9.3 per cent by the end of 2001: this latter figure was the most positive since 1989. The drop in unemployment was mainly a female phenomenon (female unemployment fell from 16.2 per cent in 1995 to 14.5 per cent in 2000).

Despite these positive signs, the most deeply rooted features of the Italian labour market remained largely unaffected: youth unemployment (among 15-24 year-olds) remained at a particularly high level overall during this decade (from 30.4 per cent in 1993 it rose to 31.1 per cent in 2000); the employment rate for the over-55s decreased from 32.3 per cent in 1993 to 30.8 per cent in 2000; figures for the long-term unemployed also fell (61 per cent of total unemployed in 2000 compared to 48 per cent in 1993), especially in the south (68.5 per cent in 2000 compared to 57.4 per cent in 1993); and the deep divide between north and south remained largely intact (in 2000 the unemployment rate reached 27.6 per cent in the south against 4.9 per cent in the north) (Istat, Forze di lavoro 1993-2000).

In such a situation, the achievement of the quantitative targets fixed by the European Union during the Lisbon and Stockholm summits in March 2000 and March 2001 – according to which the total and female employment rates should respectively reach 70 per cent and 60 per cent by 2010, while the unemployment rate should go down to 4 per cent – seems rather unrealistic given that the current gap in employment amounts to 15 per cent for the total working population, 20 per cent for the female population and 22 per cent for workers over 55. Even if we take into account the black economy, which if 'legalised' would push up the employment rate by 7-8 percentage points, the road to European standards appears a long and hard one.

Nevertheless, the effort put into policy reform was quite remarkable – as we have already shown – especially compared with the little that had been achieved during previous decades[8]. The main innovations introduced during this decade can be grouped into three areas: a) the privatisation and decentralisation of employment services; b) the introduction of policies for local development; and c) the strong promotion of flexible labour contracts.

The reform of employment services still constitutes (in 2003) one of the main challenges for Italy, and in particular for the country's regional and local governments. Legislative decree no. 469 of December 1997, following article 1 of Delegated Law no. 59/1997 on administrative decentralisation, provided for three main changes: institutional decentralisation (that is, the transfer of placement powers from the Ministry to the regions and local government[9]); the promotion of a preventive approach to placement instead of the old bureaucratic one; the entry of private organisations into the field of provision of employment services, after fifty years of public monopoly.

Between 1998 and 1999, Italian regional governments were involved in passing regional laws implementing national prescriptions. Job centres were set up throughout the country at the provincial level (one for each 100,000 inhabitants), thus giving the provinces back their former political and administrative status, which has been further reinforced after the revision of Heading v of the Constitution in March 2001 (Constitutional Law no. 3/2001)[10] broadening the regions' individual and joint competencies.

At the regional level, a new body governing and co-ordinating employment measures was created under a variety of different names (Labour Agency, Employment Authority, etc.). The new agency employs personnel from the former Regional Agencies for Employment (governed by the Ministry and the former regional labour departments) and has considerable organisational problems due to the heterogeneity of the skills and expectations of its staff. Besides their control and supervisory functions, Labour Agencies have the duty to provide technical support to the provinces implementing the reform, through the co-ordination of the Computerised Employment Information System (*Sistema Informativo Lavoro*) – an electronic data set covering labour demand and supply – through the development of research into the local dynamics of the labour market, and through the monitoring and evaluation of labour policy impact.

Furthermore, Decree 469/1997 set up two important bodies for integration and concerted action: the Tripartite Regional Commissions (*Commissioni regionali tripartite*) and the Inter-institutional Co-ordination Committees (*Comitati interistituzionali di coordinamento*). While the former include representatives of regional public institutions, trade unions and employers' organisations, the latter include representatives of the various levels of local government (regional, provincial and municipal). Compared to the old Regional Employment Commissions (*Commissioni regionali per l'impiego*), these new bodies should be more involved in the planning and implementation of labour policies, thus avoiding possible conflict. Similar tripartite commissions were also established at the provincial level.

In addition to decentralisation, the main innovation of the 1997 reform was a brand new approach to placement, more in keeping with European recommendations. Placement was seen as a fundamental part of active labour market policies and not just – as in the past – as a series of purely administrative functions (Varesi 1998; Ghirotti 1998; Reyneri 1998). In accordance with the preventive approach widely adopted in northern European countries, employment centres should go beyond the mere bureaucratic certification of unemployment and provide consultancy, orientation and pre-selection services designed to get the unemployed into the labour market as soon as possible (within 12 months in general and within 6 months in the case of those who receive unemployment benefit, as stipulated by Legislative Decree 181/2000). The main beneficiaries of such services should be those people often excluded from the labour market (the young, women and the long-term unemployed), thanks to a series of measures directly linked to the needs of local areas. The provinces are thus free to draw up and implement specific measures in the fields of job creation, counselling and orientation with the supervision and technical support of the regional governments.

Another policy innovation in the sphere of employment services has been the admission of private organisations into the field of job placement services. Notwithstanding the formal requisites that have to be satisfied, private organisations (unions, employers' associations, non-profit-making associations, etc.) were allowed to set up their own employment centres, which compete with the existing public ones. The liberalisation of employment services was also accompanied in 1997 by the introduction of temporary employment, after two European Court of Justice rulings against the Italian government for failing to comply with EU directives. Moreover, in 2001 the new Berlusconi government (cf. *infra*) announced the abolition of the 'sole purpose' constraint, that is private agencies' duty to restrict activity exclusively to one single mission, i.e. placement, which means that private agencies can now provide a range of different services (placement, orientation and selection) and that competition between public and private institutions is further encouraged (the subject of heated debate, together with claims and protests made by regional and provincial governments, worried that they might be deprived of their central functions)[11].

At the beginning of 2003, placement reform still does not appear to have been achieved in full. In the northern regions, the implementation process has been more rapid and efficient, while in the southern regions some delays and inefficiencies – especially in terms of staff competencies – continue to jeopardise the reform. The shift from a bureaucratic culture to a preventive, result-oriented approach appears to be slow. It is not surprising that the European Commission has repeatedly urged the Italian government to complete the reform according to specific quality standards.

Localism and territorial autonomy were also the goals of new local development policies, the second big innovation characterising the 1990s, and provided for in Law no. 662/1996 following the Employment Agreement signed by Prodi, the unions and the business associations. Under the heading 'negotiated planning' (*programmazione negoziata*) one can find a wide range of policy measures designed to foster local entrepreneurship, valorise local resources and institutional capabilities, and create new jobs. The numerous programmes are primarily based on a mixture of training and job creation, qualification and work. The most widespread and significant measures are territorial pacts and area contracts. Both of them are designed to encourage employability in depressed areas. These policies can hardly be considered mere labour policies, given that they incorporate the wider concept of integration in the labour market, based on local, urban and industrial development, or on the revitalisation of the territory as a whole. This new approach has been seen as the new answer to the socio-economic problems of the Italian south after the demise (in 1992) of the state's top-down special measures, which had failed to achieve the expected results. The shift from top-down subsidised industrialisation to bottom-up local autonomy constitutes the new answer to the south's traditional problem of social and economic development.

Territorial pacts consist of operative procedures and bargaining tools designed to promote the development of businesses, co-operatives and employment measures in a given area, through the utilisation of productive and natural resources that characterise that area. Bargaining does not rely upon the traditional triangle of unions, employers and the government, but on a wider network of private and public subjects (such as banks, chambers of commerce, non-profit-making associations, etc.), who are to share common policy problems and jointly fund the various measures. In 2000, more than a hundred territorial pacts had been submitted to the National Committee for the Economy and Labour (*Comitato Nazionale per l'Economia e il Lavoro* – the body competent for recommending public funding: CNEL), 71 for the south and 38 for the centre-north. Ten of these pacts are 'European pacts', that is, they are financed by special European funds (Ministero del Lavoro 2001).

Area contracts have the same goal as territorial pacts: i.e. to encourage employability in under-developed areas. They differ from the pacts in that they cover areas where industry already exists (albeit in crisis). They are signed in order to avoid mass redundancies. Unions are prepared to waive the national contractual standard and to agree to wage and administrative flexibility. Furthermore, area contracts are becoming increasingly common, with 15 in 2000 (13 in the south and only 2 in the north), corresponding to 16,328 new jobs (*ibidem*).

The third main line of governmental action in the 1990s was the encouragement of flexible and atypical employment contracts, mainly during the second half of the decade, thus further developing a process that had already begun in the 1980s. During the 1990s, policy-makers quickly became aware of the success of flexible labour contracts as a key channel for labour market entry. Numbers soon proved them right. In the 1998-2000 period, the percentage of part-time jobs grew from 4.9 per cent to 8.1 per cent, while temporary work – two years after its initial introduction – accounted for 399,289 jobs: fixed-term contracts rose from 5.1 per cent to 9.3 per cent, continuous and co-ordinated employment contracts (a widely used form of temporary contract) jumped from 6.9 per cent to 9 per cent, and in-work training contracts and apprenticeships finally surpassed the 8 per cent mark (*ibidem*).

The promotion of greater flexibility in the labour market began with the legalisation of temporary work in June 1997 – as we have already mentioned. The so-called Treu Law (from the name of the then Employment Minister) officially dismantled the existing public monopoly on job placement established in 1949 (Law no. 264). Temporary employment was progressively extended to the various branches of the private sector, and subsequently to the public sector (from August 2000 onwards) both for highly skilled and unskilled jobs. Large urban centres in northern Italy have been the main areas of expansion of this new form of employment, and male workers and young workers below the age of 40 have been its main protagonists. Temporary work agencies – both national and international – have been proliferating all over the country in recent years.

Another measure designed to encourage temporal flexibility was the revision of norms on part-time working, which had never been very successful in Italy. In April 1999 a decree law provided tax benefits for employers who wanted to avail themselves of part-time work in order to hire new employees, particularly in small and medium-sized enterprises. The law was specifically designed for working women with families and young workers below the age of 25. The measure was modified in February 2000 by Legislative Decree no. 61 which, as a response to EC Directive 97/81, introduced the so-called 'elastic clauses' for the flexible organisation of company production: it also gave employers the chance to take on part-time employees within the limits fixed by collective bargaining (part-time work could account for up to 10 per cent of weekly working time). The following year, in February 2001, Legislative Decree no. 100 further modified rules on part-time employment, shortening the period of notice required (from 10 days to 48 hours) for each change made in the organisation of working time and reducing overtime payments.

European law and recommendations also played an important role with regard to fixed-term contracts. In 1993, Law no. 221 made a combination of temporary contracts and mobility allowances (a state subsidy in case of collective dismissals) possible. Four years later, in 1997, Law no. 196 abolished the automatic conversion of temporary contracts into life-long contracts in those cases where employees continued working, replacing it with wage compensations. All of these innovations were considered to encourage employability. Then Legislative Decree 386/2001 finally implemented EC Di-

Table 4.2 Major employment policies, 1981-2001

1981
Early retirement pensions (Law no. 155)

1984
Solidarity contracts (internal and external – Law no. 863)
Training and employment contracts (Law no. 863)
Part-time work (Law no. 863)

1986
Young entrepreneurship (Law no. 44)

1987
Regional Agencies for Employment (run by the Ministry) and partial liberalisation of placement procedures (Law no. 56)

1991/92
Promotion of female employment (Law no. 125/1991 and Law no. 215/1992)

1992/93
Abolition of automatic wage indexing and reform of collective bargaining

---

1995
Territorial pacts (Law no. 341)

1996
Area contracts (Law no.662)

1997
Temporary work, revision of fixed-term contracts, work fellowships, continuous training (Law no. 196).
Decentralisation of employment services and active labour policies, privatisation of placement functions (Legislative Decree no. 469)

1998-onwards
Yearly National Action Plans for Employment

1999-2001
Revision of part-time and temporary employment contracts as a consequence of EC directives

---

1999-2001
Promotion of the new economy, social inclusion policies and equal opportunities measures

---

rective 70/1999, liberalising application, eliminating the need for employers to demonstrate their reasons for fixing the term of a contract, and weakening the role played by collective bargaining in establishing the maximum percentage of workers who could be employed on temporary contracts.

As for the so-called quasi-employment contracts (*lavoro parasubordinato*), in February 1999 the Senate passed a bill which tried to regulate the considerable numbers of quasi-subordinate or quasi-autonomous workers still deprived of any form of social protection: this it did by establishing some basic rules concerning employment rights, dismissal and work organisation (Altieri and Carrieri 2000). Given that the Law remains to be approved, quasi-subordinate wages have been tied to subordinate workers' wages by the 2000 Budget, while collective bargaining retains its central role here.

It is widely recognized that the promotion of atypical contracts contributed to the employment growth of the second half of the 1990s (especially in the period from 1995 to the spring of 2001) when 1,500,000 new jobs were created (Sestito 2002). Most of these new workers are to be considered flexi-workers, i.e. people (in particular women and first job seekers) who entered the labour market with a working time formula that was always less than full. At the end of the 1990s, the diffusion of flexibility seemed to be an incontrovertible trend of the Italian labour market even though the risks of precariousness and jobs' bad quality were emphasised in the national debate.

As we shall see, this emphasis on flexibility has intensified with the arrival of Berlusconi.

5   The impact of the European Employment Strategy on domestic policy making

The reforms illustrated so far have been partly inspired in their general goals by the European Employment Strategy (EES). The latter has exerted a significant impact also on the organisational dimension of employment policy-making – especially in terms of capacity building[12].

As is well known, the EES was officially launched with the Amsterdam Treaty of 1997 (article 128), even though the White Book on Growth, Competitiveness and Employment of 1993 and the conclusions of the Essen Council in 1994[13] were important precedents. Though remaining an exclusive competence of national states, employment policies have become part of a wider process of multilateral governance, based on horizontal co-ordination and control relations among the member states and on vertical relations with EU institutions, involving general policy orientation, monitoring and evaluation (Bonoli and Bertozzi 2002; Trubeck and Mosher 2003).

The EES consists of various elements and stages. Each year the Council of

Ministers is called to draw up a series of guidelines on the basis of the general situation of the labour market and of specific proposals of the Commission, the Parliament and the Economic and Social Committee. In the second stage, these guidelines have to be converted into specific policy aims by the member states within 'National Action Plans (NAPs)', which in the third stage of the process have to be submitted to the Commission for assessment. The results of such assessment are presented in a Commission and Council joint employment report, which may include individual recommendations to national governments. The EES is therefore aimed at fostering convergence among national labour markets, without however imposing hard regulations. Through the principle of subsidiarity and the instruments of soft laws, incentives and opportunities are offered to national governments that hold their legislative powers intact (Balboni and Buzzacchi 2003).

The Amsterdam Treaty provisions received formal (and anticipated) ratification during the extraordinary 'jobs summit' held in Luxembourg in November 1997. On that occasion, four main principles (or pillars) were indicated as the core objectives for national labour market policies: a) employability (i.e. the promotion of new skills and incentives); b) entrepreneurship (the creation of new firms and businesses); c) adaptability (the modernisation of working conditions and the promotion of company flexibility *vis-à-vis* external challenges); and d) equal opportunities (especially in terms of reduction of the gender gap in the labour market). The four pillars were further specified during the European Councils of subsequent years: greater emphasis was placed on the policies for social inclusion, on the employability potential of the knowledge economy, and on the problem of the quality of jobs.

If the most explicit goal of the EES is to drive national policies towards common strategic priorities and standards (i.e. to make them converge), another related purpose is that of affecting the modes and styles of the labour policy-making process as such. One clear aim on this front has been the promotion of dynamics of policy learning and change based on experience: past failures and success in each country have become the basis for cross-national benchmarking and peer review exercises, in the framework of the open method of co-ordination (De la Porte and Pochet 2002).

For Italy, responding to the demands of the EES raised multiple problems. The strategy took shape within Anglo-Saxon and northern European policy paradigms and values, resting on the primacy of prevention, active measures and efficient public employment services. On the contrary, the Italian model of labour policy was traditionally marked by the dominance of passive policies, by a hyper-bureaucratic system of placement and by the lack of evaluation and monitoring capabilities. The organisational structure of the Ministry of Labour, characterised by high internal fragmentation and by the juridical culture of its staff, did not favour any development of problem solving and ex-post evaluation skills. When the EES took off, the Italian government had virtually no institutional equipment for collecting and analysing data and thus for formulating articulated empirical diagnoses of the existing challenges and elaborating policy solutions along the general lines set by the European strategy. In 1987 a General Direction for the Labour Market Observatory had been created, and the exigency to set up a Labour Market Information System providing on line information to employment offices had slowly emerged. An ad hoc commission had been established, but the political and material support to such initiatives remained weak, and thus little progress had been made. Scarcely formalised was also the representation of the Ministry of Labour in international bodies and decision-making arenas. The relationships with institutions like the OECD, the ILO and the European Union were carried out on the basis of personal ties and contingent events.

In addition, the pressures coming from the EU combined with domestic reforms and in particular with the launching of administrative decentralisation (discussed in the previous paragraph), whose consequence for the Ministry was the gradual loss of important competencies and responsibilities: the reforms foresaw for the Ministry only a role of general orientation, control, supervision and international representation. Domestic decentralisation dynamics inaugurated a phase of institutional transition, which made the response to the new EU soft laws more difficult and complicated. This notwithstanding, a slow process of structural adjustment (concerning the organizational network responsible for employment policies) and cognitive learning (concerning the norms, beliefs and preferences of the various actors of this network) began to develop – a process characterised at first by extemporaneity and improvisation, but which subsequently led to institutionalised innovation and change.

In order to draw up the first NAPs, those for 1998 and for 1999, two ad hoc commissions were set up inside the Ministry, composed of a small group of external experts, without any direct involvement of the Ministry's staff, which indeed opposed various bureaucratic obstacles to these new initiatives. The 1999 NAP was marked however by a broadening of the circle of actors: the Presidency of the Council (held by D'Alema) got involved in the preparation of the plan through its economic department, which precisely in those months had undertaken an internal re-organisation with a view to equipping the Prime Minister's office with greater policy capabilities in the most crucial sectors. The 1999 experience taught an important lesson: the NAPs not only need to be prepared and packaged in order to submit them to Brussels, they also need to be defended within the peer review processes and bilateral meetings with the European Commission that take place after their formal submission: they must be accompanied all the way through the Luxemburg process, all the year round (and especially when the Joint Employment Reports are drafted). In 1999, despite the institutional investment made in its preparation, the Italian NAP was not adequately supported in the follow-ups of the official presentation: the expert Committee responsible for the document disbanded after the formal deadline, and the ministerial bureaucracy felt neither involved nor was it capable of performing the task. The change of Labour Ministers during the summer of 1999 (Bassolino left his post to Salvi, both from the DS party) did not improve the situation: the 'experts' committee system revealed itself as an inadequate organisational response to the increasingly articulated demands of an increasingly institutionalised process of multi-level governance of European labour markets and domestic employment policy regimes. Another lesson that had to be learnt in the critical juncture of 1999 was the urgent need to develop monitoring and evaluation skills in order to respond not only to the 'declarative' demands of the EES (what are your plans), but also to its 'accounting' demands (have you reached your targets).

The turning point in Italy's participation to the Luxembourg process came in 2000. In the winter of that year, a new unit called 'Monitoring Group' was established within the Ministry's cabinet with the task of collecting an updated data set on labour market trends and policies. The Group operated as an inter-service committee of administrators belonging to various directorates and ministries (Presidency of the Council, National Institute of Statistics – ISTAT, National Institute of Social Insurance – INPS, Institute for Labour and Training – ISFOL, etc.). This was indeed a relevant step in the overall reorganization of the policy-making process: a new actor capable of providing empirical data and technical knowledge on the real dynamics of the labour market appeared on the scene – with firm roots in the central administrative apparatus – and it began to play a pivotal role in the existing, loose and inconclusive employment policy network. Soon after its creation, the Monitoring Group started to produce a series of Monitoring Reports on labour market trends and policies, which have rapidly established themselves as the standard reference source for knowledge and analysis and thus as a reliable basis for policy planning and evaluation. If compared to the 1997 status quo, the progress made by Italy in terms of capacity building appears remarkable, as explicitly recognised also by recent Joint Employment Reports.

In the wake of such progress, starting from the third round of the Luxembourg process (2000), the Italian government has begun to play a more active role not only in the 'descending' phase (guidelines application, new NAP formulation, old NAP evaluation), but also in the 'ascending' phase (guidelines' definition, NAP's defence, contents of the Joint Employment Reports). From a technical point of view, a small but dynamic epistemic community (including not only the Monitoring Group but also the Italian delegates to the Employment and Social Protection Committee and some economic advisors of the Labour Ministry and the Presidency of the Council) gradually formed itself and started to perform brokerage functions between the national arena and the supranational one. From the political point of view, both Salvi (as Minister for Labour) and D'Alema (as Prime Minister) mobilised to shape the agenda of the Lisbon European Council (spring 2000), seeking alliances with other countries on issues considered relevant for Italy. One of the achievements of this strategy was the recognition of the importance of the regional dimension of the labour market (and thus of employment policies) in the conclusions of the Lisbon summit and in the 2001 guidelines.

The elaboration of the 2001 NAP (the fourth round) was also assigned to an ad hoc committee co-ordinated by a technician, but this time the expert committee worked in close contact with the Monitoring Group. The May elections and the change in government (from Amato to Berlusconi) played as disturbing events for Italy's participation to the 2001 round of the EES. At the end of the summer, the new government submitted to Brussels an addendum to the May NAP, putting greater emphasis on flexibility. But that same addendum also included, for the first time, some quantitative targets, based on the scenarios elaborated by the Monitoring Group. Starting from 2002, the whole 'NAP-empl' process at the national level has been internalised within the executive machine. External experts have lost their prominence, and the process (including of course the actual drafting of the plan) is now managed by the Labour Ministry, under the close supervision of one of the undersecretaries (i.e. deputy ministers). In sum, between 1997 and 2003 the Luxembourg process has been fully incorporated within Italy's policy-making system, and there can be little doubt that this incorporation has prompted a marked upgrading (in some areas, the creation ex novo) of crucial policy capabilities.

However, some dark spots remain in the picture. As stated above, institutional adjustment and capacity building at the national level has taken place in a context of increasing administrative decentralisation. This culminated in the Constitutional reform of 2001, which has delegated most competences in the field of employment to regions and local governments. The institutional capacities of these new actors are still relatively weak and extremely varied throughout the national territory. While regions such as Piedmont, Lombardy, Emilia-Romagna and Tuscany have made significant efforts to equip themselves with the skills to perform the new tasks (and some have even started to experiment with Regional Action Plans for employment, in full syntony with the EES), most southern regions are lagging far behind – while facing at the same time the highest problem loads in terms of unemployment and labour market modernization. The new framework of centre-periphery relations rests on co-ordination and support mechanisms which are still in a fluid state and poorly effective. Thus, what has been gained in terms of policy capabilities at the national level since 1997, in the wake of the EES, has been partly offset by the centrifugal dynamics of administrative decentralisation. As we shall see in the final chapter, this problem affects a wide range of public policies and raises some serious doubts about the stability and sustainability of the new institutional constellation laboriously put in place by the reform cycle of the 1990s.

6   A sequence of reforms in the welfare state

After a decade of chaotic attempts at retrenchment, in the sphere of social protection the 1990s witnessed the emergence of a more coherent policy of re-structuring and modernization. Several legislative interventions were passed in the field of pensions. The first one dates back to 1992. While maintaining the overall architecture of the system established in 1969 (occupational schemes and earnings-related formulas), the 1992 Amato reform introduced a number of significant innovations in a restrictive direction after decades of ameliorations. The main provisions of this reform can be summarised as follows: elevation of the retirement age from 55 to 60 for females and from 60 to 65 for males (private employees), to be phased in by the year 2002[14]; gradual elevation of the minimum contribution requirement for old-age benefits from 10 to 20 years; gradual extension of the reference period for pensionable earnings from the last 5 years to the last 10 years (and to the whole career for new entrants in the labour market); elevation of the contribution requirement for seniority (i.e. early retirement) pensions of civil servants with a very gradual phasing in; a new increase of contribution rates and a restrictive reform of the general indexation mechanism, which abolished wage-indexation.

The Amato reform did face at first harsh opposition from the trade unions. The climate of financial emergency of the summer of 1992 and the negotiational style of Amato eased the reform process, however. In September and October 1992 a number of strikes were declared, in which union leaders were publicly contested for their willingness to negotiate. Amato's concessions were able however to defuse this upsurge of protest: in particular, Amato dropped the proposal of elevating the minimum contributory requirement of seniority pensions for private employees from 35 to 36 years as well as the proposed freezing of indexing for 1993; in addition, all workers with at least 15 years of contributive seniority were exempted from the new rules.

As a follow up of the 1992 reform, new provisions for supplementary pensions were passed in 1993. The 'second pillar' had been traditionally underdeveloped in Italy, due to the presence of a highly generous first pillar and of generous rules regarding severance payments. The latter (the so-called *trattamento di fine rapporto* – TFR) play a very prominent role (almost 2 per cent of GDP). Employers are obliged to set aside ca. 7.5 per cent of gross wages, with a guaranteed yield of 1.5 per cent per year, supplemented by 75 per cent of the yearly inflation rate. Workers obtain the sum set aside for them when they change jobs or when they retire. Thus, the TFR scheme operates largely as a second pillar pension scheme in disguise and partly as a sort of unemployment insurance. At the beginning of the 1990s, the idea emerged that the TFR should gradually be transformed into a fully fledged and explicit second pillar scheme. The new provisions introduced in 1993 made some first steps in this direction: they introduced a co-ordinated legal framework and fiscal incentives for the establishment of occupational supplementary funds and foresaw the possibility of diverting the TFR contributions into such new funds. The Ciampi government, which took office in 1993, decided in its turn new penalisations on seniority pensions as well as controls on the beneficiaries of disability benefits, to contain the above-illustrated frauds.

The impact of the Amato reform was not insignificant, both in terms of cost-containment (cf. Figure 4.1 below) and in terms of equity, especially thanks to its provisions on civil servant's 'baby pensions' (i.e. their traditional entitlement to retire with only 20 years' contributions, at very early ages). But the persisting crisis of public finances, the continuing increase of pension expenditure (in spite of the cuts) and the pressures of international agencies such as the IMF, the OECD and EU institutions convinced the government in the course of 1993/1994 that a more incisive reform was needed. In the fall of 1994 the Berlusconi government, voted in office in the spring elections, disclosed a new reform plan resting on very severe measures: high penalties for seniority pensions (a 3 per cent reduction per each year of retirement prior to the legal pension age), a reduction of the replacement rate from 2 per cent to 1.75 per cent per year for those workers who had not been affected by the Amato reform and a switch from actual to programmed inflation in the indexing mechanism of all pensions. Not previously negotiated with the unions, Berlusconi's plan raised massive protests: on October 14, 1994, a first general strike was called, and two weeks later as many as one million workers crowded the streets of Rome in one of the largest popular manifestations since decades. The issue of pensions raised unprecedented tensions between the executive and the President of the Republic, Mr. Scalfaro, who recommended separating pension reform from the financial law for 1995, that needed to be approved by the end of 1994. The issue also originated irremediable strains within the majority, with the Lega North (opposed to reform) precipitating a cabinet crisis. As an emergency measure, Berlusconi was able to enact a more rapid schedule for the phasing in of the new retirement age as well as a temporary freeze on all seniority benefits (Cazzola 1995). After the approval of the financial law in December 1994 Berlusconi fell and was replaced by Lamberto Dini's technical cabinet. The trade unions agreed to negotiate into force with this government a new broad reform by the first semester of 1995. In May 1995 the new Dini government succeeded in striking the agreement with the trade unions, which was approved by Parliament the following August.

The new co-operative approach of the trade unions can be explained by at least four factors. First of all, the trade unions had undergone an internal process of maturation: the reform-oriented components of the movement grew stronger, supplying an articulated platform of proposals to the national leadership. The second factor was the concerted style of policy-making introduced by Dini (who was 'technically' supported in the Parliament also by left parties), very different from the adversarial style adopted by Berlusconi (Natali 2001). The third factor was the significant number of concessions granted to the trade unions by the Dini cabinet about the phasing in of the pension reform. Finally, there were the very concrete spurs of the international markets. As a consequence of the political crisis and the ensuing loss of credibility of the Italian government, interest rates started to soar in the winter of 1995, and the lira witnessed an alarming fall against the Deutschmark. The unions thus learnt that refusing the reform was not equal to maintaining the status quo, but making things much worse. In other words, they somehow understood by means of a 'negative re-enforcement' that the arguments of the governments and of the Bank of Italy in favour of pension reform were well grounded and accepted the bet proposed by them.

We will return to the characteristics and significance of these learning processes in the next chapter.

The main novelty of the Dini reform has been the introduction of a new contribution-related formula in place of the earnings-related formula in force since 1969. The pension is no longer related to pensionable earnings, but to the total amount of contributions paid in throughout the working career. Since this change represents a sort of Copernican revolution not only as regards the Italian welfare state, but also within the general context of European pension systems, it deserves a closer analysis.

Since 1975 (including the 1992 Amato reform) the Italian pension formula linked the pension amount to previous earnings, counting 2 per cent of the latter for each year of insurance seniority. For example, if pensionable earnings amount to 100 and the years of insurance seniority are 40, the pension amounts to 80 (2 per cent x 40). Thus, what mattered was only the *duration*, not the effective *amount* of contributions paid in. The 1995 Dini reform, on the contrary, has directly linked the pension to this amount. To calculate future pensions, the total amount of contributions effectively paid by an insured worker will be divided by an actuarial coefficient that depends on the age of retirement (the pensionable age can vary between 57 and 65). This coefficient will be revised every ten years in order to take into account demographic and economic trends. The contributory rates can be revised too, depending on the same trends. The new contribution-related pension will be indexed to inflation, and the elderly without sufficient contributory rights and below a specific income threshold will receive a social allowance financed by fiscal revenues. A series of 'credits' are foreseen for contributory interruptions due to parental and care leaves, i.e. such periods count as if contributions had been paid. Even if it simulates the logic of a funded system, the new system will maintain a pay-as-you-go type of financing: contributions paid in by active workers will not add up to a cumulative fund, but will be immediately used to pay current pensions.

Apart from new contributory formula, the Dini reform has introduced other important novelties: a new flexible retirement age for both men and women (57-65); the phasing out of seniority pensions by 2008; the gradual standardisation of rules for public and private employees; the graduation of survivor benefits according to income; and finally stricter rules on the cumulability of disability benefits and incomes from work, as well as tighter controls on beneficiaries.

Besides changes on the benefit side, the Dini reform also rationalised and raised contribution rates and widened the contribution base by extending compulsory pension insurance to special categories of self-employed workers[15]. The reform included also new provisions on second pillar pension funds, establishing the conditions for setting up these funds also for civil servants and strengthening the tax incentives for diverting the TFR contributions into the funds. According to estimates made at the time of the reform, the Dini provisions were to produce savings on the order of 0.6 per cent of GDP per year between 1996 and 2005. A revision of the key parameters of the system was foreseen in 1998 in the event of savings falling short of expectations (Mira d'Ercole and Terribile 1998: 192)[16].

The autumn of 1992 also marked an important turning point as regards health care: the 'reform of the reform' was finally approved. This transformed the local health units (USL, the basic structure of the SSN) into 'public enterprises' with ample organisational autonomy and responsibility. The USLs are no longer to be run by elective political committees but rather by a general manager appointed by the regions based on professional qualifications and with a private contract, renewable after five years if performance is satisfactory. Larger hospitals, formerly acting as branches of the USL, can now establish themselves as independent public hospitals agencies, with autonomous organisation and administration. These public hospital agencies must operate with balanced budgets. Budgetary surpluses can be used for investments and staff incentives, and unjustified deficits will jeopardise their autonomy. The reform also brought changes in the financing regulations. The central government maintains overall planning responsibilities; that is it pays for a standard set of services that must be guaranteed to each citizen in each region. In this way, each region will continue to receive a predetermined amount of resources by the centre, in accordance with its own population (with some corrections). However, whatever remains to be paid in each region in addition to its standard yearly endowment must be covered with regional resources (higher co-payments or taxes). The regions and the USL managers will thus be encouraged to actively participate to contain costs and promote an efficient use of resources within their jurisdictions. The implementation of the 1992 reform started in 1994; it must also be added that rather severe restrictions were introduced in 1993 and 1994 regarding co-payment regulations and the system of exemptions, also with a view to discouraging frauds and abuses on the side of both patients and physicians.

The 1992-1995 reforms represented major breakthroughs with respect to the institutional legacies of the past. They were also, however, the result of social and political compromises in which the government had to make a number of concessions with regard to its own original plans. The most evident concession regarded the introduction of the new pension formula: the

Dini reform exempted all workers with more than 18 years of insurance seniority by August 1995 from the application of that formula (i.e. the same cohorts that had already been exempted from the Amato reform three years earlier).

But the approximation of the EMU deadlines was keeping Italian authorities under acute budgetary pressures: soon after each one of these compromises, the government thus relaunched its reformist efforts, even widening the scope of its ambitions. In this vein, the new centre-left 'Olive Tree' coalition led by Romano Prodi and voted into office in the spring of 1996 made a comprehensive reform of the *stato sociale* one of its highest priorities. In January 1997 Mr. Prodi appointed a Commission of experts to draft a broad plan for reform. An articulated report was submitted by this Commission (known as the Onofri Commission, after the name of its chairperson, a Bologna economist). The Commission elaborated a comprehensive plan of reforms: an effort that had not been repeated since the early 1960s (when the CNEL drafted its own plan, as illustrated in Chapter 11). Considering the relevance of the Onofri Commission's proposals, a closer look at them is useful.

Acknowledging the 'double distortion' which characterises Italian social expenditures (with respect on the one side to the risks protected, and on the other to the beneficiaries), the Onofri Commission pointed out first of all the general path to follow within the process of reform: the aim of the reform was not to reduce expenditure levels (which were substantially in line with those of other EU countries, according to the data for 1994), but to promote an incisive internal re-equilibration (with some savings in the short term, to facilitate entry into the EMU). As the Commission's Final Report states, the two main objectives of the internal re-equilibration were to be:

> 'On the one hand the reduction of the resources directed to ensure similar
> levels of income for middle income groups at work as well as after retire
> ment, through public pensions (the hyper-protection of the economic
> risk of old age) and the redeployment of such resources for the economic
> risk of unemployment/lack of income, now underprotected. On the other
> side, the generosity of certain provisions on behalf of 'standard' employ
> ment has to be corrected in order to increase (or introduce *ex novo*) the
> protection of the really weaker social categories' (Commission for the
> analysis of the macro-economic compatibility of the social expenditure,
> Final Report, 1997:11).

In order to achieve this double objective, the Commission articulated a series of more specific proposals, grouped into four main chapters:

1 *The introduction of additional measures of retrenchment and rationalisation of public pensions.* Despite a positive evaluation of the basic principles and elements of the Dini reform, the Commission also pointed out its weaknesses, with particular regard to the scope of application of those principles and elements, which was considered too limited. According to the analysis of the Commission, the phasing in of the new system was too slow, burdening the younger generations with the costs of change. The Commission therefore proposed, in order to consolidate the new regime more rapidly, to overcome the remaining elements of iniquity and to introduce a new pillar of supplementary pensions. The specific proposals were:

a. a complete and quick implementation of all the parts of the Dini reform, with particular regard to the harmonisation of the rules about pensionable age, minimum contributory seniority, pensionable earnings, evaluation of working career, yearly yield of contributions, maximum pensionable amount, cumulation, inability and invalidity pensions;

b. a clear separation between social insurance and social assistance, identifying those provisions belonging to social assistance and managed by the National Institute of Social Security (INPS) in order to shift their financing to general taxation;

c. the introduction of new measures to complete the design of the new system, i.e. more specifically: unification (and not only mere harmonisation) of all existing pension schemes or, alternatively, recognition of financial and managerial autonomy only if certain specific pension schemes can prove to be self-sufficient based on long-term technical financial projections; universal application of the contributory formula, without any exception; revision of the coefficients of conversion according to automatic procedures; increase of the minimum pensionable age, in order to reduce the rates of contribution;

d. the acceleration of the transition to the new regime by means of the elimination of existing differences of treatment, particularly with respect to seniority pensions;

e. the resolute acceleration of the development of supplementary pensions, also with respect to the public sector.

2 *An articulated reform of unemployment benefits and employment promotion schemes:* acknowledging that the existing system of unemployment benefits and active labour policies was 'incoherent and almost ungovernable', the Commission proposed a reform aimed at establishing three different tiers of protection:

a. first tier in case of temporary suspension of employment with job preservation: here the instrument of protection should be an insurance scheme similar (but more circumscribed) to the existing ordinary *Cassa Integrazione;*
b. a second tier in case of job loss: here, in line with the main European systems, the instrument should be a 'general unemployment benefit', unifying all different forms of unemployment benefit within the Italian welfare system; and finally
c. a third residual tier in case of exhaustion of the right to insurance benefits.

With regard to labour policies, the Commission also proposed to centre public policy upon active measures, empowering both vocational training and placement services.

3 *A further rationalisation of the incentive structure within the National Health System.* In this case proposals were made with regard to the financing of the national health system (acceleration of the law on the self-financing of regions) and to the provision of services (revision of the division of competences between central administration and regions). Also, the Commission put forward several suggestions with regard to organisational innovations (for example in the hospital sector) and recommended a swift introduction of supplementary health insurance schemes.

4 *The reform of social assistance,* based on the following principles: a balanced mix between universalism, with respect to beneficiaries, and selectivity, with respect to the provision of benefits; a redefinition of needs and benefits centred upon citizenship in general (not only the elderly, not only cash transfers); empowerment of local governments within a national legislative and programmatic framework. More in detail, the Commission proposed:
a. the rationalisation and unification of existing cash transfer schemes, and the introduction of new schemes: a minimum income scheme and a Fund for dependent persons in need of long-term care;
b. the empowerment of local administrations;
c. the establishment of standardised and reliable procedures in order to perform the means and asset-test.

The Onofri report was the object of a rather heated debate in the summer and autumn of 1997. In the budget law for 1998, the Prodi government tried to adopt many of the Commission's recommendations. The fierce opposition of the Refounded Communists (whose votes were crucial for reaching a majority in parliament) and the difficult negotiations with the social partners forced the government, however, to substantially scale down its ambitions. In the field of pensions, Prodi was able to introduce some cuts of seniority pensions, especially for public employees: their contributory requirement for claiming a seniority pension was fully aligned with that applying to private employees, thus tightening the Amato provision of 1992. Contributions for the self-employed were raised, a temporary freeze on the indexation of higher pensions was introduced, and some steps were made on the 'harmonisation' front. However modest (with respect to the government's original ambitions), these cuts had the advantage of being immediately effective and thus gave a small contribution (0.2 per cent of GDP) for reaching the budgetary targets for 1998. The most important recommendation of the Onofri plan, i.e. a much faster phasing in of the new pension formula introduced in 1995, could not be adopted, and by opening a cabinet crisis the Refounded Communists were able to obtain the exemption of blue-collar workers from the cut in seniority pensions[17].

No reform was passed in the field of unemployment insurance either. But the government was able to push through some important innovations on the social assistance and 'selectivity' fronts. More transparent rules for the financing of social assistance were introduced, and the budget law for 1998 – which was approved in December 1997 – delegated the executive to take measures in two important directions: 1) the introduction of a new 'indicator of socio-economic conditions' (ISE), based both on income and asset criteria, to be used as a yardstick for all means-tested benefits; and 2) the introduction of a new (experimental) scheme of 'minimum insertion income' or RMI, i.e. a last resort guaranteed safety net administered by local governments. Both the ISE and the experimental RMI were actually introduced in the course of 1998[18].

In the field of health care, finally, a third reform (after the 1978 and the 1992 reforms) was introduced in June 1999. This established new rules with respect to the financing competences of the centre and the periphery, a new regulation of the relationships between hospital doctors and the National Health Service (imposing on hospital doctors the incompatibility between full-time employment and private activities outside the hospital), and a new regulatory framework for supplementary health insurance funds.

This sequence of reforms has not fully eradicated the distributive and allocative distortions of the Italian welfare state that have been described in Chapter II. They have, however, made significant steps in this direction. More importantly, they have planted promising institutional seeds for a dynamic of recalibration (see Table 4.3).

Table 4.3   Main reforms of social protection, 1983-2000

1983
First measures of retrenchment of public pensions
New user charges for health care

1984
New rules on invalidity pensions INPS

1992
'Amato' pension reform
Health care 'reform of the reform'

1995
'Dini' pension reform

1997
'Prodi' pension reform

1998
Introduction of a new 'indicator of socio-economic conditions' (ISE) for means-tested benefits
Introduction of a new (experimental) scheme of 'minimum insertion income'

1999
Third reform of SSN
Allowances for families with many children, and maternity allowances for women not covered
by compulsory insurance

2000
New framework law on social services and assistance

On the one hand, the setting of more transparent and clear-cut boundaries between social insurance and social assistance as well as the consolidation of new instruments such as the ISE and the RMI will work to strengthen that safety net of means-tested and need-based benefits and services which has been historically lacking (or very weak) in Italy[19]. In this vein, the D'Alema government formed in October 1998 decided to raise social and minimum pensions and to introduce two new means-tested benefits: an allowance for families with three or more children, and a maternity allowance for women not covered by compulsory insurance. In its turn, the Amato government (the last 'Olive Tree' cabinet, in office until June 2001) introduced in the autumn of 2000 a broad 'framework law' of social services and assistance. This law is very important and highly innovative in that it sets rather articulated standards of service that must be guaranteed by all regions. Moreover, just before the end of its mandate (June 2001), the Amato government proposed a comprehensive National Action Plan against poverty and social exclusion, in the wake of the new 'inclusion process' launched by the EU.[20]

Figure 4.1 Pension expenditure projections, 1995-2045

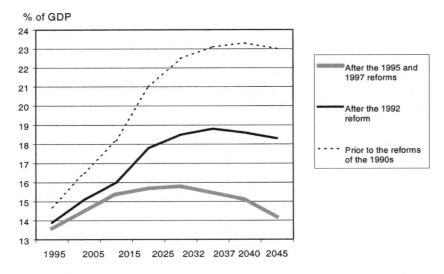

% of GDP

Source: Ministero del Tesoro (1998)

On the other side, the new architecture of the pension system will work to gradually downsize, or at least to contain, the further expansion of a sector that has been historically oversized. It is true that, in spite of the reforms, at the beginning of the 2000s, Italy still displays one of the highest ratios of pension expenditure/GDP in the whole OECD area and that the situation is still going to worsen for at least two decades (cf. Chapter VI below). But if we look at the internal structure of social expenditure, we can see some promising developments. Between 1996 and 1999, for the first time in several decades, the share of old age and survivors pensions out of total expenditure declined slightly (from 65.9 to 64.0 per cent). The share of family benefits, on the contrary, increased slightly from 3.5 to 3.7 per cent (Eurostat, Depenses et recettes de protection sociale, Luxembourg 2000), while in 1999 the function 'social exclusion and housing' registered a figure different from zero, i.e. 0.2 per cent. These are only decimal variations, but they are in any case encouraging. Furthermore, the significance of the 1992-2000 reforms must be appreciated in contrast with the status quo. According to the estimates of the Ministry of the Treasury (1998), in the absence of reforms, pension expenditure would have reached the impressive peak of 23.2 per cent of GDP in the year 2040, before starting to decline. As we shall see in the concluding chapter, after the reforms, the peak is expected to reach 'only' about 16 per cent of GDP in the year 2033. The virtual stabilisation of pension expenditure may not have been enough to cure the long-standing disease of Italy's unbalanced welfare state. But it has certainly contained its fatal aggravation (see Figure 4.1). The reforms of the 1990s have also started to give the Italian pension system a more balanced architecture, putting in place some pre-conditions for the development of the second pillar, thus relieving the first from its functional overload. Last but not least, such reforms have significantly enhanced the overall equity of the pension system. This has been achieved in several ways: by eliminating the legal privileges of civil servants and the de facto advantages enjoyed by the self-employed after the 1990 reform; by abolishing the premium enjoyed by workers with more dynamic careers (typically white collar and managerial staff) under the earnings-related formula, linking benefits to last or best years; by increasing social and minimum pensions.

Of course, the appreciation of the path followed during the last decade should not make us neglect what remains to be done: the recalibration of the Italian welfare state is far from complete. For the most part, the agenda is still that of the Onofri plan: streamlining pensions and consolidating social assistance. But the successful continuation of the reform process is linked to the dynamics of Italy's political system. It is to these dynamics that now we turn our attention.

V   Reforms as Outcomes of Institutional Learning

In Chapter 1 we already presented the analytical perspective that we find most promising for explaining the sequence of reforms that took place in Italy during the 1990s. While we recognize that such a sequence rested to some extent on the traditional logics of 'political exchange', i.e. *quid pro quo* bargains struck between governing authorities and the social categories most affected by the reforms, we wish to emphasise in our explanation the role played by learning dynamics, i.e. processes through which salient policy actors come to modify their preferences under the spur of unforeseen events, past policy failure, sudden constraints, and a particular kind of interaction, based on argument and persuasion. In Italy the years between 1992 and 1998 witnessed a combination of internal and external developments that offered a peculiarly fertile ground for the unfolding of such dynamics. The fall of the 'First Republic', on the one hand, and the Maastricht process, on the other, drastically changed the overall policy-making constellation: new actors appeared on the scene; the rules of both the domestic and the EU games underwent a sudden and significant alteration; the cost and benefits of the various policy options (and thus their distributive implications) became very hard to quantify and predict, also in the wake of the extremely high volatility of financial markets. Political exchanges remain always possible in such unstable constellations, but they get more difficult: actors become more uncertain about what exactly to demand of whom. They thus mature an interest in a common search for policy solutions that can stabilise the constellation as such, rather than bring specific advantages to their part. Of course partisan consideration continues to be salient also during this search. But a distinct *fil rouge* (which can be traced back to a 'learning logic') will run through the actors, interactions and policy-making in this type of environment: a thread consisting of genuine puzzling exercises (often joint, cross-actor exercises) around the nature of the crisis, the possible path(s) of institutional stabilisation and the technical solutions to policy challenges.

In this chapter we will illustrate how this syndrome operated during

Italy's journey into the EMU, breaking the vicious circle of the past and paving the way for a novel, reform-oriented virtuous circle. Building on the factual reconstruction offered in the previous chapters, we will restate in a more articulated fashion our 'anchoring' argument (i.e. how and why the Italian élite opted for European convergence) and will then focus on the political logic that inspired the 1992-1998 reforms.

1   The vicious circle: spoils-sharing governments, inefficient bureaucracy and distributive policies

Up until the 1980s the high institutionalisation of the Keynesian welfare state and of the regulated labour regime centred on passive-distributive policies, on a disproportionate protection for the insiders and a persisting exclusion of the outsiders, originated a highly resistant vicious circle, sustained by an interest coalition including powerful industrial unions, centre-left governments and weak employers' associations.

Why did the (distorted) 'welfare capitalism Italian-style' survive and indeed consolidate throughout the 1980s, despite its manifold perverse effects of an allocative and distributive nature and its increasing mismatch with respect to a rapidly transforming social and economic environment?

As has already been mentioned, the answer lies primarily with the 'political logic' of the 'First Republic' and more particularly with four interrelated ingredients: a) a spoils-centred model of party government; b) a weak and inefficient public administration; c) a highly institutionalised system of political relations between the government and organised interests; and finally d) the distributive nature of labour and social policies. All of these factors were embedded in the context of proportional representation (epitomised by the electoral system), which fostered interest fragmentation and a particularistic distribution of benefits. In the 1980s some efforts to modify these ingredients were attempted, but their effectiveness was not very high, owing to the strong resistance of the supporters (and obviously main beneficiaries) of the status quo.

As is well known, the Italian political system was characterised – at least until the end of the First Republic – by high party fragmentation and lack of competition (Sartori 1982; D'Alimonte 1978; Cotta 1987). Multiparty coalition cabinets were not based on clearly defined and shared programmes, but rather on the proportional distribution of offices and spoils (cf. par. 2 of Chapter II). These unstable executives were led by Prime Ministers with a weak role of co-ordination, while the ministers who borrowed their legitimisation directly from political parties enjoyed high autonomy. The lack of vertical co-ordination between the Prime Minister and the other ministers was reflected moreover in weak horizontal inter-ministerial co-operation. In such a fragmented context, the capacity to introduce innovative public policies was hindered by interest group pressures and partisan vetoes (Fabbrini 2001). The best strategy of survival for the various cabinets was to respond to all the inputs and micro-demands coming from social and political groups by formulating on the one hand general, ambiguous and therefore ineffective public policies and on the other hand by multiplying particularistic laws and regulations in order to distribute advantages and benefits to those social categories whose electoral support seemed to be particularly important. The continuous and cost-irresponsible reception of all particularistic claims had dramatic consequences on public finances, bureaucratic efficiency and the quality of policies and services.

This micro-sectional style of policy-making, characterised by a very low degree of overall substantive coherence, intersected with a system of public administration marked by high centralisation, a top-down, hierarchical implementation style and weak problem-solving capacity (Freddi 1989; 1990; Capano 1992). Up until the 1990s the structure and functioning of central ministries remained virtually unchanged with respect to the nineteenth-century tradition: staff immobility, low decentralisation, a legalistic culture and the obsessive respect of formal rules were the main features of this system, which remained almost impervious to the logic of efficiency and efficacy.

In this fragmented political environment, occupied by a multitude of political actors, unstable and multiparty coalition governments and an ineffective public administration, a thick network of exchanges and negotiations between the government and interest groups was bound to flourish. This is especially true for the major trade unions: after the 'hot autumn' of 1969 the unions acquired an informal guarantee of involvement in social and economic policy-making. In the 1980s, a paradox emerged: labour unions considerably weakened, but their inclusion in policy-making grew deeper roots. It was the executive that, in a period of alarming economic crisis, searched for union approval and help, in order to legitimise its actions and programmes (Gualmini 1997b; 1998). In the 1990s, this tight relationship found a more formalised structure in the practices of *concertazione* and incomes policy that were officially introduced by the 1993 Ciampi agreement (cf. par. 5.). Interestingly enough, the employers' associations (Confindustria in particular) did not contrast the development of corporatist policy-making. In the 1960s and 1970s, when employers were still weakly organised, they accepted trilateral agreements in order to restore peace in industrial relations and at the plant level. In the 1980s, in a period of increased employer power, they supported and participated in corporatist practices, since they had the opportunity to influence the government and obtain favourable legislation, such as industrial subsidies and tax privileges.

Another important factor for the institutionalisation of welfare capitalism Italian-style was the content itself of social and labour policies. This content can be referred to as micro-distributive: highly concentrated (selective) benefits and widely dispersed costs. Micro-distributive policies were the 'poisoned gift' of the economic miracle of the 1950s and 1960s and of the political strategies pursued by the centre-left governments of the 1960s and 1970s, which were inclined to incorporate a growing number of social categories in the welfare state (cf. *supra*, Chapter 11). Distributive policies are indeed particularistic; contrary to universalistic policies, they encourage fiscal irresponsibility and create loyalty and rising expectations in their beneficiaries (Pierson 1993; 1994; Ferrera 1998). They generate incentives for client groups to organise and mobilise in defence of their entitlements.

It is important to remark that the vicious circle we have described so far – vicious because it assured the perpetuation of an unsustainable policy path and hindered every attempt at reform (North 1990) – was a fully coherent system from an internal perspective, a 'tightly coupled' system (Weick 1976). Beneficiaries were obviously keen on supporting it, unions agreed on distributive policies, employers received appealing incentives, and the governments of the *Centro-sinistra* or of the *Penta-partito* could meet the demands of their voters and distribute spoils among the various coalition partners.

But around 1990 the castle began to crumble, under the pressure of growing claims on the side of outsiders, the explosion of costs and the radical transformations of the external economic environment. And starting in the early 1990s the first timid signs of a new virtuous circle began to emerge. We now turn our attention to this new circle.

2   Towards the Second Republic: from vices to virtues?

In the early 1990s, the transformation that in the domestic debate was defined as 'the transition from the First to the Second Republic' together with strong pressure to meet EMU deadlines shook the old model of Italian-style welfare capitalism to its roots. The two dynamics combined to produce a virtuous chain of policy reforms.

During the first half of the 1990s, the Italian party system underwent some rather dramatic and sudden changes. First and foremost was the discovery of a dense, all-pervasive network of political corruption involving prominent political leaders and party members, which led to a snowballing delegitimisation of the ruling class. As a result of the 'Clean Hands' (*Mani pulite*) investigation (a name coined by the pool of judges working in Milan), an extensive network of illegal financing and fiscal fraud involving both politicians and well-known businessmen was brought to light, thus underlining the very close (and risky) connection between politics and business. In the 'Tangentopoli' storm (Milan was depicted as 'Bribesville'), several employers and political leaders were convicted by the courts, and a large section of the First Republic's ruling élite subsequently retired from public life.

The dramatic effects of Tangentopoli intersected with major changes in the structure of the political system. In 1991 the positive results of the referendum on the 'single preference vote' – which reduced the number of candidates for the lower Chamber that voters could choose in their ballot from four to one – opened the way to the reform of the electoral system, which was transformed from an almost pure plurality system to a new majority-rule system (i.e. first past the post). This reform was officially passed after the results of the electoral referendum held in April 1993.

One year later, for the first time ever in Italy, two large party coalitions stood against each other to gain electoral support. The bipolarisation of the political contest marked the end of the so-called *conventio ad excludendum* (agreement to exclude) in relation to the communist party, whereby the communists had been isolated and forced into permanent opposition. This was also a consequence of the end of the 'Cold War', so clearly symbolised by the fall of the Berlin Wall. The 'pro-system/anti-system' cleavage – which had moulded and ossified the Italian party system – began to lose salience, and opposition parties gained increasing credibility with regard to their governing credentials. Moreover, in the very same year, 1989, under Occhetto's leadership, the Italian Communist party had taken a fundamental step in the direction of a more 'liberal' philosophy, much closer to that of the existing European social-democratic parties. This step was symbolised by the change in party name from the Communist Party to the Left Democratic Party (PDS) and later Left Democrats (DS).

Let us now take a closer look at the profound transformations that the political system underwent during this period. In the first place, after the 1994 elections the old political parties were hit by an irreversible electoral and organisational crisis. The cornerstones of the five-party coalition, i.e. the Christian Democrats, the Socialists, the Social Democrats, the Republicans and the Liberals, practically evaporated into thin air. Secondly, the crisis of these political parties brought about another crisis, one concerning the entire party system and its above-mentioned characteristics: its polycentric structure, the lack of competition, the predominance of centre-based coalitions, its weak leadership capacity. Thirdly, the crisis marked the nadir of an entire political class. In 1994, 71 per cent of deputies were elected for the first time. There were many reasons for dissolution of the old political élite besides Tangentopoli: the emergence of numerous internal party conflicts, the loss of control over the executive, the inability to change and the entry of new competitors into the political arena (Cotta and Verzichelli 1996; Fabbrini and Vassallo 1999). The fourth factor was the setting up of new parties and movements. After the electoral success of the Northern League (Lega Nord) back in 1992 (a party whose main aim was to eliminate strong state centralisation and its suffocating system of taxation), 1994 saw the birth of a new centre right political movement led by Silvio Berlusconi, Forza Italia, which in the space of four months managed to organise itself and win the election.

Other important factors that characterised this period of transition included the gradual process of separation of the national executive from the grip of political parties, and the consequent changes in inter-institutional relationships. In fact, the demise of the First Republic changed the nature of relations between the various different political institutions. Relations between the executive and the President of the Republic shifted in favour of the latter, while relations between the executive and Parliament moved in favour of the former, and finally the relationship between the judiciary and the general political system was marked by the dominance of the judges.

A stronger national executive made the introduction of structural reforms easier. The technical cabinets headed by Amato, Ciampi and Dini (cf. Table 1, above) were allowed to work in the absence of any strict party control and could thus enjoy greater autonomy and have a more direct say in governing the policy-making process.

This autonomy, on the contrary, was rather limited in the case of the Berlusconi government, formed in May 1994 after the first election had been won with the new majority-rule electoral system. This executive did not, however, last long due to inner conflict and tension. The coalition was in fact based on two different alliances: Forza Italia and Alleanza Nazionale (the renamed neo-Fascists) in the south, Forza Italia and the Lega Nord in the north. The presence of the Lega Nord in the government brought with it a non-conventional opposition between the independentist, entrepreneurial claims of the North and the State-centred culture of southern Italy, which overlapped with the more traditional political contrast between right and left. Furthermore, Berlusconi's government was constantly subjected to the strict control of the President of the Republic, Scalfaro, mainly due to the yet unresolved conflict between the Premier's business interests and his public office. After only six months, the Berlusconi government fell due to the withdrawal of the Northern League from the majority, basically on the pension issue (cf. Chapter IV), which touched upon this party's electoral interests in the North. The Berlusconi government was replaced by a technical coalition led by Dini.

In April 1996 Berlusconi tried to repeat the victory of 1994, but was defeated by the leader of the centre-left 'Olive Tree' coalition, Romano Prodi. The new executive included some innovative elements which made observers believe that the period of institutional transition had come to an end: the rules of turn-over and alternation had worked; the government was strengthened in relation to Parliament[1]; and the role of the Prime Minister was reinforced against that of his ministers (Fabbrini 2000; 2001). But the events that occurred during the entire centre-left legislature (1996-2001), characterised by the formation of four different governments, showed that the shift to a real majority-rule democracy was still underway.

A few months after victory (in January 1997), the 'Olive Tree' coalition set up the third parliamentary commission for constitutional reform under the guidance of D'Alema, the leader of the coalition's biggest party (the Democratic Party of the left which was about to change name once again – at the 1997 congress in Florence – becoming the party of the Left Democrats – DS). The D'Alema commission was established together with the leader of the opposition, Berlusconi, with the aim of introducing extensive reforms of the country's system of government (towards a majoritarian format), of the structure of the Italian state (in a federal direction) and of the working of parliament (involving the abolition of a perfect bicameral system, the simplification of law-making, the creation of a regional senate, etc.). Like its predecessors (the Bozzi commission and the De Mita commission in 1983 and 1993, respectively), the D'Alema commission ended up by producing a bill which got sunk in Parliament under the weight of vetoes and conflicts between various parties both inside and outside the majority, which in particular failed to see eye-to-eye on the multiplicity of governmental models (from the purely presidential to the purely parliamentary).

Notwithstanding the failure of the bicameral commission – which, as a matter of fact, the Prime Minister remained somewhat distant from – during the Prodi government some important reforms were passed by means of ordinary policy-making procedures: reforms such as the establishment of administrative federalism thanks to the so-called 'Bassanini laws' (59 and 127/1997) and the (related) reform of government ministries (legislative decree 300/1999).

The Bassanini reform reorganised the distribution of political and administrative power between central and local levels, introducing a wide-ranging devolution of competencies from central ministries to regional and local governments. This transfer of power took place in a number of crucial policy sectors, like commercial activities, labour policies, welfare and transportation. This process meant the decisive reorientation of the role of subnational levels of government, inducing a clear degree of differentiation among the performance and institutional capacities of the various different Italian regions. The provinces and municipalities saw their role strengthened, even with respect to the regions, contrary to what had happened in the past[2].

The reform of the ministries was the other side of the decentralisation coin, and the new provisions were designed to be implemented as of the following legislature. The reduction and merger of ministries (from 18 to 12), the clear separation between political and management functions, the introduction of departments and executive agencies within the ministries together er constituted the main goals of the reform, which tried to imitate the British managerial experience of the 1980s[3] (Gualmini 2003).

In October 1998, an increasing divergence within the governing coalition between the Premier and Rifondazione Comunista (a 'hard left' party originating from the old Italian Communist Party – the PCI – who supported the coalition but had not entered the majority and the executive) emerged over the 1999 financial law, leading to the fall of the Prodi government. The executive was defeated, 313 votes against 312, but was nevertheless the Italian Republic's second longest-lasting executive after the Craxi government of the 1980s (August 1983-August 1986).

The first (October 1998 - December 1999) and second (December 1999-April 2000) D'Alema governments, supported by the new party set up by the former President of the Republic Cossiga (UDEUR) and including certain fugitives from Berlusconi's Forza Italia party, marked the confirmation once again of political parties' weight in the distribution of office, and of Parliament's strength to the disadvantage of the Prime Minister. The number of technical ministers and technical undersecretaries fell significantly, the ministries were shared out among seven different parties compared with five in the previous executive, and the role of D'Alema, notwithstanding his efforts to maintain a presidential style, was simply one of *primus inter pares*. As a result of all this, the fragmentation of the centre-left coalition grew significantly.

Furthermore, the second government headed by D'Alema inevitably fell early on (April 2000) due to the negative performance of the centre-left coalition in the 2000 regional elections, notwithstanding the international legitimisation gained by the Premier during the diplomatic events preceding the war in Kosovo.

A well-known figure on the Italian political scene, Giuliano Amato was appointed by the new President of the Republic, Ciampi, to form a new government without calling elections: its explicit task was to pass the Budget and to conclude the reform of the electoral system. Amato led the government until May 2001, without succeeding in completing the said reform (since the referendum of May 2000 on the final abolition of proportional representation did not achieve the quorum). Nevertheless, it did manage to take another step towards federalism. The Constitutional Law of March 2001 (no. 3) – which was finally approved by a consultative referendum in October 2001[4] – broadened the number of exclusive and joint powers held by sub-national governments. More in detail, it turned over the logic of article 117 of the Constitution where regional competencies were listed, defining in the first place the exclusive legislative powers of the state (foreign policy, defence, immigration, citizenship, justice, financial and monetary policy), in the second place the subjects for joint state-regions competency (education, work safety, pensions, health, trade, etc.) and finally delegating all remaining matters to the exclusive competence of the regions.

The debate on the autonomy and legislative role of sub-national governments continued to remain a central issue within the second Berlusconi government, elected in May 2001. The project on devolution, strongly supported by Bossi, which should further empower regional and local governments in the field of education, health and local security, worked as an important pay-off for the participation of the Lega Nord in the centre-right coalition. But the second Berlusconi government and its main policy strategies will be the subject of the next chapter.

3   Financial adjustment in the name of Europe: what should be done?

It is within the two aforementioned contexts (the old vicious circle and the emerging virtuous one) that the process of structural adjustment, described in Chapters III and IV, has taken place and shape. How can we interpret this process in terms of learning? As mentioned in Chapter I, in order to answer this question, we have to distinguish between two different challenges to which the adjustment has responded. The first challenge was of a substantive nature and has essentially regarded 'what to do', both in terms of goals and instruments. The second challenge was of an essentially political nature and has regarded 'how to get the reforms passed', given the obstacles of the decision-making process and the social resistance to change. These two challenges presented themselves with a slightly different timing: substantive puzzling (i.e. the analysis of problems and the search for possible solutions) came prior to 'powering' (the orchestration of consensus and the actual exercise of power to change things). In part, the two exercises have also involved different actors: a more restricted circle of *architects* of the adjustment, with the Bank of Italy and the Ministry of the Treasury as main protagonists, in the first case; a wider circle of *builders,* including also political actors at the highest levels of government and parliament, and major interest group and party leaders, in the second case. Yet the overall process remained relatively integrated, with strong interdependencies and links between the two circles and levels of action. And if we try to reconstruct the main lines of this process, we can see that it took place through a sequence of approximations, through various trials and errors, within the typical logic of 'operational conditioning', which, as argued above, is one of the classical and most efficient modes of learning[5].

From a substantive point of view, the first step consisted of the elaboration of a correct diagnosis of the new problems originated by the shocks of the 1970s, acknowledging the failure of the status quo in various sectors of public intervention. On the basis of this diagnosis, a slow process of institutional design and planning was started – both with regard to the objectives and to the instruments of governmental action – outlining an increasingly richer and more articulated reformist agenda. The irreversible anchoring to Europe – and in particular to the emergent European monetary system – imposed itself as the overarching priority of this design. This choice should not be taken for granted at the time when it was made: between the 1970s and the 1980s, there was still much scepticism and uncertainty about what to do even within those circles that were most favourable and open to the external world and to Europe (Radaelli 1999). But the 'European pin' gradually managed to reinforce itself, and a strong advocacy coalition gathered around it in order to spell out and underline all the implications of the external constraint (the *vincolo esterno*) with regard to the contents, modalities and timing of domestic policy-making, obviously starting from monetary and budgetary policies[6]. For the most part, it has been a coalition that crossed traditional ideological and party cleavages, made up of a central nucleus of professors from academic, political and administrative environments, accustomed to international meetings and exchanges[7]. Even if these actors elaborated substantially original projects, we have to take into account that numerous solutions to domestic problems were determined by a process of comparative learning, that is emulating and adapting solutions already experimented with by other countries. The speed of these processes has been ever accelerating. Not only did the various actors start to learn faster and with more effectiveness, but the target itself (the European Community, and then Union) started to move: after twenty years of relative institutional stability, between the 1970s and the 1980s the integration process began to walk faster, originating three constitutional revisions (the 1986 Single Act, the 1992 Maastricht Treaty, and the 1997 Amsterdam Treaty) and three enlargements (firstly to Greece, then to Spain and Portugal, and finally to the Nordic countries and Austria). Thus, in correspondence with each advancement of the European building, the project of institutional adjustment and internal modernisation had to be renewed and accelerated.

In the previous chapters we have described the programmatic confrontations and institutional innovations, trials and errors through which the different decision-makers (starting from those defined as 'architects' of the financial adjustment) learnt what to do in order to 'Europeanise' Italy progressively, with particular reference to public finances, welfare and labour markets. Before turning to the second challenge (and therefore to the specific dynamics of political learning), we will elaborate on two important phases/aspects of the anchoring process: the decision that made this process virtually irreversible, i.e. the entry into the EMS in 1978; and its 'external side', i.e. the contribution given by the Italian architects to the development of the European institutions and rules, and thus of the so-called *vincolo esterno*. These questions deserve our attention in the first place since they are not well known, but also because they allow us to understand unexpected connections between the old circle of 'vices' and the new circle of 'virtues', in the dynamics of the First and the Second Republic.

As we have shown in the second chapter, the entry into the EMS in December 1978 was the result of an exceptional performance of the fourth Andreotti executive, followed by the breaking off of the so-called 'national solidarity' pact between Christian Democrats and Communists. Busy as it was in searching for a third way between Western-type capitalism and Soviet-type socialism, the Communist Party strongly opposed entry into the new monetary regime. The periodical 'Rinascita' (linked to the PCI) stamped it as an attempt to bind Italy's hands to those countries 'still more crudely class-centred than our own'. Constrained by the main ally of the coalition (the PCI), the Christian Democrat Prime Minister Andreotti was forced to say 'no' to Brussels, when on the 5th of December 1978 the other member states (with the exception of the United Kingdom and the Republic of Ireland) signed the agreement. But once back in Rome, Andreotti searched for votes within Parliament and found them on the right. On the 13th of December, 270 members of the Parliament voted in favour of the agreement (including neo-Fascists and liberals), 218 voted against. How was this dramatic choice forged, foreboding virtuous implications for the Italian economy? A detailed account of this story still has to be written[8]. We know that the Bank of Italy (i.e. the circle of architects) played an important role, but when the game became tougher (and the executive was on the verge of a crisis) Andreotti and foreign minister Forlani (i.e. two historical leaders of the DC) were the ones who decided to go ahead. Were they inspired by far-sightedness, noble intentions and incorruptible Europeanism? Maybe, but it is possible that they acted to pursue specific political advantages. The embrace with the Communist Party was becoming politically stifling and more and more costly in terms of economic resources and international credibility. To choose a 'European' issue to break with the Communists was not very risky in terms of electoral support (indeed, it could have positive implications), while the activation of a rather strict external constraint would help to keep the Socialist Party (PSI) in check, which was an ally necessary to form any government coalition, but was also undisciplined in political and programmatic perspective – also because of the competition coming from the left. Craxi was not enthusiastic of the EMS, and embraced the cause of austerity only when he was elected Prime Minister. If this interpretation is correct, then we need to highlight a connection, even if it is a weak one, between the logic of functioning of the First Republic and the process of financial adjustment that took off seriously only after the end, paradoxically, of the First Republic itself: the political 'yield' of the European choices of the parties which governed that Republic (and in particular the DC) was a precondition of the virtuous circle and the dynamics of substantive and procedural learning that have anchored Italy definitively to the European Union.

The external side of this anchorage is not very well known or appreciated either. It is true that the flux of ideas (values, knowledge, institutional techniques, and so on) from Europe to Italy has been much more intense and relevant than the flux in the opposite direction. Yet the rhetoric that has depicted Europe as a constraint has had the effect of obfuscating the tiring and complex game of attack and defence (mainly the latter) played by many Italian political actors (within both circles mentioned above) since 1979 onwards, in various EC *fora* of decision-making. We are referring, for example, to the enervating negotiations on the lira's re-alignments within the EMS during the 1980s, or to those on the contents and timing of implementation of the long series of directives aimed at the completion of the Internal Market.

The decision-making process that led to the Single Act and some of its contents were also substantially conditioned by the Italian initiative: it was Craxi who started the process during the Council of Ministers in 1985 in Milan (which had to decide upon the launching of constitutional revision through an intergovernmental conference), isolating a recalcitrant and furious Thatcher. Also, on this external front of Europeanisation several diagnoses and projects were necessary to protect Italian interests. Furthermore, it was essential to learn what to do (and how) in order to condition the EC agenda, to avoid its definition solely on the side of other countries, not so much against Italian aspirations as against Italy's institutional capacities.

The most difficult challenge occurred at the beginning of the 1990s, during the negotiations on the Maastricht Treaty and on the Economic and Monetary Union in particular. Ciampi (as Governor of the Bank of Italy), Carli (as Minister of the Treasury), De Michelis (as Minister of the Foreign Affairs) and, once more, Andreotti (as Prime Minister) had to pursue two different and – in a sense – contradictory objectives: 1) to define rather rigid and specific deadlines and procedures with respect to the realisation of the third phase of the EMU, so as to introduce a credible commitment towards the deepening of integration on the side of the stronger countries (such as Germany, above all) and, at the same time, to forge an external constraint strong enough to stimulate the financial adjustment of the weakest countries; and 2) to avoid the establishment of too prohibitive criteria, which could mean the relegation of Italy into a sort of Europe of second division (Ferrera 1991; Dyson and Featherstone 1996). To reach the first objective, the Italian negotiators first of all had to defend themselves against the British proposals: Mrs. Thatcher pushed for the consolidation of a system based on the competition between currencies and opposed any formal commitment to move towards a common currency. The British resistance was wisely circumvented in the second quarter of 1990, when Andreotti, as President of the European Council, managed to isolate Thatcher (once more) in the Rome Summit, which established that the beginning of the second phase of the EMU was the 1st of January 1994. A short while later, however, during the negotiations on the Treaty, the strongest countries formed a new front against the establishment of an 'automatic' deadline for the third and decisive phase. The efforts of the Italian negotiators on this front (with their French allies) were decisive: it was for the most part the pressures exercised by Andreotti and Mitterrand during the last round of negotiations before Maastricht that determined the establishment of the 1st of January

1999 as the ultimate 'automatic' deadline for the creation of the Euro. Retrospectively, considering the hesitations of Germany in the course of 1997, we need to appreciate the importance of that decision.

In order to reach the second objective (i.e. to avoid overly strict convergence criteria, given the general conditions of Italian public finances) the Italian negotiators had to contrast the powerful fire of the Bundesbank, which aimed at creating a sort of Germanised Union with respect to its targets (price stability, absence of public deficits, and so on) as well as institutions (an independent European Central Bank, free from any political conditioning), and at imposing the Deutschmark as the anchor of the EMS. On this front, an important battle was fought against the proposals advanced by the Dutch Presidency in 1991. These proposals called for a set of convergence criteria based on automatic thresholds which were completely out of reach for Italy, and suggested that the third phase start in 1997, with the agreement of only six countries. This, in practice, meant that Italy would have been excluded. Carli brought a vigorous attack against the Dutch plan (which was also supported by Germany), defining as 'aberrating' the idea of an automatic inclusion/exclusion, based on arithmetic criteria, without taking into account the real size, and thereby the actual relevance of a specific country within the context of the EC. Carli and De Michelis also opposed the quorum of six countries for the 1997 deadline. Although they accepted the principle of quantitative convergence criteria, the two Italian ministers insisted on the interpretation of the criteria in evolutionary rather than static terms. They asked, in other words, that variables such as inflation or deficit be considered not at a certain moment, but that their evolution over time be taken into account. This would have allowed those countries that followed a path of convergence to be included, even if they didn't comply exactly with the quantitative requirements. Carli also insisted that the quorum necessary for the launch of phase III be raised from six to seven countries. This would increase the chances of inclusion for Italy. The proposals of Carli, supported by France and the Commission, were eventually included in the Treaty (articles 104c and 109j). In conclusion, it was Andreotti's last executive that shaped the EMU so that Italy could realistically join the Euro-group – even if by means of impressive efforts.

As in the case of the EMS, the story of the Italian initiatives (proposals, attempts, mistakes, re-elaborations) aimed at influencing the decisions of the European Union during the last, delicate twenty years of deepening and widening still has to be written. It is likely that such a reconstruction could confirm, in general, the impression of a less enterprising and effective member state than its role of 'big fourth' could potentially involve. But the Italian voice, at least in some critical conjunctures, has been loud and successful. That *vincolo esterno* which played such an important role in Italy's adjustment cannot be thought of as totally *exogenous*. And since in some occasions Italy's opinions were voiced by protagonists of the First Republic, we may observe here a further connection between the circle of 'vices' and the circle of 'virtues'.

4   The political dilemmas of the 'Olive Tree' coalition

The second process of learning involved the question of how to get the reforms passed. As we have previously noted, the project of financial adjustment 'in the name of Europe' began to be implemented in the 1980s: the divorce between the Central Bank and the Ministry of the Treasury, the new budgetary procedures, the measures of financial management of health care, and so on. The first measures introduced were the least visible, as they were aimed at affecting the capacity to govern economic policy as a whole, rather than the deficit spending due to specific policies or to the rigidity and bad functioning of the labour market. The attempts to intervene on the latter fronts were much less effective: this is why earlier we referred to the 'chaotic' restructuring of welfare and to the 'uncertain' deregulation of the labour market in the 1980s. Indeed, for the government only one clear-cut signal came from the hard game of politics: keep your hands off the welfare state, don't touch social benefits! At the end of the 1980s, the 'public expenditure party' (largely criss-crossing the official party lines) was still very strong: in critical conjunctures of policy-making, it commanded enough resources to veto any substantial alteration of the distributive status quo.

The window of opportunity to introduce more incisive changes opened up in 1992, due to the external and internal dynamics we have already described. The feeling of urgency created by the financial crisis of that summer and by the new European deadlines, the delegitimation of the old establishment, the restructuring of the party system and the reinforcement of the executive led to a series of wide-ranging reforms. After the victory at the level of ideas, the coalition of architects of the financial adjustment obtained new resources to implement their objectives within a few months. In the public policy arena the game based on ideas is always a power game too: as Müller writes (1995), the *prise de parole* is at the same time a *prise de pouvoir*. In Italy in 1992-1993 this coincidence however took a very strong form: many architects were invited to enter the very shrine of executive power, i.e. the central cabinet. Repositioning of the actors in the decision-making arena obviously played an important role. But it was only the first step of a new game, explicitly aimed at influencing the material interests of wide social (and electoral) constituencies. And this game, too, may be read in terms of learning: 'puzzling on how to power', using the formula discussed in Chapter 1. There is an evident dynamic of 'operational conditioning' that led the architects of financial adjustment (many of whom in the meanwhile had taken up roles of political leadership: Ciampi, Dini and Prodi, to name only Prime Ministers) to shape the contents, modalities and timing of the reforms, taking into account their political and social feasibility. On the other hand, the dynamic of 'operational conditioning' persuaded the advocates of the status quo (and the trade unions in particular) to accept these same contents, modalities and timing, acknowledging the negative consequences of a strategy based on vetoes and thus altering their very preferences.

After the fall of the Berlusconi government, in December 1994, it became clear that also in the new institutional context the reforms could not be made by means of antagonistic politics, consisting of direct confrontations with organised interests. It was therefore essential to work out certain compromises with these interests. The post-Berlusconi governments began two different strategies in order to build up the necessary consensus: on the one hand, they stressed all the medium-term advantages of the entry into the Euro, and particularly the advantages for trade unions and employers; on the other, they elaborated a new discourse in support of financial adjustment, in order to further delegitimise the status quo, and make the reform more acceptable to the trade unions at the symbolic level.

The first effort (which may be considered an example of policy-making aimed at a form of 'sequential equity': first the stick, and then the carrot) (Barney and Ouchi 1984) led to the acceptance of a large number of subtractive policies (above all restrictions on social benefits) in exchange for more or less specific promises for the medium-to-long term (such as the use of the savings on the debt-service due to the Euro in order to develop and relaunch employment, particularly in the South, the reduction of social and fiscal burdens for the employers, etc.). As we will see in more detail in the next section, the Amato, Ciampi and Dini agreements (1992-1995) represent the subtractive part, while the Pact for Work of the Prodi government and the D'Alema Pact for Development (1996-1998) represent the compensatory part of this strategy.

The second effort aimed at adding arguments in terms of equity to those based on considerations of efficiency (such as the entry into EMU to adjust public finances and restoring the whole Italian economy to health): welfare reform was to be pursued because it would restore a new balance between categories which are well protected (the *garantiti*) and those not protected, between 'fathers' and 'sons', between 'compensations' and 'opportunities', and so on. Even if these statements were sincere and their arguments objectively relevant, if we consider Italy's welfare system in comparative perspective[9], we have to acknowledge that this new discourse had an important communicative and co-ordinative function (Schmidt 2000) not only in order to publicly legitimate the reforms, but also to consolidate relations between the government and the trade unions.

The Dini and Prodi governments in particular are responsible for this operation of symbolic and normative redefinition of the *risanamento*. Both governments were backed by the main party of the left – who had its own ministers within the Prodi cabinet, for the first time in the history of the Republic. Thus, both Dini and Prodi had the possibility of passing reforms that were unpopular in the eyes of the trade unions. It is a syndrome known within the literature on welfare as 'Nixon goes to China'. Just as it took a hyper-conservative politician such as Nixon to persuade the American Congress to normalise relations with China, it is easier for left-wing parties to persuade trade unions to reform the welfare state (Ross 1998). When they try to push through reforms, such parties can also take advantage of a relatively benign treatment on the side of the opposition: the centre-right can speak for bolder reforms but would find it difficult to adopt a strategy of boycott. During the 1990s, the 'Nixon goes to China' approach was adopted by many other European centre-left governments, which justified their reforms as measures aimed at substituting past 'vices' (overly generous pensions, passive unemployment benefits, poverty and unemployment traps, and so on) by means of new 'virtues' (such as a contributory pension formula, funded forms of financing, active labour policies, fight against social exclusion, etc.) (Levy 1999a; 1999b). Of course, such operations were (and are still) very problematic. Welfare reform 'from the left' needs a number of contortions at the ideological-programmatic and political-electoral level. It also means taking a difficult path, step by step (with some steps backwards), by means of repeated attempts, revisions, and revisions of revisions: with obvious consequences in terms of coherence, efficiency and effectiveness of the reforms. But alternative political paths were and still are extremely difficult in all 'consensual' democracies – which are the norm in Europe. It is no coincidence that the only two countries in which conservative governments carried out important and incisive welfare reforms in the 1990s are majoritarian democracies such as the United Kingdom (where the Conservatives were in power until 1997) and New Zealand: that is, democracies with a very limited number of veto players in the decision-making process. Within consensual democracies, the passing of social reforms during the Maastricht decade seems to have been easier in the presence of 'lib-lab' coalitions, inclined to reconcile the reasons of efficiency and innovation with those of equity. The protagonists of the Dutch miracle of the 1990s were 'purple' governments led by socialists (represented by the colour red) and liberals (represented by the colour blue). "The Third Way" project, which became so popular among centre-left governments in the second half of the 1990s, can after all be seen as an attempt at recasting the dilemmas of welfare reform in a symbolic frame resting on a virtuous combination of efficiency and justice, competitiveness and solidarity (Giddens 2001), also with a view to smoothening trade union opposition to welfare reforms.

But let us return to the Italian case. The efforts described above, making the restrictive provisions more palatable, allowed the Dini and Prodi governments to get ever closer to the trade unions and obtain their confidence. The unions, on their part, took some steps towards compromise, abandoning the strategy of vetoes, softening up their position and eventually converting themselves to a reformist path. The turning point occurred in the winter of 1995, during the negotiations on the Dini pension reform. As we have already explained, in those frantic months the trade unions changed their position rapidly, elaborating their own articulated platform of initiatives. Dropping the Berlusconi draft reform plan, the Dini government actually took the union draft reform as the starting point for negotiations, and union experts informally assisted ministerial technicians in each phase of the drafting of the final bill (Regalia and Regini 1998). But it was under the blows of the international markets – that worsened the lira's exchange rate day after day, obliging the Bank of Italy to raise interest rates, with heavy consequences for the public budget – that the trade unions ultimately convinced themselves that the status quo was no longer sustainable. During the first three months of the Dini government (January-March 1995), the spread between interests on Italy's and Germany's state bonds (the 'BTP' and the 'Bund') reached an impressive peak of almost seven base points, up from three base points of only a year before; in the same months, the probability assigned by markets (e.g. JP Morgan's 'EMU calculator') to Italy's admission into the EMU by 1999 was as low as 0.127 (Chiorazzo and Spaventa 1999). In other words, the lesson for the trade unions was: there is no status quo, but a declining trend that is rapidly leading to an abyss unless we agree on a credible pension reform capable of re-assuring the markets on Italy's *risanamento*. In the first months of 1995, Italian economic and social policy-making started to function as a sort of 'Skinner box', where the international markets produced stimuli in terms of variations of the lira's value and of interest rates[10]. In this case too, the logic of operational conditioning pushed the trade unions towards compromise. In May, Law no. 335/1995 (the Dini reform) was approved. The opposition (i.e. Berlusconi) abstained from the final vote: but during the negotiations it displayed a reasonably collaboratively stance (Cazzola 1995). The reform was positively received by international markets. In early 1996, the BTP/Bund spread had dropped to four points, and the probability of EMU entry had increased to 0.527. After Prodi's new reform in the autumn of 1997 (in the framework of the financial law for 1998), the spread reduced further to less than one point and the probability of admission jumped to 0.96. Between 1995 and 1997 the average cost of public debt declined from 9.2 to 7.9 per cent of GDP[11].

In addition to the factors mentioned above, the dynamics of political learning of the 1990s were sustained and fed by the system of rules and decision-making practices that is called concerted action (*concertazione*). Concerted action primarily promoted an environment of trust among the different actors, enabling them to discover mutually advantageous paths of change – or at least to avoid turning a single actor into a firescreen against popular discontent. Let us complete our interpretative reconstruction by examining in greater detail the system of concerted action and its contribution to the process of financial adjustment.

5   The return of concerted action in the 1990s

Within the mainstream literature on neo-corporatism, Italy has always been considered the least corporatist country in Europe. During the 1970s debate, it was conceived as a case of weak corporatism, at the bottom of international classifications, lacking in all the essential functional requirements: a strong state, cohesive and centralised interest groups monopolising the representation of interests, and a pro-labour government (Schmitter 1974; Lehmbruch and Schmitter 1984; Streeck and Schmitter 1985). A second generation of studies then tried to rehabilitate the cases in which corporatism seemed absent, showing how concerted action can develop even without these functional requirements, as in the United Kingdom at the end of the 1970s, or in Italy during the 1970s and the 1980s (Goldthorpe 1984; Regini 1989; 1991).

More recently a good number of scholars have concentrated their attention on the wave of corporate agreements that spread throughout Europe during the second half of the 1990s, after the debate had spoken of the death, or anyway decline, of corporatism (Schmitter and Grote 1997; Wiarda 1997; Gualmini 1997a; 1997b; Salvati 2000). The idea of a new 'social contract' (Rhodes and Meny 1997), centred upon an unusual combination between deregulation and cost containment, on the one hand, and the maintenance of consensus, on the other, led to a sort of 'third way' of welfare regulation: this was situated somewhere between unrestricted capitalism and state management, and was favoured by several European leaders. The Dutch model, based on a combination of concerted action, flexibility, welfare reform and wage moderation became a benchmark.

Some writers compared this to the tireless efforts of Sisyphus, characterised by constant, wave-like movement (Schmitter and Grote 1997). The idea of waves, that is periodical swings between concerted action designed to produce a mixture of co-ordination, control and consensus, and a strategy of deregulation, designed on the contrary to remove the restrictions imposed by institutions (Regini 1999), seems to fit the Italian case quite nicely: agreements employed as tools, constantly available in the tool box of various governments, and dusted down to be used during periods of socio-economic crisis.

In Italy concerted political action, rather than being associated with the political hues of government cabinets (which did not actually change very much throughout the entire lifetime of the First Republic), has always been a response to the aggravation of economic conditions, and as such a specific reaction to the need to construe consensus in order to get ordinary and extraordinary policy decisions passed. Furthermore, the chronic inefficiency of the parliamentary arena with regard to the provision of laws aimed at problem-solving led to the search for functional replacements. The Italian Parliament has always suffered from an extreme sluggishness in the policy-making process. This is due not only to the high fragmentation and internal divisions of party coalitions, but also to certain structural elements: in particular, the duplication of the legislative process between the two Houses (the Chamber and the Senate) as a result of the 'perfect bi-parliamentary' model, and an intense activity of obstructionism. The latter was a perverse effect of parliamentary regulations granting veto powers to all minor parties and fostering cross-house alliances between the majority and the opposition. The slow decision-making process of the Parliament, frustrating as well as distant from the real social and economic problems of Italy, produced sectorial provisions and regulations. Concerted action to some extent substituted the Parliament for the elaboration of the main reforms of economic and social policy. It had a strong pragmatic and contingent orientation, in the absence of alternative decision-making circuits[12].

This particular mix between the logic of political exchange and the logic of problem-solving (i.e. of mutual information and learning) – as we have already underlined in Chapter 1 – particularly suits the Italian case where trade unions and business associations were able, especially in the 1990s, to provide the governments (weakened as they were by the events of Tangentopoli) strategic and relational information (Culpepper 2002) on the possible solutions to emergency problems. The dialogic capacity of interest groups was exercised both internally and externally, i.e. towards their rank-and-file in order to make them accept the contents of negotiated reforms, and towards the government in order to support it in the formulation and design of effective policy recipes.

However, action varied throughout the decade. Agreements emerged from a series of trials and errors producing two kinds of results. On the one hand, this sequence spurred a learning process, transferring to the actors involved the capacity and experience to plan effective solutions to the problems on the agenda, on the basis of their technical know-how as well as their capacity to persuade and mobilise their members; on the other hand, it induced a gradual institutionalisation of the architecture and logic of functioning of that specific model of decision-making, by means of the strengthening of the democratic procedures of the unions' internal decision-making, which allowed increasing participation and discussion by the rank-and file (Baccaro 2002). As a first effect, then, the stability of the decision-making context, the need to maintain the promises already made, the character of a repeated game, based on an agreement that originates other subsequent agreements – i.e. a series of conditions guaranteed by concerted action – produced a sense of loyalty and reciprocal commitment among the participants, reducing the possibility of defection and free riding, while fostering the activity of reform[13]. As a second effect, concerted action worked somehow to regenerate itself; starting from the Amato, Ciampi and Dini agreements on labour costs and social security, right up to the D'Alema agreement in 1998, more and more specific rules were formally introduced, reinforcing not only the development of a model of policy-making based on pacting, but also its rhetoric and its legitimation in political discourse.

But let us take a closer look at the sequence of negotiations that took place during the 1990s and its process features. It is possible to identify two distinct phases marked by different economic contexts, contents and power relationships among the participants (see Table 5.1). The first phase can be defined as 'emergency political exchange ', encouraged by the technical governments of transition, covering the Amato, Ciampi and Dini agreements (1992-1995). During this phase the first moves were made by the technical governments, which intentionally searched for the help and support of the

Table 5.1 Concerted action in the 1990s

	Emergency political exchange	*Institutionalised political exchange*
	1992-1995	*1996-1998*
Actors	technical governments (*first movers*) trade unions and business associations absence of parties	pro-labour political governments larger no. of trade unions and business organisations partial return of political parties
Contents	subtractive policies (wage moderation, welfare cuts) forced financial adjustment	policies for local and economic development active labour policies 'shared' financial adjustment

social partners, since they could not turn to Parliament (seriously delegitimated by the events of Tangentopoli)[14]. Organised interests tended to replace political parties at that time, and were given the chance to openly do what they had been doing in a more secret manner up until then: provide the keys and formulas of economic and social policy (in lieu of parties), using informational resources and mediating powers developed and put to the test inside the associations themselves. The contents of the agreements were for the most part subtractive: wage moderation, restriction of the automatic wage and social benefit indexation, and the freeze on hirings in the public sector, all designed to fall in line with the EMU[15]. As has been shown by Baccaro (2002), workers accepted to comply with these agreements since they had been involved in internal discussions and in deliberative referenda at the plant-level.

The second phase, highly connected to the first one (indeed, impossible without the first one), can be defined as 'institutionalised political exchange'. Power relationships among the actors and contents of the pacts changed: political prime ministers (Prodi and D'Alema) leading the first pro-labour governments took the place of technical prime ministers; economic conditions were no longer alarming, with the emergence of the first benefits of the efforts made over recent years. Political parties started to reorganise themselves and take more active part in the debate on employment policies (as was clearly evident in the Parliamentary battles concerning the approval of the Treu law or the introduction of the 35-hour week). The number of representative organisations signing the agreement grew (reaching a total of 32 for the so-called Christmas Pact of 1998)[16]. This modified scenario allowed for the continuation of consensual co-operation, adopting diversified targets: concerted action turned from restrictive policies to policies of development (active labour and local promotion policies), which became a sort of reward for previous sacrifices (still in an overall dynamic of learning through trial and error or rather through sacrifices and compensations). The problem of workers' legitimation and involvement was paradoxically less important in this second phase – since the agreements did not subtract but tried to distribute resources. But at the same time the lack of a widespread mobilisation and internal collective discussion within firms somehow lessened the symbolic and substantive strength of the agreements. This is especially true of the Christmas Pact signed with the D'Alema government, which was bound to remain largely unimplemented.

Concerted emergency action began in 1992, amidst a national outcry over the Tangentopoli scandal, the ensuing renewal of the entire political class, and a sudden fiscal and monetary crisis. This situation constituted the background to the first consensual pact, ten years after the last experience of triangular political exchange (1983-1984). A technical government led by Amato summoned trade unions and business associations in order to work out a solution to the economic crisis and the increasingly difficult process of European integration. As we have already shown in Chapter III, within a few months Amato had passed one of the biggest financial adjustment measures of the entire post-war period. Thanks to this manoeuvre, for the first time in years a stop could be put to the rise in debt service; the lira was in the wake of a heavy devaluation, the government, trade unions and business associations signed a wide-ranging agreement designed to reduce inflation and slow wage claims. The most visible results of the social pact were the abolition of the *scala mobile* (indexing wages to the cost of living) and a wage freeze in 1992 and 1993. The Amato agreement, like that in Wassenaar in the Netherlands ten years earlier, represented a watershed with regard to industrial relations and the decision-making style of the previous decade, and led to protest among workers, who saw the abolition of the *scala mobile* as the end of an era, the end of a symbol of the trade union movement for half a century. The agreement was in fact signed on the 31st of July, but it forced the CGIL leader Trentin to resign. As was the case in 1984, a fierce opposition rose inside the CGIL, especially on the side of self-organised groups of rank-and-file (the so-called '*autoconvocati*'). Their protest was related on the one hand to the hierarchical and scarcely democratic style of policy-making produced by concerted action and on the other to the ban of plant-level bargaining. In some cities of the north, this part of the agreement was declared invalid, and union representatives were able to force management to sign decentralised company-level agreements. The national leader of the CGIL decided to sign the agreement all the same, before exiting from the scene.

Just one year later, the overall industrial relations scenario radically changed, and the signature of the Ciampi agreement was both politically accepted and substantially feasible. Despite the monetary storm in September 1992, Ciampi followed in his predecessor's path with a further extraordinary budgetary manoeuvre and wage negotiations. The Ciampi pact confirmed the abolition of the wage index, completely reformed the structure of collective bargaining, and established a strict incomes policy. Incomes policy, indeed, became a fundamental instrument of economic policy designed to achieve a more equitable distribution of incomes by containing labour costs, inflation and nominal incomes, and promoting job creation and firm competitiveness. The two budgetary sessions (May/June and September), in fact, were to guarantee the link with the Document of Economic and Financial Planning (DPEF) and the financial law (cf. Chapter III).

Notwithstanding some internal tensions, the 'autoconvocati' movements did not mobilise this time, because of the higher attention to union democracy. The reform of the factory-based union representatives' election was included in the pact with the aim to pursue regular turnover and binding consultations among the workers on the most important economic and social matters.

The same emergency approach which led to the return of concerted action within the labour market and industrial relations was applied to pension policy. As already illustrated above, the reform of welfare appeared on the political agenda between 1992 and 1993. The 1992 Amato decree regarding pensions had introduced some important modifications but had not changed the most important features of the pension system. Thus, a complete reorganisation of the pension system had to be negotiated with the unions and business associations. The involvement of the latter, and their admission to the decision-making arena, was necessary in order to avoid the devastating effects of serious social conflict. Once again, it was Ciampi who made the first move, in the form of dialogue and mediation with the trade unions and the Confederation of Italian Industry, in order to map out a consensual platform for the revision of the pension system (Ciampi 1996).

The Ciampi government, however, did not last very long since the reform of the national voting system was approved and paved the way for new elections, and Ciampi's successor, Berlusconi, opted for an alternative approach to concerted action, introducing provisions designed to abolish seniority pensions into the 1995 financial law. Trade unions rose up in arms against this unilateral move, and the subsequent general strike led to the removal of such provisions. Trade unions, therefore, offered a further demonstration of the powerful role they continued to play in economic and social policy-making, not only as joint decision-makers, but also as leaders of the opposition to the centre-right government. Once again, Parliament was literally bypassed.

It was no coincidence that another technical government, the Dini executive, started to bargain with the unions and business associations once again. The consensus obtained by Dini regarding pension reforms was only a partial one, since the Confederation of Italian Industry did not sign this agreement, which it saw as doing too little in terms of economic and financial reform.

The unions on the contrary engaged themselves in the organisation of a wide wave of assemblies and debates among the workers (about 42,000) that eventually led to a secret ballot referendum. In addition, they tried to reach a compromise with the government, accepting the reform of the pension formula and rejecting the abolition of seniority pensions for strenuous and hazardous jobs. Almost four and a half million workers voted, and 64 per cent declared themselves in favour of the reform (Baccaro 2002).

With the advent of the first centre-left government, led by Romano Prodi, certain significant changes were made to the exchange between government and the unions and business associations. On the one hand, the experience of previous years could not be radically disrupted, of course, by a government that was substantially pro-labour; on the other hand, however, the state of the economy and public finances were already displaying the first positive results of the decisions taken up to that moment (the public debt service and inflation were already falling). The only thing to do was to continue with concerted action, which the parties involved were already used to, and to improve its form and content. The Prodi government's Employment Agreement (1996) and the D'Alema government's Economic Development Agreement (1998) introduced other innovations in addition to the usual policy of wage moderation: these included active labour policies and local development policies, in particular in favour of the south of Italy. Power relationships within the decision-making arena now changed: the dominance of trade unions, as a result, of business associations was partly weakened by the return of political parties, whose leaders engaged in a hard battle over the question of employment flexibility.

The role of unions seemed to be less crucial than in the emergency period. The innovations introduced by the Employment Agreement – above all on vocational training – were largely agreed upon, with the exception of temporary work which was strongly contrasted in Parliament by Rifondazione Comunista and by some parts of the CGIL[17].

In order to introduce it in the Treu Law of June 1997, the government had to satisfy the demands made by Rifondazione Comunista and provide conspicuous funds for subsidised welfare provisions in the southern regions (work fellowships and socially useful jobs).

Consequently, the revival of political parties and a friendly government, on the one hand, and an institutional framework ready to be used for the purposes of concerted action, on the other, enabled government, the unions and business associations to continue to co-operate in an atmosphere of growing loyalty and reciprocal trust.

The development of concerted action came to its apex and at the same time to its last act with the D'Alema agreement regarding the economy and economic development (December 1998 – the so-called 'Christmas Agreement'), which represented a sort of final balance of the long series of exchanges and negotiations of the 1990s, and established the rules and regulations to empower the concerted modalities of policy-making. The concerted action approach emerged strongly reinforced, in keeping with the guidelines of the 1993 agreement, and now extended to numerous representative associations besides the three main trade union confederations (CGIL, UIL and CISL), and covered a number of issues which had previously been debated only at the local level. The agreement was defined as the new Constitution of concerted action, just as the 1993 agreement had been seen as the new Constitution of industrial relations (Carinci 1999).

Three different levels of concerted action were established: the first regarded negotiations on the welfare state based on the government – trade unions – employers triangle; the second level concerned those relations between workers and companies that do not require the intervention of government; the third level covered the domestic implementation of European directives. The scope of concerted action was therefore widened; it was designed to intervene during the so-called ascending and descending stages of European decision-making, in the formulation of national laws, in the setting up of regional and local policies, and in the design of social, environmental and development policies (D'Alberti 1999).

However, notwithstanding great expectations and the promises made, the D'Alema agreement was the final instance of Italian corporatism seen up to the end of 2001. It was never really implemented; very few measures were translated into law, and the new consensual style of decision-making suddenly came to an end. Entry into the EMU seemed to be the last issue on which consensus was needed; after that, no other shared goal appeared on the political stage (Bellardi 1999; Ghera 1999), not even under the aegis of a pro-labour government, with Amato taking over from D'Alema. Moreover, the change of the rules of the concertation game within the D'Alema's pact, that is the widening of the circle of actors involved (which meant the weakening of the role of federal unions), somehow suspended the experience.

The arrival of the centre-right governing coalition in May 2001 has opened a new phase for the *concertazione* and, indeed, for the whole national system of policy-making.

VI   Rescued, but Still Free to Harm Itself

1   A new virtuous circle: but how stable?

If what matters, in the history of a country, are the big turning points, i.e. the evolutionary junctures through which a specific path is chosen instead of another one, then the turbulent 1990s were a successful decade for Italy. Through an impressive sequence of reforms, the country was able to improve the conditions of its battered public finances and start an incisive modernisation of its backward bureaucratic apparatus, its rigid labour market and its unbalanced welfare state, without jeopardising either social peace or the overall competitiveness of its economy in the global context. The dynamics of internationalisation and (especially) European integration were crucial in instigating this quantum leap in institutional capabilities: indeed, the Italian experience shows that internationalisation may well be a *solution* rather than a *problem*.

Naturally, internationalisation and European integration have not been the only factors behind this process of institutional modernisation. Other factors have played a significant role: the sudden waning of endogenous blocks to change (the demise of the First Republic), the rapid de-ideologisation of the political culture (in the wake of the fall of the Berlin Wall), as well as its traditional pro-European-integration leanings, the emergence of new actors (fresh politicians, experts, a new 'technocratic' élite), new styles of policy-making (concerted action) and – as a result of all this – an accelerated dynamic of social and institutional learning.

As we have illustrated in the second chapter, a major fault of the original constellation of welfare capitalism 'Italian-style' was the fundamental weakness and 'porousness' of the *state* (a deficit of legality coupled with a deficit of efficiency and normative integration). Perhaps the 1970s and the 1980s represented the apex of a perverse syndrome where the state acted primarily as an instrument of creation and an arena of distribution of spoils on behalf of various social and political groups. The solution of collective problems by means of any sort of 'goal-oriented rationality' was only a secondary function, so to speak, of the state apparatus. The most important effect produced by the exogenous shocks and the European convergence process upon the Italian political and institutional system has been exactly to encourage the 'hardening' of the state and of its institutional capabilities: the state (but also social) élite have learned that to face collective problems and solve them effectively is a more important task (and surely a prerequisite) than contending for the spoils of power on behalf of their own specific parties and social clients.

The notion of 'learning' (both at the level of ideas and of political and social behaviour) is particularly useful, we believe, for capturing the nature of the changes that occurred in Italy and, above all, the internal dynamic of the process of change. At first, in the 1970s, a belief matured that Italy needed an incisive process of financial adjustment in order to catch up with a virtuous path of economic growth and social modernisation; and the firm anchorage to the (then) European Community was seen as the best way (and maybe the only way) to achieve this objective. This conviction changed into a more precise *institutional project* during the 1980s, when its implications were fully understood, and a wide-ranging agenda of reforms was set up. The project was principally elaborated and supported by the technical circles of the Bank of Italy and the Ministry of the Treasury, and started to spread on various sectoral policy networks. The process of convergence started at Maastricht, and the 1992 monetary crisis persuaded a wider circle of actors that failing the 'financial adjustment in the name of Europe' would have led to very dangerous consequences. A real campaign was launched, aimed at persuading the various interest groups (and in particular the trade unions) to accept the reforms in view of the long-term advantages of financial adjustment: economic growth, lower debt service, and hence new precious opportunities to reduce taxes and requalify public expenditures. As we have shown in Chapters IV and V, the campaign was successful. The reforms have been introduced, the Maastricht criteria have been satisfied, and a new 'public discourse' on economic-social themes has started to develop in the country: a discourse based on knowledge and reasoning, formulated in terms of efficiency and equity instead of the old ideological clichés.

True, our positive diagnosis is predicated on the peculiarly bad shape in which Italy found itself not only in the 1975-1990 period, but even at the heyday of the so-called golden age of welfare capitalism. Measured against this domestic historical record, the whole process of financial adjustment and the final seal of EMU membership cannot appear but a remarkable achievement. If we adopt a more exacting perspective of analysis, we must admit that the reforms of the 1990s have not fully eradicated the old vices.

In national public debates it is widely recognised that *la transizione* is not over yet and that the innovative dynamics that emerged during the 1990s have not reached a firm point of political and economic equilibrium. In the remainder of this chapter, we will present and discuss the most recent phase of the uncompleted transition, which opened with the alternation in government in 2001.

2   Enter Berlusconi

On 13 May 2001 Silvio Berlusconi won the elections at the head of the House of Freedom coalition (*Casa delle Libertà*) for the second time in a decade. Compared to 1994, i.e. the first Berlusconi government, the political scenario had changed remarkably. Some new elements were in fact appearing on the stage, all suggesting a strengthening of 'bipolar democracy' in Italy, i.e. a political system resting on the (possibility of) alternation in government between two opposing coalitions. These new elements were: a) the large size of the majority won by Berlusconi in both Chambers; b) the inner cohesion of the coalition; c) the unchallenged leadership of Berlusconi; and d) the fragmented and quarrelsome state of the opposition, especially after the election.

The number of seats gained by the centre-right coalition was large both in the lower Chamber and in the Senate, and the Berlusconi second executive was the first in Italy to be formed as the result of a complete turnover of the governing team. Overall, the *Casa della Libertà* gained 55.9 per cent of the seats in the Senate and 59.1 per cent in the Chamber as against 40.6 per cent and 39.2 per cent of the Olive Tree coalition. Within the centre-right coalition the success of Forza Italia (Berlusconi's own party) was considerable, while the other parties of the coalition suffered a decline: Forza Italia gained 29.4 per cent of the vote compared to 20.6 per cent in the 1996 elections (1996), while Alleanza Nazionale (the right-wing party led by Fini) declined from 15.7 in 1996 to 12 per cent in 2001, the CCD-CDU (the centre-moderate party, composed of former Christian Democrats) shifted from 5.8 per cent in 1996 to 3.2 per cent in 2001, and the Lega Nord (led by Bossi) fell to 3.9 per cent compared to 10.1 per cent in 1996 (Diamanti and Lazar 2002: 61). These data reveal that Forza Italia was able to capture the largest share of centre-moderate voters and to fill the vacuum left by the First Republic governing parties (like the Christian Democrats and the Socialists).

The second new element of the Berlusconi government is the internal cohesion of the coalition itself. The downsizing of the allied parties and especially the remarkable drop of the Lega Nord meant that – in contrast with 1994 – the risk of blackmail and vetoes was much lower. The seats of the Lega Nord are no longer essential for government stability (while in 1994 Bossi's demands were the main cause of the government's fall). The formation of the executive and the distribution of posts reflected the power relationships among the parties: nine ministries were assigned to FI (four without portfolio), four to Alleanza Nazionale (one without portfolio), three to the Lega Nord (one without portfolio) and two to the CCD-CDU (both without portfolio). It must be noted that in order to satisfy each party's expectations Berlusconi had to bypass the rules introduced by the former government, which in 1999 had reduced the number of ministries from 18 to 12: Berlusconi increased this number to 14. The vice-premiership was assigned to Gianfranco Fini, the leader of Alleanza Nazionale, the Presidency of the Senate to Marcello Pera of Forza Italia and the Presidency of the Chamber to Pier Ferdinando Casini of the centre-moderate party of the coalition (CCD-CDU).

The third element of novelty is the undisputed centrality of Berlusconi as a leader of the coalition. No other figure within the House of Freedoms has ever succeeded in challenging Berlusconi, and the electoral campaign was mainly focused on his personal characteristics and political strategies – both on the side of the centre-right coalition and on the side of the opposition, which did not hesitate to consider Berlusconi as its main enemy and thus target.

A few days before the elections, on 8 May, during a popular TV show broadcast on the main state channel, Berlusconi signed a 'contract with Italians', indicating the main priorities of his programme: tax reduction and fiscal discounts to firms in case of reinvested profits, incentives for the emergence of underground work, abolition of the tax due for successions and donations, administrative simplification, a tax amnesty for capital repatriation from abroad, new rules for the conflict of interest. After the elections, many of these policy priorities were translated in the so-called '100 days law' (no. 18/2001), including a host of measures to be implemented in the first three months of the legislative term.

The fourth factor – no less important – of Berlusconi's success was, as mentioned, the internal weakness and negative performance of the Olive Ttree coalition, which was not able to repeat the 1996 results. The main factors at the basis of the Olive Tree's defeat have been clearly identified by the post-election debate. The slump of the Left Democrats (from 21.1 per cent in 1996 to 16.6 per cent in 2001) was an unexpected major event. After the collapse of the First Republic, the Left Democrats found themselves as the

biggest party in Italy; in May 2001 they had become the smallest left reformist party in Europe. The drop was partly the result of the tensions and
conflicts inside the coalition and partly the consequence of the low visibility
of the DS leaders. The President of the party and former Prime Minister
D'Alema, who was perceived inside the Olive Tree as the main culprit of the
Prodi government's fall, maintained a low profile during the electoral campaign, mainly in his constituency in Gallipoli (Apulia), while the national
secretary Veltroni had already been appointed as centre-left candidate for
the mayoral elections in Rome, after Rutelli (the incumbent mayor) had
been selected as the leader of the Olive Tree. Giuliano Amato, the incumbent
prime minister, also maintained a low profile, in order not to disturb Rutelli.
Another important reason of the Left Democrats' defeat was the significant
success of the so-called *Margherita* (Daisy alliance) which assembled five
centre-left moderate parties: the Popular party, the Dini list, Prodi's Democrats and the Union of Democrats for Europe (UDEUR). This electoral car-
tel, led by Rutelli, who was also the direct opponent of Berlusconi, scored
14.5 per cent (only two points behind the Left Democrats). Beside the shift
of votes from the left to the centre-left of the coalition, the Olive Tree
seemed to be in great difficulty trying to contrast the centre-right leader on
the communicative point of view, valorising the positive results of the legislative term that was coming to an end (like Italy's entry into EMU): a gen-
eralised sense of defeat already appeared to be widespread in centre-left circles before the elections. According to a provocative diagnosis of a protagonist of the Olive Tree experience, the self-inflicted weakness of the centre-
left coalition finds its roots in the incomplete 'cultural' conversion of the
Italian Left (and the DS in particular) to a genuine, pragmatic, European-
style social reformism (Rossi 2002). As we have seen in the previous chapter, the second half of the 1990s did witness a significant discursive turn on
the side of the Olive Tree (including many DS) leaders, and this turn was essential in forging the necessary consensus for the reforms. But the cognitive
and normative re-orientation did not fully percolate throughout the whole
party apparatus, leaving significant parts of it basically unconvinced about
the new programmatic course.

The defeat of the Olive Tree must also be taken against the background of
Italy's new electoral system. As a matter of fact, the seats gained by the
Olive Tree, added to those of Rifondazione Comunista and of Di Pietro's
movement (one of the main judges of the 'Clean Hands' investigation that
had brought down the First Republic) might have become a victory, just as
had happened in 1996. However, an alliance with Rifondazione Comunista
– even only for electoral purposes- was impossible, in the wake of RC's re-

sponsibility in the fall of Prodi and of the ensuing radicalisation of this party's ideological and programmatic profile: another macroscopic symptom of the legacy of 'polarised pluralism' and of the incomplete cultural transformation of the Left.

The gradual consolidation of the rules of alternation and bipolarism in Italy mixed with persisting ambiguities and contradictions within the second Berlusconi government both in terms of the characteristics of the executive and of public policy performance.

As for the style and nature of political steering, the leadership of Berlusconi in the first two years of the legislative term swung between a presidential and parliamentary model of co-ordination (Verzichelli and Cotta 2003). On the one hand, the degree of autonomy and the steering capacity of the Premier made observers underline the presidentialistic traits: for instance, the high concentration of decision-making in the hands of the executive and the signature on behalf of Berlusconi of most of the laws submitted to Parliament. On the other hand, however, in many specific circumstances the Premier's ability to intervene and co-ordinate executive action seemed very weak, and the logic of parliamentary democracy seemed to prevail (e.g. the management of the very turbulent G8 meeting in Genoa in June 2001, or the management of two ministerial resignations, that of foreign minister Renato Ruggiero in December 2001 and that of the Minister for the Interior Scaiola in the spring of 2002).

But it is above all in terms of policies that ambiguities have to be highlighted and examined. In the first place, the gap between Berlusconi's programmatic declarations and actual achievements has proved rather large. The size and stability of its parliamentary majority would have allowed the executive to push through incisive changes; on the contrary the contents and objectives of the policies introduced have appeared rather modest. During the two first years of office, 160 measures were introduced (53 government's draft bills, 5 delegation laws, 44 decree laws and 58 treaty ratifications) (*ibidem*); at least 50 per cent of these initiatives brought rather marginal policy changes, while the remaining part included very controversial reforms, the majority of which has still to be implemented (e.g. those on devolution, education and university, infrastructure, judiciary organisation, telecommunication systems). As we shall see, very little has been made in the crucial area of welfare state reform.

In addition, the first year of the Berlusconi government and a major part of the second were occupied by some legislative initiatives which were stigmatised by the opposition (as well as by the international press) as directly connected with Berlusconi's private interests: i.e. the laws on company accounts falsification, on international rogatories, on 'legitimate suspicion' as a reason to relocate judicial trials and the one still being discussed at the lower Chamber on the so-called 'conflict of interests' – i.e. rules on the compatibility between private interests and public offices. The new discipline on company budget falsification (no. 366/2001) has significantly reduced (from 10 to 3-5 years) the prescription years for the offence and the related penalties; that on international rogatories (367/2001) has invalidated international inquiries and investigations which do not respect some specific formal rules, and the one on legitimate suspicion (no. 248/2002) allows defendants to appeal to a High Court in order to transfer a trial in case of suspicion about the partiality of the judges or of local conditions supposed to disturb the proceedings. All of these initiatives can interfere with the legal action in which Berlusconi is still currently involved.

But the issue which was mostly debated inside and outside the Parliament is the so-called 'conflict of interest', originating from the problem of the compatibility of Berlusconi's private empire, including telecommunications (three highly popular national TV channels), publishing, cinema production companies, insurance and his political role as Prime Minister. A law proposal on the conflict of interests was already presented in the former legislative term by the centre-left coalition, but it was not approved[1]. The law project (no. 1206) presented by the second Berlusconi government has given rise to a hot political dispute; in the centre-right's opinion it is the best possible solution, while according to the opposition it is a 'save Berlusconi' law. Article 2 of this project introduces the incompatibility between public offices and business activities but not an incompatibility with the mere ownership of such activities, thus legitimating the current situation of the Premier, who has entrusted the control of his empire to third parties. The proposed new law confers monitoring powers to the Antitrust Authority, which can signal to Parliament possible situations of conflict. The Authority can also recommend to Parliament measures to remedy such situations. The Olive Tree opposition contests in particular the weakness of the sanctions foreseen (basically, symbolic reprimands) and the absence of a real incompatibility rule between ownership and public offices. It is however true that the opposition lost its chance to legislate a more effective discipline when in office between 1996 and 2001. The conflict of interest issue will continue to cast a dark shadow on Italy's incomplete institutional transition. The issue is a very delicate one in abstract terms (there are no univocal remedies in terms of normative theory and/or institutional engineering), and finding a solution to it under the premiership of Berlusconi – the most prominent and immediate target of any possible solution – is a truly daunting challenge for the still fragile Second Republic.

On economic policy grounds, the aims of the new Berlusconi government were promptly presented in the first Document of Economic and Financial Planning (DPEF) for the period 2002-2006, whose title was 'From decline to development'. According to the document, development should mainly follow from tax reductions and a simplification of the tax system, new investment in infrastructure, labour market reform and increases in lower pensions. The negative international conjuncture and the deep economic crisis following September 11, 2001, together with the need to comply with the constraints of the European Growth and Stability Pact, have made it very difficult for the government to embark on its reform plan. In the new scenario, Berlusconi's agenda has been watered down, and the Finance Minister, Giulio Tremonti, has been forced to resort to traditional 'patch up' measures in order to meet the budgetary targets for 2001 and 2002 (e.g. the freezing of recruitment in the public sector and one of the largest tax amnesties of Italian history). Despite the difficult international context of 2002, Italy has been able to maintain its public deficit below 3 per cent in and to slightly reduce its public debt (106.5 per cent). However, it remains to be seen whether in the absence of structural reform (or in the wake of destabilising structural reforms, e.g. on fiscal federalism, as we shall see) the *risanamento* of the 1990s will be able to sustain itself in the coming years.

3   Labour market reform: from concerted action to 'social dialogue' and flex-security?

Soon after its establishment, the Berlusconi government tried to inaugurate a new phase in the realm of 'concerted action' with the trade unions. In October 2001 a White Book on the Labour Market was published, which criticized the *concertazione* for its low effectiveness and innovation potential. Rather than new trilateral, corporatist agreements, the White Book advocated a new method of interaction with the social partners, dubbed as 'social dialogue' (a term explicitly borrowed from the EU jargon), and basically consisting of milder forms of consultation and preventive negotiations on economic and social policy, in which the executive reserved for itself wider margins of manoeuvre and the role of 'ultimate' policy-maker. As we shall see, mindful of its 1994 failure precisely on this front, the Berlusconi government did not adopt a completely confrontational and adversarial style *vis-à-vis* the unions. However, it has clearly embarked upon a strategy of reshaping the system of relationships with the social partners, bringing it more in line with the changed conditions of the political system and the new logic of bipolar and 'quasi-majoritarian' democracy – in a post-emergency financial climate.

As we have explained in the previous chapters, the increasing salience of *concertazione* as a policy-making method during the 1990s was the result of three elements: 1) the historical legacy of a hyper-proportional and 'consensual' model of democracy, in which polarised pluralism virtually blocked alternation in government, but allowed at the same time numerous veto points in policy-making; 2) the crisis of the First Republic and its main institutions (especially parties and Parliament), in combination with pressing European demands and deadlines for fiscal discipline; and 3) a self-sustaining dynamic of institutionalisation, once the first social agreements were struck and started to produce virtuous outcomes. After the 2001 elections, the first two elements lost their systemic relevance. The House of Freedoms considered its own victory as a seal on a new model of majoritarian democracy, primarily resting on electoral (rather than corporatist) legitimation. The parliamentary stability and internal cohesion of the new government, on the one hand, and the less constraining EU environment on the other hand induced Berlusconi to claim a primacy for executive action both *vis-à-vis* Parliament and the social partners that has no precedent in post-war Italy and that presupposes a downsizing of corporate channels of influence. Against this background it is not difficult to understand why the new government has embraced a strategy of de-institutionalisation of the *concertazione*, aimed at partially dismantling the complex procedural framework foreseen by the 1998 Christmas Pact and resting on a sort of *divide et impera* tactic. According to the new 'social dialogue' approach, the social partners are not completely deprived of policy-making functions, but these functions must be exercised within the objectives and priorities set by the government and within a perimeter of policy guidelines and solutions set – at least in a preliminary and general way – by Parliament (Mania and Sateriale 2002).

The unions (and especially the CGIL) certainly did not welcome Berlusconi's new approach. They reacted very negatively to the White Book, both to its procedural and to its substantive proposals, mainly oriented towards further steps of liberalization and flexibilization of the labour market. Criticism soon snowballed into an overt battle when the government asked to Parliament for a broad delegation of powers for labour market reform, including the modification of article 18 of the Workers' Statute of 1970 (cf. *supra*, Chapter II). As shown in Box 1, this norm has created one of the most protective labour regimes in Europe, and already during the 1990s a debate had started on how to change it[2]. What upset the unions in the autumn of

BOX 1

Article 18 of the Workers' Statute: how it actually works

If a judge finds that a dismissal is 'unjustified', the worker is automatically re-integrated into his or her job, and the employer is sentenced to pay all the wages matured until the ruling, as well as the social security contributions and a penalty which added together virtually double the payment. This outcome may originate from the first ruling, but also from a ruling after the fourth possible appeal (6-10 years after the opening of the case). A single negative ruling (out of the possible five) is sufficient for defeating the employer, with damages proportional to the length of the trial. Even when the initial negative ruling is invalidated after a few years, the employer is not allowed to get back the wages and contributions paid in the meantime, which remain with the worker who is provisionally re-integrated and to INPS, respectively. There are no statutory limits to the amount an employer must pay. Labour judges are responsible for interpreting the rightfulness of the cause of dismissal. Since a single ruling of the whole proceeding may determine the overall outcome for the employer, the intensity of the protection regime based on article 18 does not depend on the average orientation of labour judges, but on the orientation of those who are less benevolent to employers.

The procedures of article 18 apply to firms with more than 15 employees and thus cover less than 10 million workers (of which 3.5 million are public employees). The remaining 12.5 million workers of Italy's labour force are not covered and can be fired with no compensation.

(Summary from Ichino 2002)

2001 was, however, the sudden appearance of this issue in the delegation draft bill, without any prior discussion (not even the White Book had mentioned this as a priority). The unions took this move as a clear signal of hostility on the side of Berlusconi, with the employers' backing.

The government's proposal was not particularly radical. It suggested a derogation from article 18 in three cases: if a company with more than 15 employees 'came out' from the black economy with a view to regularizing its position (starting of course from the contractual and social security position of its employees); if a company decided to pass the threshold of 15 employees with the hiring of new regular staff; if a company transformed temporary workers into permanent ones. In these three sets of circumstances, article 18 was to be suspended for an experimental period of three years. However, the unions declared that they could not in principle accept any change of the status quo. On 23 March 2002, the CGIL called a general strike that mobilized about three million workers around the country under the slogan 'no to firing, yes to entitlements'. In the following months the main Italian union radicalised its opposition against any kind of labour market reform. But the other two unions, the CISL and the UIL, softened their stance and opened negotiations with the government, which in its turn manifested an openness to compromise that had not been shown in 1994. The negotiation led to a new social agreement: the *Patto per l'Italia* (Pact for Italy), signed in July 2002 by the CISL and the UIL with Berlusconi and Confindustria, the employers' association. The Pact contained a watered-down version of the government's proposal regarding article 18³: an agreement to substantially improve both the replacement rate (from 40 per cent to 60 per cent) and the duration (from 6 to 12 months) of the ordinary unemployment benefit; the implementation of most of the liberalising proposals of the White Book; the government's commitment to launch various initiatives for the development of the *Mezzogiorno*, the upgrading of human capital, the support of lower income workers and pensioners. The CGIL did not sign the Pact: after the summer of 2002 its secretary general, Sergio Cofferati, left his post to Guglielmo Epifani and has subsequently become a prominent political figure of the centre-left opposition.

After the July agreement, parliamentary discussions on labour market reform resumed, and in March 2003 a broad delegation law on the labour market was approved by Parliament. This law is referred to as the 'Biagi law' (no. 30/2003), after the name of the well-known Bologna professor and technical advisor of many Italian executives (from Prodi to Berlusconi II), who had inspired the White Book and who was tragically killed by the resurrected Red Brigades on 19 March 2002. The main provisions of this law, which has been acknowledged by the legislative decree no. 276 of 10 september 2003, are listed in Box 2. As can be seen, to a large extent these provisions constitute further steps down the road opened by the Treu law of 1997- which according to most observers have indeed started to unblock Italy's labour market, allowing the creation of more than 1.5 million jobs, especially for women and the young (Sestito 2002). Besides flexibility measures, the Biagi law foresees a further modernization of employment services – the traditional Achilles' heel of the Italian labour market. But, again, it remains to be seen whether this part of the law will be actually and effectively implemented, in parallel with the ameliorative reform of unemployment insurance. Without effective employment services, decent unemployment protection and serious vocational training institutions, the Italian labour market is bound to remain for too many workers 'a repulsive and dangerous place' – to use the crude but appropriate metaphor coined by Ichino (2002). A change in article 18 will also have to be introduced at some point in the future, in order to fully modernize Italy's labour market along

BOX 2

The Biagi Law (no. 30/2003 and d.lgs. 276/2003) on labour market reform: main provisions

–Placement reformed. Full liberalization of employment services: not only public agencies, but also private agencies, private consultants and universities. Establishment of a national placement information system.
–New forms of contract introduced: job on call, job sharing and jobs linked to special projects.
–Staff leasing introduced: firms can lease workers from specialized agencies.
–Part-time work made more elastic, both horizontally and vertically.
–Regularization of outsourcing practices.
–Training: reform of work and training contracts and of apprenticeships; closer link between training and the fruition of unemployment benefits.

the lines recommended by the European Employment Strategy. It must be remembered that, despite recent progress, Italy's employment rates are still far behind the targets set by the Lisbon strategy: in 2001 the total employment rate was 54.5 per cent (Lisbon target = 70 per cent), and the female employment rate was 40.9 per cent (Lisbon target = 60 per cent) (cf. Table 1.1. in Chapter 1).

The events of 2002 have not only de-institutionalised the *concertazione* but also produced a rather deep split within the unions. This is not the first time that the unions have divided themselves into two camps: in Chapter IV we discussed the divisions of the early 1980s on the *scala mobile* issue. Given the presence and long-term persistence of union pluralism in Italy, such splits should not be regarded as an anomaly, let alone a tragedy. It would be a great pity, however, if such divisions should disperse the capital of the problem-solving culture developed by all Italian unions during the 1990s, i.e. their capacity to seriously puzzle on economic and social dilemmas, to elaborate innovative proposals and to exercise forms of dialogic persuasion. True, union pluralism works differently when a centre-right government is in office: to paraphrase the metaphor used in Chapter V, in such case 'it is no longer Nixon who goes to China', there is less trust and less willingness to co-operate on both sides. But certainly the new political context allows for more options that just a fierce power confrontation between juxtaposed and rigid interests. And, more generally speaking, a *divide et impera* strategy on the part of the government and a split response on the part of the unions is not the only possible game of a bipolar democracy. The new epoch of 'social dialogue' may be a transitory phase, to be sooner or later followed by a further re-configuration of industrial relations, possibly linked to supranational and/or sub-national developments (Mania and Sateriale 2002). In June 2003, after the failure of a national referendum on article 18[4], encouraging signs have emerged of a more civilised 'social dialogue' between the government and the social partners – including the CGIL. If in the near future unions and government reach a (further) agreement to make the Italian labour market less 'repulsive and dangerous' for the millions of outsiders through additional measures of desegmentation, this transitory phase may even turn out to be healthier than the phase of *concertazione* – certainly of its post-1998 developments. Admittedly, it is a big 'if'. But it is not out of reach, provided that an appropriate balance of flexibility and security is actively and seriously pursued. This requires not only a prompt implementation of the Biagi law and of the remaining parts of the *Patto per l'Italia*, but also further reforms of the welfare state, to which we now turn.

4   Still a pension state? An unfinished recalibration

At the end of Chapter IV we suggested a positive assessment of the reforms of the 1990s (at least in terms of fiscal bankruptcy avoidance), but also argued that the internal recalibration of the Italian welfare state was far from complete: to a large extent the agenda is still that of the 1997 Onofri plan, i.e streamlining (if not further downsizing) pensions and improving family benefits and social services. This diagnosis seems to be widely shared among commentators and experts – also within the Berlusconi government itself. But since 2001 very few concrete steps have been made in this direction.

Two important reports on pensions have been produced during the 2001-2003 period: the report of a governmental commission (the Brambilla Commission), appointed with the task of 'verifying' the state of implementation of the 1995 Dini reform and of trends in expenditure (Ministero del Welfare 2001); and the national strategy on pensions submitted to the EU by the Italian government in the framework of the new 'pension process' launched in 2002 (Ministero del Welfare 2002). Both reports recognize the progress made through the reforms of the 1990s on three fronts: 1) short-term cost containment and the long-term financial sustainability of the pension system; 2) the reduction of institutional fragmentation and of unjustified disparities of treatment across occupational categories; and 3) the transition towards a more balanced, multi-pillar pension system, offering incentives for the development of supplementary schemes.

When the new system introduced by the Dini reform will become fully operative (around 2035), Italian public pensions will become much less generous: the replacement rate will be cut from 76.9 (2000) to about 65 per cent[5]. An important change is expected to take place in the same period. The so-called 'TFR' (end-of-contract payment) should transform itself into a fully fledged supplementary pension, hopefully providing approximately another 17 per cent of earnings (Ministero del Welfare 2002). After reaching the steady state (i.e. when most pensions in payment will be based on the new formula), the system should be able to stabilise and sustain itself, with an incidence of pension expenditure on GDP of ca. 13.6 per cent (2050). However, this scenario poses two major problems. In the first place, the transition to the steady state is going to be very slow. The old pre-Dini formula will be phased out gradually, i.e. it will continue to operate fully for all those workers who had paid at least 18 years' contributions in 1995. In combination with demographic trends (the retirement of the baby boomers), this will produce an increase of the incidence of pensions over GDP from 13.8 per cent (2000) to 16 per cent in 2033: only thereafter will spending start to decline again. This *gobba* (hunch) in expenditure trends raises serious financial preoccupations. The second problem is the actual take off of supplementary pension funds: a development which cannot be taken for granted given the existing legal framework and the sticky preferences of Italian workers and employers, who are very reluctant to abandon the TFR system[6].

Various proposals have been made (e.g. by the Brambilla Commission) in order to tackle the first problem and the financial challenge linked to the projected *gobba*: a faster phasing-in of the Dini formula (especially as regards the notorious seniority pensions), 'hard' disincentives for encouraging workers to postpone the decision to retire, higher contributions for the self-employed and a complete harmonization of rules for all groups, tighter links between the conversion coefficients of accrued contributions and demographic developments, etc. As to the second problem, i.e. the rapid transformation of the TFR into a proper second pillar, there are different technical views on how precisely to achieve this aim: but the aim itself is widely supported, as is its temporal urgency.

As in the case of labour market reform, already in 2001 the Berlusconi government had asked Parliament for a delegation of powers to pass a new pension reform. The *delega* on pensions encountered harsh opposition from the trade unions, and everything remained blocked during the controversy on article 18, discussed above. After the *Patto per l'Italia* agreement, discussions and negotiations resumed also on this front, and, after lengthy debates, the government submitted to Parliament a law of delegation on pen-

BOX 3

The delegation law on pensions (no. 2145/2001, amended by the Act of Senate of 27/10/2003, no. 2058): main provisions:

First phase (till 2007)
– workers who mature the right to a seniority pension and opt for staying at work will receive a tax free bonus equal to the amount of their pension contributions (i.e. 32.7% of their earnings)
– extraordinary contribution of 3% levied on very high pensions
– further measures of harmonization across various professional schemes
– stricter controls on disability pensions
– workers with disabled relatives who opt for part time work will receive figurative contributions as if they worked full time

Second phase (since 2008)
– Single unified requirement for obtaining an old age pensions: either 65 years of age (60 for women) or 40 years of contribution
– Seniority pensions with 35 years of contributions and 57 years of age still possible, but calculated with the less favorable contribution-related formula introduced by the Dini reform
– Exceptions/exemptions for 'debilitating' jobs, working mothers and workers who started prior to the age of 18
– Further incentives for the development of supplementary pensions (also for public employees) and the transfer of TFR contributions into pension funds
– Possible reduction of up to 5% of contributions for newly hired young workers – without prejudice to their future benefits

sion reform. The latest version of this law – submitted to Parliament in the context of the financial law for 2004 – is summarized in box 3. As can be seen, the government proposes a two-step reform process. During the first phase (till 2007), the main measure will be a set of incentives to encourage later retirement, even if the entitlement to a seniority pension has been matured based on the transition rules set out by the Dini and Prodi reforms. The second phase will rest on 'structural' changes: a higher age of retirement for old age pensions and substantial penalties for seniority pensions – with exceptions and exemptions. In the projections of the Treasury, the savings estimated from this reform could amount to ca. 1% of GDP per year, thus substantially lowering the spending curve in the critical years between 2010 and 2040.

The government's new plan has encountered harsh opposition by all trade unions – reuniting their front after the split of 2002. A general strike in October 2003 brought millions of protesters to the streets. The government has responded by saying that the specific content of the reform can be changed (even after Parliament's approval of the delegation bill) through negotiation, as long as its structural effects on spending trends are maintained.

Expert comments on the reform plan are mixed[7]. Criticisms focus in particular on the sudden character of change in 2008 (as opposed to a softer phasing in period) and on the proposed reduction of contributions, which is seen as a violation of the whole logic of the Dini reform[8]. But it is largely recognized that a new structural intervention is indeed needed to confront the upward trend of spending projections.

Meeting the 'hunch' challenge in the field of pensions through new restrictive measures would also be a pre-requisite for a wider strategy of welfare recalibration, aimed at enhancing standards and levels of protection in other areas of social protection, most notably family policy and social assistance. In 2000, the share of social spending devoted to the 'family and children' was still attested at 3.8 per cent, and the share of spending for 'housing and social exclusion' was stuck at 0.2 per cent. These percentages are the lowest in the EU, and progress 'by the decimal' is not enough for seriously tackling the functional and distributive problems originated by Italy's distorted pattern of social spending: declining fertility, great difficulties for women to reconcile paid and unpaid work, low female participation rates, low territorial mobility, high incidence of poverty (especially among couples with two or more children and particularly in the south), etc. The improvement of family benefits and services is an essential component of the 'flex-security' strategy mentioned above in the context of labour market reform. Italy's social expenditure was still below the EU average in 2000 (25.2 per cent as against 27.3 per cent). The room for significant spending increases in the future is, however, severely restricted by the high incidence of the debt service in a context of rigid budgetary constraints and tax-cutting priorities. The only way for making room for higher spending on non-pension benefits is containing pension costs and/or the cost of public employees (Boeri and Perotti 2002).

The Berlusconi government seems to be aware of the predicament. In February 2003 it published a White Book on Family and Family Policy that contains a detailed diagnosis of Italy's problems in this area (Ministero del Welfare 2003). This document highlights the dramatic decline of fertility and its negative long-term implications for the country's social and economic system. It also recognises the functional overload of Italian families (and women in particular) and the persisting challenge of poverty. The White Book is nevertheless very reticent in terms of policy solutions, especially as regards spending commitments. Its main proposal is increasing tax deductions for low-income and large households. Very little is said about other measures, such as family services, and nothing is said about child benefits. The government also seems inclined to discontinue the experimental program of guaranteed minimum income introduced in 1998 by the D'Alema government (Sacchi, Bastagli and Ferrera 2003), replacing it with a vaguely defined income guarantee of last resort.

In summary, despite its rhetoric on 'policy innovation', the Berlusconi era does not seem to be promoting any substantial and rapid advancement on that 'recalibrative agenda' of Italy's unbalanced welfare state that emerged around the 1990s and that started to be watered down after 1998. The bet of the new government was that of solving fiscal problems (including those of the *stato sociale*) through a big economic boost, prompted by a mix of tax cuts, labour market flexibility and a more employer- and business-friendly climate. But the worsened international conjuncture has closed off this option, 'sandwiching' Berlusconi back into the familiar corner of hard constraints and unpopular policy choices – a corner in which the Premier is very likely to remain for the rest of his legislative term. Without further reform, however, the new institutional constellation put in place in the 1990s may not be able to sustain itself, and the 'devolution' campaign on which the new government has embarked upon is unlikely to make things easier.

5   'EU-friendly' internal federalism: is it feasible?

As was illustrated in the previous chapters, the Italian political system has undergone a far-reaching institutional reconfiguration in recent years that has markedly remodelled the relations between levels of government, in the wider EU framework. This reconfiguration has been the outcome of two interrelated dynamics: the dynamic originated by the sphere of politics proper (especially after the appearance of the Lega Nord and its impact on the electoral market) and the dynamic linked to the sphere of public policies (the functional pressures for adjustment and institutional modernization). The intensity of the latter dynamic was strongly reinforced by the external constraint and especially by the creation of EMU.

Three main lines of development in this institutional reconfiguration can be noted. The first has been a strengthening of regional and local governments which – after the acceleration impressed by the 'Bassanini' laws of 1997 – culminated in the reform of Heading Five of the Italian Constitution (i.e. the provisions on the internal articulation of the Republic). This reform, which was approved in May 2001 and confirmed by a popular referendum in October 2001, has significantly widened the range of policy areas in which the regions have exclusive or joint competence (basically all social policy except for cash benefits administered by INPS). The second line has been the restructuring of the national executive and, more generally, of the whole system of relationships between the executive and the legislative. The main outcome of this development has been the strengthening of the Presidency of the Council and a reform of the ministries (which has reduced their number and made them organisationally more efficient) that has been implemented for the first time with the formation of the Berlusconi government in June 2001 (cf. above). The third line has been a restructuring of the whole system of relationships between the central and regional/local governments. The most important development in this respect has been the effort to establish a greater symmetry between 'upward' rules (i.e the rules and processes disciplining the relations between the Italian government and the EU) and 'downward' rules, i.e. those disciplining the relations between the government and regions/local authorities. The most emblematic example of this search for a greater symmetry has been the introduction of a Domestic Stability Pact in 1998, which makes the regions and the municipalities share responsibility for the compliance with the EU Stability Pact of 1997 (Maino 2002).

As argued in the previous chapters, this threefold reconfiguration has produced some important results in terms of institutional performance. But a number of questions remain open. Even if correctly oriented towards greater symmetry and inter-level cooperation, the new system of relations does not contain all the elements that are needed in order to really work in a virtuous fashion. The national executive has been strengthened: but – in spite of Berlusconi's presidential style – it still lacks stable steering capacities on both substantive (i.e. in terms of priority setting) and organisational grounds. The absence of a truly federal Chamber – where the regions can bring their claims but are also encouraged to reconcile them with each other, with a view to producing policies of a nation-wide scope – is originating a sort of tug of war between levels of government that often creates confusion and stalemate. As a consequence of these two deficits, there are no established procedures for monitoring and evaluating regional and local policy performance – especially in those areas which have become the semi-exclusive competence of decentralised governments such as health care, social assistance and services, education and training. As the EU experience teaches us, the key for a successful 'management by objectives' is the presence of diagnostic capabilities at the centre – capabilities resting on the inputs and collaboration of the peripheries. Of the whole federal issue (at the supranational but also national level), the presence of such capabilities is one of the most fundamental elements: only if adequately steered and monitored, does a federal (or multi-level) framework operate in a virtuous fashion, encouraging politicians and policy-makers at all levels to adopt (or privilege) a problem-solving logic.

As shown by theories on subsidiarity, the latter is a two-way street: lower levels of government act first, but the higher levels can (indeed, ought to) intervene if the former fail. It is true that there are no magic formulas to operationalize subsidiarity: as a matter of fact, in all existing federations, the issue is the object of frequent and heated controversies (on 'who', 'what', 'when', 'how'), that can only be resolved, in the end, through political negotiations (McKay 2001). But it is equally true that without systematic forms of monitoring, capable of encouraging empirically grounded arguments and discussions, inspired by efficiency, effectiveness and equity considerations, political controversies may easily degenerate into brute power confrontations. Moreover, it is only in a framework of adequate information and co-operative co-ordination that the principle of 'substitutive powers' (i.e. the right of the centre to intervene *vis-à-vis* a periphery that fails to act) can find an effective application. Again, this principle is a tenet of all federal doctrines and is explicitly foreseen by the recent Italian reforms. Are the Italian regions willing to partake in periodical rounds of comparative evaluation, based on a national frame of guidelines and indicators that the regions themselves would contribute to defining, in the wider framework of the EU social policy agenda? Is the Berlusconi government willing to pursue this institutional objective?

In the aforementioned White Book on Family and Family Policies published in February 2003, the Ministry of Labour has made concrete proposals about establishing an 'open method of co-ordination' in the realm of all social policies, involving the central government, the regions, local governments and representatives of the stakeholders (Ministero del Welfare 2003). Such a domestic OMC should be closely linked with the various EU ongoing processes, and in particular the employment process and the social inclusion process. The idea is promising, but the regions have not shown any enthusiasm about it. The real stake for them is the new draft bill on 'devolution', which the Lega Nord is trying to push through, further extending the exclusive powers of the regions and formally creating a Federal Republic. Not surprisingly, one of the most delicate issues of such a bill is its financial implications: according to technical estimates, the bill would create severe strains in Italy's public budget and very likely to worsen the relative position of poorer regions[9]. Inter-regional transfers and solidarity, in a context of an increasing, but poorly monitored fiscal federalism, are bound to become a very controversial matter in Italian politics in future years: a challenge that, if not adequately managed, may seriously endanger the fragile achievements of the *risanamento* and re-aggravate the never-solved southern question (La Spina 2003; Viesti 2003).

6   Conclusion

In a recent article on the relationship between Italy and Europe, Tommaso Padoa-Schioppa has argued that with the creation of EMU the European game has become less favourable for Italy – a country still characterised by serious shortcomings in terms of administrative capabilities and by a low 'national determination' in the pursuit of international success.

> There are no incentives from Brussels or from other member states to adopt 'winning' behaviour. The EU architecture forces each member state to grant access to foreign competitors, without discrimination; it commits each member state to not harming the other partners; but it leaves each country free to harm itself by not being competitive, by being inefficient, hostile to the forces of production, incapable of guaranteeing security and order (Padoa-Schioppa 2001: 99).

If, in many respects, the changes of the 1990s have led to institutional and behavioural progresses that can now be considered as sufficiently rooted (this is the main argument of our factual reconstruction), in the new European and international context Italy continues to display a high degree of vulnerability, especially if its capacity to solve collective problems through policy innovation remains inferior to that of its partners. As we have shown in this chapter, there seem to be no signs so far that the new Berlusconi era is making any serious advancement on this front, thus confirming the *decalage* already initiated after 1998.

In this book we have essentially interpreted Italy's adjustment in terms of a 'rescue by Europe'. In this reading, what has allowed for the quantum leaps of the 1990s has been the combination of a focusing event (the EMU deadline) with anticipated sanctions (higher interest rates and currency depreciations whenever international markets thought that Italy would not make it) – in the presence of an articulated institutional project, weakened veto points in policy-making and a widening advocacy coalition for the *risanamento*. For two or three years, this combination of factors (especially the first and the second) radically altered the interactive constellation among policy players: what disappeared from the field was the status quo. In most decision-making processes, if an agreement is not reached, things remain as they are. But in the Italy of 1995-1998, not reaching an agreement meant suffering immediate and heavy financial sanctions – a pale anticipation of the heavier ones that would have followed from an exclusion of the country from EMU. This was the most powerful spur behind the various *coups de reins* of the Dini and Prodi governments. After 1998, this spur has gradually been disappearing: the cost of non-reform has become more opaque and its implications less immediately clear and perceivable. Entry into EMU has certainly rescued Italy from a potentially very serious and 'systemic' crisis. But far from being an easy trail towards success, the new scenario is that of a rugged path requiring more reforms, which must be undertaken by mobilising all available institutional capabilities and by rapidly building new ones. 'Europe' is still there, of course, with its various sticks and carrots. But it has become a softer Europe – one in which 'failure' is less clearly recognizable and in which an inefficient status quo can be maintained without immediate and explicit penalties. Capacity-building and capacity mobilization must come from within. Something that, after the 'glorious' 1990s, has certainly become easier for Italy, but that still risks being easier said than done.

Notes

Notes Chapter I

1 The table also includes three reforms undertaken in 1999-2000, as these reforms were elaborated in the previous years in the framework of EMU convergence and were enacted by the last Olive Tree governments.
2 The degree of 'stateness' – i.e. the strength, autonomy and cohesion of public administration *vis-à-vis* political institutions (Heper 1987) – notwithstanding a pervading and highly institutionalised system of administrative law was therefore quite low, compared to some other continental bureaucracies like the French and the German one.
3 The literature on policy learning and policy change is quite extensive. In particular, cf. Heclo (1974); Hall (1993); Sabatier and Jenkins-Smith (1993); Haas (1992); Visser and Hemerijck (2001). A review and a critical analysis are offered in Gualmini (1995).
4 On the concept of 'institutionalization' in political science and policy analysis see Hall and Taylor (1996); Immergut (1998); March and Olsen (1989; 1995); Pierson (1993; 1994).
5 The other basic form of conditioning is classical or 'Pavlovian': here the subject is more passive and learns to associate stimuli and answers based on a logic of continuity: the sound of a diapason, immediately followed by food, ends up with causing the dog's salivation even without feeding him, by means of a conditioned reflex.

Notes Chapter II

1 It must be noted that at the end of the 1960s the pension formula for civil servants was already more generous: it allowed for replacement rates of 100 per cent and for early retirement at any age after 20 years of service. This very generous provision had been originally introduced by the fascist regime in favour of some categories of public employees, and then extended to all public employees in the 1950s.

2 In 1987 a ruling of the Italian Constitutional Court (n. 497) found that the amount of the allowance (corresponding to 800 Liras, i.e. 0.4 euros per day!) was not in line with the cost of living. In 1988 Law no. 160 modified the mechanism of calculus bringing it to 20 per cent of previous earnings, later raised to 40 per cent (Gualmini 1998).

3 Confindustria is the national employers' peak association, mainly representing big firms.

4 When we speak in general of trade unions, we refer to the three main Italian workers' peak associations, that is the CGIL, the biggest Italian left-oriented union, the CISL, traditionally connected with Catholic movements and the Christian Democratic party, and the UIL, the smallest one, traditionally linked with minor lay parties.

5 Contrary to the logics of incomes policy, in the period 1969-1975 earnings growth was disjointed from productivity gains and from inflation dynamics. Real and nominal wages increased outside of any legal or bargaining regulation.

6 In the period 1970-71 nominal wages increased by 19.9 per cent and in the 1973-75 period by 22.7 per cent (compared to 6.8 per cent in 1968-69). In 1970 real wages rose by 15 per cent (Rossi 1998). One of the most innovative achievements of the unions was the separation of wage dynamics from productivity trends; just to mention an example one should consider that in the manufacturing from 1969 to 1973 per capita real earnings rose by 36 per cent compared to an increase in productivity of 23 per cent (Signorini and Visco 1997). The ensuing rise in the cost of labour was particularly strong in the first half of the 1970s.

7 Indexation had always been a fundamental element of the Italian earnings regime. The so-called *scala mobile* had been introduced early in 1945 to safeguard wages against inflation. Its functioning was simple: the level of wages was periodically adjusted to the level of the cost of living (which was measured on the basis of a pre-defined 'basket of goods'). In 1975 the employers were basically forced to agree on the new instrument (which was clearly going to push up wages) in exchange for the stopping of conflicts and strikes in the firms. But what was supposed to be a temporary agreement became a permanent feature of the Italian wage system - and an object of heated controversy until the early 1990s.

8 The indexation dynamic was not in fact perfectly aligned with the consumer prices trend. If in period 'A' the inflation had risen, wages would have grown in the period immediately following, that is in period 'B', when inflation had possibly fallen. And if wages had risen, this was an opportunity for firms to push up prices; employers had no hesitations in doing this since they could rely on the lira devaluation mechanism. The 1975 agreement ended up by offering the basis for an uncontrollable wage-inflation rise. It was not a coincidence that from 1970 to 1979 the percentage of wage increases due to indexations grew from 13.5 per

cent to 79.7 per cent (Somaini 1989). The earnings dispersion between the median and first decile (D5-D1) declined from 1.96 in 1979 to 1.50 in 1989 (Scharpf and Schmidt, 2000, vol. 1, app. Table A.21).

9 From 1965 to 1976 the total outlays of government rose from 34.2 per cent of GDP to 43.4 per cent; in the same years the revenues remained basically unchanged, moving from 30 per cent of the GDP to 31.2 per cent.

10 The term 'civic culture' was coined in the 1950s by Almond and Verba (1963) to designate positive traits in the citizenry such as trust in government, willingness to comply with the law, unreadiness to engage in non-conventional (and especially violent) forms of political participation, etc. From Almond's and Verba's pioneering comparative research (essentially based on survey data) Italy stood out for its relatively low scores on most indicators of 'civicness'. For a discussion and updated analysis of Italy's political culture, cf. Sani (1980), Sani and Segatti (2001) and Putnam (1993).

11 Ministero del Tesoro (1981), Ministero del Lavoro (2000).

Notes Chapter III

1 In 1990, 58.2 per cent of exports was addressed to EC countries, 4.9 per cent to Eastern Europe and 14.7 per cent to developing countries (Onida 1993: 192). The Italian share of world export also increased from 3.8 per cent in 1980 to 4.7 per cent in 1989 (World Trade Database 1980-1994).

2 In the period 1980-1985 family allowances rose, even though the number of beneficiaries fell; the average amount of pensions increased more rapidly than the per capita GDP; the growth of school teachers surpassed that of pupils and the number of hospital employees significantly expanded (for a discussion, cf. Rossi 1998: 69).

3 In 1993 the first loss of employment in the tertiary sector, after more than 30 years of positive growth, was registered (from 59.9 per cent in 1992 to 59 per cent in 1993) (Gualmini 1998).

4 The adjective 'technical' refers to the presence in the cabinet of at least some ministers chosen for their substantive competence and professional reputation (matured in the private sector or in the Bank of Italy or in academia), with only weak partisan ties. In 'political' executives, ministerial positions are instead typically occupied by career politicians and party leaders.

5 The manoeuvre included also a wide-ranging plan of privatisations, more realistic and feasible than that proposed by Andreotti one year before (Verzichelli 1999).

6 The high propensity of Italian families to save and their preference for state

bonds (instead of stock market equities) has always been a characteristic feature of the Italian economic and social behaviour and culture.

7 We will come back to these points in more detail in Chapter V.

8 In December 1996, at the Dublin summit the Growth and Stability Pact was approved, concerning the constraints and conditions for the countries which were to join the EMU in order to maintain stability and fiscal responsibility. These conditions were to be more precisely stated in the Amsterdam Treaty of June 1997 and in the EC regulations of July 1997.

9 The same law established the merging of the Ministry of the Treasury and the Ministry of the Budget within a wider Ministry for the Economy.

10 The main arguments of the debate can be found in: Barca and Visco (1992), Bodo and Viesti (1997), De Nardis and Galli (1997), Deaglio (1998), Micossi and Visco (1993), Onida (1993), Cominotti and Mariotti (1997), Garrett (1999), Lange and Struggs (1999), Lawrence (1996) and Barba Navaretti (2002).

11 This is especially relevant for the implementation of the Uruguay Round and, more decisively, for the elimination of the Agreement on Multifibres. This process will gradually remove the trade barriers which have so far favoured the Italian producers. More generally, the growing supply of workforce of developing countries, in a context of global trade liberalisation, will have a deeper influence on the Italian trade conditions than on other industrialised countries (Faini *et al.* 1999). In other words, the 'niches advantage' which helped Italy in the international economy will be gradually lost.

12 In 1999 Italian social expenditure as a share of GDP was – in addition – lower than in Germany (29.6 per cent), France (30.3 per cent), United Kindgom (26.9 per cent), the Netherlands (28.1 per cent), Denmark (29.4 per cent) and Sweden (32.9 per cent) (Eurostat, Social Protection in Europe 2002).

Notes Chapter IV

1 The *Cassa Integrazione* scheme is statistically measured in terms of the number of 'paid hours', rather than compensated workers.

2 The pre-retirement scheme had an exceptional success: every year, between 1981 and 1987, 30,000 workers got access to pre-retirement benefits, at a cost of 30,000 billion liras (15,000 million euros) (Capellari 1989).

3 For discussion cf. Amendola, Caroleo and Garofalo (1997).

4 We use the term 'income testing' rather than means-testing because assets were not considered in the early provisions of the 1980s.

5 These data were reported by 'Il Sole 24 Ore', 21 March 1996.

6   In spite of the huge increase in contributions, the transfer of the central government to finance social protection rose by 76 per cent in real terms between 1980 and 1990, increasing from 5.0 per cent to 7.1 per cent of GDP (OECD, Social Expenditure Statistics 1996).

7   The historical series is considered from 1993 onwards, since in 1992 the method for data collection and analysis was changed by the National Institute for Statistics (ISTAT). The employment and participation rates are calculated on the population aged between 15 and 64. Where not mentioned the source is the National Institute for Statistics, ISTAT, Forze di lavoro, 1993-2001.

8   On the innovations of the 1990s cf. Esping-Andersen and Regini (2000); Treu (2001) and Sestito (2002).

9   The decentralisation process involved also the competencies for active labour policies which were devolved to the regions (completing the process initiated in 1978 with vocational training).

10   The Law was finally approved by a national confirmative referendum, called in October 2001, as the procedure for the formal revision of constitutional rules requires.

11   As we will extensively argue in chapter VI, this proposal was finally pursued through the law no. 30 of 2003, the so-called 'Biagi law'.

12   For a summary evaluation of the impact of the EES on the Italian labour market, cf. Isfol (2002). For a more articulated analysis on the impact of the EES on Italy's policy-making, covering also the regional dimension and the role of social partners, cf. Ferrera and Gualmini (2003).

13   Five main recommendations were outlined at the Essen Council: a) to improve opportunities for employability; b) to promote labour-intensive economic growth; c) to reduce labour costs; d) to develop active labour market policies; and e) to introduce specific measures for long-term unemployment. Member states were also invited to produce annual reports in order to fit convergence requirements (Goetschy 1999).

14   The Dini reform of 1995 equalised the retirement ages of men and women: cf. *infra*.

15   Such as freelance workers and other semi-autonomous workers (*lavoro parasubordinato*).

16   This revision was made in the course of 1997 and led to the new reform of the Prodi government (see *infra*).

17   For a full review of the 1997 pension reform and its financial impact, see Mira d'Ercole and Terribile (1998). For a comprehensive evaluation of the reforms which followed the Onofri Report, see the monographic issue of the review 'Politica Economica', no. 1, April 1998.

18   A more detailed discussion of these developments is contained in Ferrera (1999).

19 On the current state of the RMI and its future prospects, see however *infra*, chapter 6.

20 For an illustration of this new process of open co-ordination in the field of inclusion, cf. Ferrera, Matsaganis and Sacchi (2002).

Notes Chapter V

1 This was also witnessed by the intense use of delegation laws and of deregulation (Vassallo 2001).

2 The introduction of the direct election of mayors and of provincial presidents four years before – in 1993 – had strongly contributed to this reinforcement.

3 As a matter of fact, the new Berlusconi government, voted into office in May 2001, modified the previous government's reform by decree (D.L. 217/2001, converted into Law 317/2001), bringing the number of ministries up to 14.

4 Every single revision of constitutional rules requires a final approval by means of a national consultative referendum.

5 On the importance of the 'cognitive path' to institutional change and the new role of experts in Italy during the 1990s, see also Giuliani (1999) and Radaelli (2002). The same authors have also written an interesting review of different interpretations concerning the process of financial adjustment and the entry into EMU (Giuliani and Radaelli 1999).

6 In the 1980s the idea of an external constraint (and of a virtuous circle consisting of compliance with the constraints, their reinforcement, further alignment of national behaviours to the European norm, and so on) got progressively institutionalised, becoming a true frame of reference for the interpretation of social reality (what Müller, 1995, defines as *referentiel*). For further insights on the influence of this interpretative paradigm upon the Italian financial adjustment, see Dyson and Featherstone (1996) and Radaelli (1999). On the concept of advocacy coalition, see Sabatier and Jenkins-Smith (1993).

7 On the role of these professors within the Italian policy-making of the 1980s and the 1990s, see Regonini (1993).

8 For a summary but accurate account, see Dyson and Featherstone (1999) and Walsh (2000).

9 With regard to its 'sincere' part, the new discourse on equity is indeed part of the substantive learning we have discussed in the previous paragraph.

10 In the famous Skinner box, the animal is free to move as it wishes: but it gets food (positive reinforcement) only if it pushes a button spontaneously, by means of firstly casual and then intentional movements. Naturally, the metaphor is to be read in its weak sense: the Italian decision-makers did not suffer from passive

and purely exogenous conditionings, on the part of any 'gnome' able to manipulate them through financial markets. On the contrary, they reshaped their preferences on the basis of constraints that could not be negotiated anymore, on the one hand, and of the unsustainable status quo, on the other. The latter factor played a very important role: if the status quo is not anymore the default option, the veto power becomes not only unproductive, but also self-injuring.

11 Despite the convergence achieved under Dini and Prodi, Italy's admission into the EMU remained uncertain until early 1998. Antonio Fazio, the Governor of the Bank of Italy, has revealed that as late as March 1998 he had to threaten the lira's unilateral exit from the EMS if Italy was not admitted, despite the positive macro-economic trends. For admission, he had to take the commitment to maintain a current account surplus in order to reduce public debt (Il Sole 24 Ore, 29 November 2001).

12 On the connection between concerted action and the economic and financial policy-making, cf. also Paganetto (1999) and Padoa-Schioppa (1998).

13 On this aspect, see Visser and Hemerijck (1997).

14 As Amato himself reveals in a book about his own experience as Prime Minister (Amato 1994).

15 It is, in fact, no coincidence that the countries in which social pacts experienced a clear revival in the 1990s were exactly those which had the biggest problems with respect to entry into the Euro-zone, that is those situated outside the Deutschmark area (Italy, Spain, Portugal, Finland and Ireland).

16 Thus, the indicators of the institutionalisation of political exchange would be: a) the larger number of actors who signed the agreements (wider diffusion of consensus and higher representativeness of the agreements); b) the presence of a pro-labour government; and c) the presence, within the agreements, of rules and principles governing the functioning of the new decision-making procedures.

17 For the parliamentary debate on the approval of temporary work (within the Treu law of 1997) see Gualmini (1998).

Notes Chapter VI

1 For a detailed reconstruction of the law projects on the conflict of interests presented from the XII to the XIV legislative terms see Gitti and Maffeis (2003).

2 Already in 1997, under the Prodi government, a draft bill aimed at changing the norms on individual dismissals – and thus art. 18 – had been presented to Parliament by a number of DS MPs led by Senator Franco Debenedetti. According to this proposal, workers must be re-integrated into their jobs only in cases of discriminatory, anti-union or 'capricious' dismissals. In all other cases, workers

must receive adequate compensation, but without re-integration (Debenedetti 2002).

3   Article 18 was to be experimentally suspended only in the second of the three cases given above.

4   A number of left-wing parties and social movements promoted a referendum in June 2003 with a view to extending its scope of application also to enterprises with fewer than 15 employees. The turnout was very low (less than 30 per cent), thus invalidating the whole initiative.

5   After 40 years' contributions and at the age of 65 (Ministero del Welfare 2002: 15).

6   For workers, the TFR can play the role of an unemployment benefit, in case of termination of a contract prior to retirement. Without the introduction of more generous unemployment benefits, it should not be surprising that Italian employees are reluctant to forego the TFR. For employers, the TFR constitute a cheap source of financing. TFR contributions are set aside by companies only 'notionally'. In practice, they remain part of the company's cash flow. Companies are obliged to pay a small contribution for bankruptcy insurance.

7   For an articulated debate and informed comments on recent developments of Italian social and economic policy , cf. the web site: www.lavoce.info.

8   The contribution rebates of the *delega* may be considered as a partial compensation to the employers for the obligatory and *real* (as opposed to notional) payment of TFR contributions into the pension funds.

9   Cf . Il Sole 24 Ore, 9 February 2003. Cf. also the debate on this issue on www.lavoce.info.

References

Accornero, A. (1992), *La parabola del sindacato*, Bologna, Il Mulino

Addis, E. (1987), *Banca d'Italia e politica monetaria: la riallocazione del potere fra stato, mercato e banca centrale*, in: 'Stato e mercato', 19: 73-95

Altieri, G. and Carrieri M. (2000), *Il popolo del 10%*, Rome, Donzelli

Amato, G. (1990), *Due anni al tesoro*, Bologna, Il Mulino

Amato, G. (1994), *Un governo nella transizione. La mia esperienza di presidente del consiglio*, in: 'Quaderni costituzionali', 3: 355-371

Amendola, A., Caroleo, F.E. and Garofalo, M.R. (1997), *Labour Market and Decentralized Decision-Making: An Institutional Approach*, in:'Labour', 3: 497-516

Ascoli, U. (1984), (Ed.), *Welfare state all'italiana*, Bologna, Il Mulino

Baccaro, L. (2002), *The Construction of Democratic Corporatism in Italy*, in: 'Politics & Society', vol 30, no. 2: 327, 357

Bagnasco, A. (1977), *Tre Italie*, Bologna, Il Mulino

Balboni, E. and Buzzacchi, C. (2003), *Le politiche comunitarie per l'occupazione e l'obiettivo della coesione economica e sociale*, in: E.Balboni, E. Gualmini and F. Timpano (Eds.), *Coesione sociale e politiche attive del lavoro nelle regioni d'Europa*, Fondazione Ruffilli, Forlì, 9-39

Barba Navaretti, G. (1999), *Is the Suspect Guilty? Labour Market Effects of Trade Liberalisation in Textile*, Discussion Paper, University of Ancona

Barba Navaretti, G., Bruno, G., Castellani, D. and Falzoni, A. (2002), *Does Investing Abroad Create or Destroy Jobs at Home? The Case of Italian Multinationals*, paper presented at the Conference on 'Labour Market Effects of European Foreign Direct Investments', Turin, 10–11 May

Barca, F. and Visco, I. (1992), *L'economia italiana nella prospettiva europea: terziario protetto e dinamica dei redditi*, Rome, Banca d'Italia

Barney, J.B. and Ouchi, W.G. (1984), *Information Cost and Informational Governance*, in: 'Management Science', 10: 47-95

Bellardi, L. (1999), *Concertazione e contrattazione*, Bari, Cacucci Editore

Biagi, M. (1997), *Mercati e rapporti di lavoro*, Milan, Giuffré

Bodo, G. and Viesti, G. (1997), *La grande svolta*, Rome, Donzelli

Boeri, T. *et al.* (Eds.) (2002), *Non basta dire no*, Milan, Mondadori

Boeri, T. and Perotti, R. (2002), *Meno pensioni, più welfare*, Bologna, Il Mulino

Bonoli, G. and Bertozzi, F. (2002), *Verso una convergenza delle politiche nazionali per l'occupazione? La costruzione di un modello Europeo attraverso il metodo di coordinamento aperto*, in: 'Rivista italiana di politiche pubbliche', 3: 31-57

Brusco, S. and Paba, S. (1997), *Per una storia dei distretti industriali dal secondo dopoguerra agli anni novanta*, in: F. Barca (Ed.), *La storia del capitalismo italiano*, Rome, Donzelli

Bufacchi, V. and Burgess, S. (1998), *Italy Since 1989: Events and Interpretations*, London, Macmillan

Cafiero, S. (1997), *La questione meridionale nella prospettiva dell'UE*, in: 'Rivista economica del Mezzogiorno', 4: 815-821

Capano, G. (1992), *L'improbabile riforma*, Bologna, Il Mulino

Capano, G. and Giuliani, M. (2001), (Eds.), *Parlamento e processo legislativo in Italia*, Bologna, Il Mulino

Capellari, S. (1989), *Le politiche di pensionamento anticipato attuate in Italia negli anni ottanta*, in: F. Neri (Ed.), *Le politiche del lavoro negli anni ottanta*, Milan, Angeli, 35-70

Carinci, F. (1999), *Alle radici della concertazione contemporanea*, Discussion Paper, Rome, La Sapienza University

Carrieri, M. (1995), *L'incerta rappresentanza*, Bologna, Il Mulino

Cassese, S. (1974), *L'amministrazione pubblica in Italia*, Bologna, Il Mulino

Cassese, S. (1984), *Il sistema amministrativo italiano*, Bologna, Il Mulino

Cazzola, G. (1995), *Le nuove pensioni degli italiani*, Bologna, Il Mulino

Cella, G.P. and Treu, T. (Eds.) (1989), *Relazioni industriali. Manuale per l'analisi dell'esperienza italiana*, Bologna, Il Mulino

Cella, G.P. and Treu, T. (Eds.) (1998), *Le nuove relazioni industriali. L'esperienza italiana nella prospettiva europea*, Bologna, Il Mulino

CENSIS, Centro Studi Investimenti Sociali (1976), *L'occupazione occulta. Caratteristiche della partecipazione al lavoro*, Rome

Centorrino, M. (1976), *Consumi sociali e sviluppo economico in Italia*, Rome, Coines

Checkel, J.T. (2001), *Why Comply? Social Learning and European Identity Change*, in: 'International Organisation', vol 55. no. 3: 553-588

Chiorazzo, V. and Spaventa, L. (1999), *The Prodigal Son or a Confidence Trickster? How Italy Got into EMU*, in: D.Cobman and G.Zis (Eds.) *From EMS to EMU: 1979 to 1979 and Beyond*, London, Macmillan, 129-155

Ciampi, C.A. (1996), *Un metodo per governare*, Bologna, Il Mulino

Ciampi, C.A. (1998), *Risanamento e sviluppo, due momenti inscindibili della stessa politica*, in: 'Info/Quaderni', Special Issue on *The Euro and the Policies for Development and Employment,* Rome, 198-203

CNEL, Consiglio Nazionale dell'Economia e del Lavoro (1963), *Osservazioni e proposte sulla riforma della previdenza sociale*, Rome, Istituto Poligrafico dello Stato

Cominotti, R. and Mariotti, S. (1997), *Italia multinazionale: tendenze e protagonisti dell'internazionalizzazione*, Milan, F. Angeli

Comitato di Studio per la Sicurezza Sociale (1965), *Per un sistema di sicurezza sociale*, Bologna, Il Mulino

Cossentino, F., Pyke, F. and Sengenberger, W. (1997), *Le risposte locali e regionali alla pressione globale: il caso dell'Italia e dei suoi distretti industriali*, Bologna, Il Mulino

Cotta, M. (1987), *Il sottosistema governo-parlamento*, in: 'Rivista italiana di scienza politica', 2: 241-243

Cotta, M. (2002), *Berlusconi's Second Governmental Test*, in: P. Bellucci and M. Bull (Eds.), *Italian Politics. The Return of Berlusconi*, Oxford, Berghahn Books, 146-166

Cotta, M. and Verzichelli, L. (1996), *La classe politica: cronaca di una morte annunciata?*, in: M. Cotta and P. Isernia (Eds.), *Il gigante dai piedi di argilla*, Bologna, Il Mulino, 373-408

Crouch, C. and Traxler, F. (Eds.) (1995), *Organized Industrial Relations in Europe: What Future?*, Aldershot, Avebury

Culpepper, P.D. (2002), *Powering, Puzzling and 'Pacting': the Informational Logic of Negotiated Reforms*, in: 'Journal of European Public Policy, vol. 9, no. 5: 774-790

D'Alberti, M. (1999), *Aspetti istituzionali della concertazione tra costituzione ed amministrazione*, Discussion Paper, Rome, La Sapienza University

D'Alimonte, R. (1978), *Competizione elettorale e rendimento politico: il caso italiano*, in: 'Rivista italiana di scienza politica', 3: 457-493

Deaglio, M. (1998), *L'Italia paga il conto*, Milan, Guerrini & Associati

Debenedetti, F. (2002), in: T. Boeri *et al.* (Eds.), *Non basta dire no*, Milan, Mondadori, 35-61

De la Porte, C. and Pochet, P. (Eds.), (2002), *Building Social Europe Through the Open Method of Co-ordination*, Brussels, P.I.E. - Peter Lang

Del Boca, A. (1996), *Prospettive di riforma degli strumenti di integrazione del reddito nell'ambito della spesa sociale*, Rome, Technical Commission for Public Expenditure

Delogu, S. (1967), *Sanità pubblica, sicurezza sociale e programmazione economica*, Turin, Einaudi

De Nardis, S. and Galli, G. (1997), (Eds.), *La disoccupazione italiana*, Bologna, Il Mulino

De Nardis, S. and Paternò, F. (1997), *Commercio estero e occupazione nell'industria italiana*, in: S. De Nardis and G. Galli (Eds.), *La disoccupazione italiana*, Bologna, Il Mulino, 151-188

Dente, B. (1989), *Il governo locale*, in: G. Freddi (Ed.), *Scienza dell'amministrazione e politiche pubbliche*, Rome, La Nuova Italia Scientifica, 123-170

Dente, B. (1991), *Politica, istituzioni e deficit pubblico*, in: 'Stato e Mercato', 33: 339-370

Diamanti, I. and Lazar, M. (2002), *The National Elections of 13 May 2001: Chronicle of a Victory Foretold – Albeit a Little Too Soon*, in: P. Bellucci and M. Bull (Eds.), *Italian Politics. The return of Berlusconi*, Oxford, Berghahn Books, 49-67

Di Palma (1977), *Surviving without Governing: The Italian Parties in Parliament*, Berkeley, Berkeley University Press

Duverger, M. (1988), *La nostalgie de l'impuissance*, Paris, Albin Michel

Dyson, K. and Featherstone, K. (1996), *Italy and Emu as a 'Vincolo Esterno': Empowering the Technocrats, Transforming the State*, in: 'South European Society and Politics', 2: 272-299

Dyson, K. and Featherstone, K. (1999), *The Road to Maastricht. Negotiating Economic and Monetary Union*, Oxford, Oxford University Press

Epstein, G.A. and Schor, G.B. (1987), *The Divorce of the Banca d'Italia and the Italian Treasure: a Case Study of Central Bank Independence*, in: P. Lange and M. Regini (Eds.), *State, Market and Social Regulation: New Perspectives on Italy*, Cambridge, Cambridge University Press, 147-165

Esping-Andersen, G. (1990), *The Three Worlds of Welfare Capitalism*, Cambridge, Polity Press

Esping-Andersen, G. (1995), *Il welfare state senza lavoro. L'ascesa del familismo nelle politiche sociali dell'Europa continentale*, in: 'Stato e mercato', 45: 347-380

Esping-Andersen, G. (1996), *Welfare States in Transition*, London, Sage

Esping-Andersen, G. and Regini, M. (2000) (Eds.), *Why Deregulate the Labour Market?*, London, Oxford University Press

European Commission (1993-1995), *Social Protection in Europe*, Luxembourg

European Economy (1999), *Italy's Slow Growth in the 1990s*, Bruxelles, European Commission

Eurostat (1999), *Depenses et recettes de protection sociale*, Luxembourg

Fabbrini, S. (2000), *Parlamento, governo e capo del governo nella transizione italiana*, in: G. Di Palma, S. Fabbrini and G. Freddi (Eds.), *Condannata al successo? L'Italia nell'Europa integrata degli anni Novanta*, Bologna, Il Mulino, 45-78

Fabbrini, S. (2001), *Tra pressioni e veti*, Rome-Bari, Laterza

Fabbrini, S. and Vassallo, S. (1999), *Il governo. Gli esecutivi nelle democrazie contemporanee*, Rome-Bari, Laterza

Faini, R., Falzoni, A.M., Galeotti, R., Helg, R., and Turrini, A. (1999), *Importing Jobs or Exporting Firms? On the Wage and Employment Implications of Italian Trade and Foreign Direct Investment Flows*, in: 'Giornale degli Economisti', vol. 58, no. 1: 95-135

Ferrera, M. (1984*), Il welfare state in Italia*, Bologna, Il Mulino

Ferrera, M. (1986/87), *Italy*, in: P. Flora (Ed.), *Growth to Limits. The Western European Welfare State since World War II*, Berlin/New York, De Gruyter, vol. 2, pp. 385-499 and vol. 4, 476-528

Ferrera, M. (1989), *Politics, Institutional Assets and Industrial Policy*, in: P. Lange and M. Regini (Eds.), *State, Market and Social Regulation in Italy*, Cambridge, Cambridge University Press, 111-127

Ferrera, M. (1991), *Italia: aspirazioni e vincoli del 'quarto grande'*, in: M. Ferrera (Ed.), *Le dodici Europe. I paesi della Comunità di fronte ai cambiamenti del 1989-1900*, Bologna, Il Mulino, 73-92

Ferrera, M. (1993), *Modelli di solidarietà*, Bologna, Il Mulino

Ferrera, M. (1996), *Il modello sud-europeo di welfare state*, in: 'Rivista italiana di scienza politica', 1: 67-101

Ferrera, M. (1998), *Le trappole del welfare*, Bologna, Il Mulino

Ferrera, M. (1999), *Targeting Social Benefits*, New Brunswick, Transaction

Ferrera, M. and Gualmini, E. (2003), *La strategia europea sull'occupazione e la governance domestica del mercato del lavoro: verso nuovi assetti organizzativi e decisionali?*, Rome, Isfol Report

Ferrera, M., Matsaganis, M. and Sacchi, S. (2002), *Open Coordination Against Poverty: the New EU 'Social Inclusion Process'*, in: 'Journal of European Social Policy', vol. 12, no. 3: 225-237

Flora, P. (Ed.) (1983), *State, Economy and Society in Western Europe*, London, Macmillan, 2 vols.

Flora, P. (1986-1987), *Growth to Limits. The Western Welfare States Since World War II*, Berlin, De Gruyter, 4 vols.

Freddi, G. (1989), *Burocrazia, democrazia e governabilità*, in: G. Freddi (Ed.), *Scienza dell'amministrazione e politiche pubbliche*, Rome, La Nuova Italia Scientifica, 19-65

Freddi, G. (1990), *Medici e stato nel mondo occidentale*, Bologna, Il Mulino

Garrett, G. (1999), *L'autonomia nazionale nell'economia globale*, in: 'Stato e Mercato', 55: 79-116

Gerelli, E. and Majocchi, A. (1984), *Il deficit pubblico: origine e problemi*, Milan, Angeli

Ghera, E. (1999), *La pratica della concertazione in Italia*, Discussion Paper, Rome, La Sapienza University

Ghirotti, M. (1998), *Il collocamento e le azioni per favorire l'incontro tra domanda e offerta*, in: 'Le istituzioni del federalismo', vol. 2, no. 3: 339-356

Giddens, A. (Ed.) (2001), *The Global Third Way Debate*, Cambridge, Polity Press

Gitti, G. and Maffeis, D. (2003), *E il conflitto di interessi?*, in: 'Il Mulino', 2: 295-316

Giuliani, M. (1996), *Italy*, in: D. Rometsch and W. Wessels (Eds.), *The European Union and Members States: Towards Institutional Fusion?*, Manchester, Manchester University Press, 105-133

Giuliani, M. (2000), *Europeanization and Italy: A Bottom-Up Process?*, in: 'South European Society and Politics', 5: 47-72

Giuliani, M. and Piattoni, S. (2001), *Italy. Both Leader and Laggard*, in: E. Zeff and E. Pirro (Eds.), *The European Union and the Member States. Cooperation, Coordination and Compromise*, Boulder, Lynne Rienner Publishers, 115-142

Giuliani, M. and Radaelli, C.M. (1999), *Italian Political Science and the EU*, in: 'Journal of European Public Policy', vol. 6, no. 3: 517-524

Goetschy J. (1999), *The European Employment Strategy: Genesis and Development*, in: 'European Journal of Industrial Relations', vol. 5, no. 2: 117-37

Goldthorpe, J.H. (1984), *Order and Conflict in Contemporary Capitalism*, Oxford, Oxford University Press

Granovetter, M. (1985), *Economic Action and Social Structure: The Problem of Embededdness*, in: 'American Journal of Sociology', 3: 481-510

Graziani, A. (1979), *L'economia italiana dal 1945 a oggi*, Bologna, Il Mulino

Graziani, A. (1998), *L'Italia nella crisi economica internazionale*, in: A. Graziani and A.M. Nassisi (Eds.), *L'economia globale in trasformazione*, Rome, Manifestolibri

Graziano, L. (1984), *Clientelismo e sistema politico*, Milan, Angeli

Gualmini, E. (1995), *Apprendimento e cambiamento nelle politiche pubbliche: il ruolo delle idee e della conoscenza*, in: 'Rivista Italiana di Scienza Politica', 2: 343-370

Gualmini, E. (1997a), *Le rendite del neo-corporatismo*, Soveria Mannelli, Rubbettino

Gualmini, E. (1997b), *L'evoluzione degli assetti concertativi in Italia e Germania*, in: 'Rivista Italiana di Scienza Politica', 1: 101-150

Gualmini, E. (1998), *La politica del lavoro*, Bologna, Il Mulino

Gualmini, E. (2003), *L'omministrazione nelle democrazie contemporare*, Rome-Bari, Laterza

Haas, P.H. (1992), *Introduction: Epistemic Communities and International Policy Co-ordination*, in: 'International Organization', 1: 1-35
Hall, P.A. (1993), *Policy Paradigm, Social Learning and the State: The Case of Econoomic Policy-Making in Britain*, in: 'Comparative Politics', 25: 275-296
Hall, P.A. and Taylor, R.C.R. (1996), *Political Science and the Three New Institutionalisms*, in: 'Political Studies', 5: 936-957
Heclo, H. (1974), *Modern Social Politics in Britain and in Sweden*, New York, Yale University Press
Heper, M. (1987), *The State and Public Bureaucracies*, Westport, Greenwood Press
Hine, D. (1993), *Governing Italy*, Oxford, Clarendon Press
Hood, C. (1991), *A Public Management for all Seasons?* in: 'Public Administration', 69: 3-19
Hood, C. (1998), *The Art of the State. Culture, Rhetoric, and Public Management*, Oxford. Oxford University Press

Ichino, P. (1982), *Il collocamento impossibile*, Bari, De Donato
Ichino, P. (1996), *Il lavoro e il mercato*, Milan, Mondadori
Ichino, P. (2002), *Ferri vecchi e strategie nuove*, in: T. Boeri *et al.* (Eds.), *Non basta dire no*, Milan, Mondadori, 13-44
Immergut, E.M. (1998), *The Theoretical Core of the New Institutionalism*, in: 'Politics and Society', 1: 5-34
ISFOL (2000), *Formazione e occupazione in Italia e in Europa*, Rome, Isfol
ISFOL (2002), *Impact Evaluation of the European Employment Strategy: Final Report*, Rome, Isfol.
ISTAT (1990-2001), *Forze di lavoro*, Rome

Kahneman, D. and Tversky, A. (1979), *Prospect Theory: an Analysis of Decision Under Risk*, in: 'Econometrica', 47: 263-291
Kahneman, D. and Tversky, A. (1984), *Choices, Values and Frames*, in: 'American Psychologist', 39: 341-350
Kingdon, J.W. (1984), *Agendas, Alternatives and Public Policy*, Boston, Little Brown

Lange, P. and Struggs, L. (1999), *Where Have All Members Gone? La sindacalizzazione nell'era della globalizzazione*, in: 'Stato e Mercato', 55: 39-78
La Palombara, J. (1964), *Interest Groups in Italian Politics*, Princeton, Princeton University Press

La Spina, (2003), *La politica per il Mezzogiorno*, Bologna, Il Mulino

Lawrence, R. (1996), *Regionalism, Multilateralism, and Deeper Economic Integration*, Washington D.C., The Brookings Institution

Lehmbruch, G. and Schmitter, P.C. (Eds.), (1984), *La politica degli interessi nei paesi industrializzati*, Bologna, Il Mulino

Levy, J. (1999a), *France in a Globalizing Economy: The Shifting Logic of Welfare Reform*, Discussion Paper, Florence, IUE

Levy, J. (1999b), *Vice into Virtue? Progressive Politics and Welfare Reform in Continental Europe*, Discussion Paper, Florence IUE

Lijphart, A. (1999), *Patterns of democracy. Government Forms and Performance in Thirty-Six Countries*, New Haven, Yale University Press

Maino, F. (2002), *L'europeizzazione della sanità. La politica sanitaria italiana tra patti esterni e patti interni*, in: S. Fabbrini (Ed.), *L'europeizzazione dell'Italia. L'impatto dell'Europa sulle istituzioni e le politiche italiane*, Bari, Laterza, 164-189

Mania, R. and Sateriale, G. (2002) *Relazioni pericolose. Sindacati e politica dopo la concertazione*, Bologna, Il Mulino

Manin Carabba, G. (1977), *Un ventennio di programmazione*, Bari, Laterza

Maraffi, M. (1990), *Politica ed economia in Italia*, Bologna, Il Mulino

March, J.G. and Olsen, J.P. (1989), *Rediscovering Institutions. The Organizational Basis of Politics*, New York, The Free Press

March, J.G. and Olsen, J.P. (1995), *Democratic Governance*, New York, The Free Press

McKay, D. (2001) *Designing Europe. Comparative Lessons From the Federal Experience*, Oxford, Oxford University Press

Micossi, S. and Visco, I. (1993), *Inflazione, concorrenza e sviluppo. L'economia italiana e la sfida dell'integrazione europea*, Bologna, Il Mulino

Ministero del Lavoro (2000), *Nucleo di Valutazione della Spesa Pensionistica: Gli andamenti finanziari del sistema pensionistico obbligatorio*, Rome

Ministero del Lavoro (1/2001), *Rapporto di Monitoraggio*, Rome

Ministero del Tesoro (1981), *La spesa previdenziale e i suoi effetti sulla finanza pubblica*, Rome

Ministero del Tesoro (1998), *Convergenze dell'Italia verso l'UEM*, Rome

Ministero del Welfare (2001), *Verifica del sistema previdenziale ai sensi della legge 335/95 e successivi provvedimenti nell'ottica della competitività, dello sviluppo e dell'equità*, Rome

Ministero del Welfare (2002), *Rapporto sulle strategie nazionali per i futuri sistemi pensionistici*, Rome

Ministero del Welfare (2003), *Libro bianco sul welfare. Proposte per una società dinamica e solidale*, Rome

Mira D'Ercole, M. and Terribile, F. (1998), *Pension Spending: Developments in 1996 and 1997*, in: L. Bardi and M. Rhodes (Eds.), *Italian Politics. Mapping the Future*, Boulder Colorado, Westview, 210-237

Müller, P. (1995), *Les politiques publiques comme construction d'un rapport au monde*, in: A. Faure, G. Pollet and P. Warin (Eds.), *La construction du sens dans les politiques publiques*, Paris, L'Harmattan, 153-179

Natali, D. (2001), *La ridefinizione del Welfare State contemporaneo: la riforma delle pensioni in Francia e in Italia*, Phd Dissertation, Florence, IUE

North, D.C. (1990), *Institutions, Institutional Change and Economic Performance*, Cambridge, Cambridge University Press

Onida, F. (1993), *Collocazione internazionale e fattori di competitività dell'industria italiana*, in: S. Micossi and I. Visco (Eds.), *Inflazione, concorrenza e sviluppo*, Bologna, Il Mulino

Onofri, P. (2003), *Un anno di politica economica del governo Berlusconi*, in: J. Blondel and P. Segatti (Eds.), *Politica in Italia*, Bologna, Il Mulino, 157-171

Padoa-Schioppa, T. (1998), *Che cosa ci ha insegnato l'avventura europea*, in: 'Il Mulino', 987-1001

Padoa-Schioppa, T. (2001), *L'Italia e l'Europa: un'interazione fruttuosa*, in: T. Padoa-Schioppa and S.R. Graubard (Eds.), *Il caso italiano 2*, Garzanti, Milan, 53-101

Paganetto, L. (1999), *Oltre l'euro. Istituzioni, occupazione e crescita*, Bologna, Il Mulino

Pennacchi, L. (1998), *La moneta unica europea fra risanamento, sviluppo e crescita dell'occupazione*, in: 'Info/Quaderni', Special Issue on the Euro and the Policies for Development and Employment, Rome, 8-30

Pierson, P. (1993), *When Effect Becomes Cause. Policy Feedback and Political Change*, in: 'World Politics', 45: 595-628

Pierson, P. (1994), *Dismantling the Welfare State? Reagan, Thatcher and the Politics of Retrenchment*, Cambridge, Cambridge University Press

Pierson, P. (1999), *The Comparative Political Economy of Pension Reform*, Discussion Paper, Florence, IUE

Pierson, P. (2001), *The New Politics of the Welfare State*, Oxford, Oxford University Press

Pugliese, E. and Rebeggiani, E. (1997), *Occupazione e disoccupazione in Italia (1945-1995)*, Rome, Edizioni Lavoro

Putnam, R. (1993), *Making Democrazy Work. Civic Tradition in Modern Italy*, Princeton, New Jersey, Princeton University Press

Quadrio Curzio, A. (1996), *Noi, l'economia e l'Europa*, Bologna, Il Mulino

Radaelli, C.M. (1999), *Networks of Expertise and Policy Change in Italy*, in: 'South European Society and Politics', vol. 3, no. 2

Radaelli, C.M. (2000), *Discourse and Institutional Change: The Case of Italy in the Euro-Zone*, Discussion Paper, University of Bradford

Radaelli, C.M. (2002), *The Italian State and the Euro: Institutions, Discourse, and Policy Regimes*, in: K. Dyson (Ed.) *The European State and the Euro*, Oxford, Oxford University Press, 212-237

Regalia, I. and Regini, M. (1998), *Sindacati, istituzioni, sistema politico*, in: G.P. Cella and T. Treu (Eds.), *Le nuove relazioni industriali. L'esperienza italiana nella prospettiva europea*, Bologna, Il Mulino, 467-494

Regalia, I. and Regini, M. (1998), *Italy: the Dual Character of Industrial Relations*, in: A. Ferner and R. Hyman (Eds.), *Changing Industrial Relations in Europe*, Malden Mass: Blackwell Publishers, pp. 459-503

Regini, M. (1983), *Le condizioni dello scambio politico. Nascita e declino della concertazione in Italia e Gran Bretagna*, in: 'Stato e Mercato' 9:353-384, Bologna, Il Mulino

Regini, M. (1991), *Confini mobili. La costruzione dell'economia tra politica e società*, Bologna, Il Mulino

Regini, M. (1999), *L'Europa tra de-regolazione e patti sociali*, in: 'Stato e Mercato', 55: 38-63

Regonini, G. (1993), *Politici, burocrati e politiche pubbliche*, in: G. Pasquino (Ed.), *Politici e burocrati*, Bologna, Istituto Carlo Cattaneo, 31-58

Reyneri, E. (1998), *Economia globale e mercati del lavoro locali: il ruolo delle politiche del lavoro*, in: 'Le istituzioni del federalismo', vol. 2, n. 3: 203-220

Rhodes, M. and Meny, I. (Eds.) (1997), *The Future of European Welfare. A New Social Contract?*, London, MacMillan

Ricciardi, M. (1986), *Lezioni di storia sindacale. Italia, 1945-1985*, Bologna, Clueb

Ross, F. (1998), *A Framework for Studying Unpopular Policies: Partisan Possibilities, Institutional Liabilities and the Anti-State Agenda*, Discussion Paper, Florence, IUE

Rossi, S. (1998), *La politica economica italiana 1968-1998*, Bari, Laterza

Rossi, S. (2002), *Riformisti per forza. La sinistra italiana fra il 1996 e il 2001*, Bologna, Il Mulino

Sabatier, P.A. and Jenkins-Smith, H.C. (1993), *Policy Change and Learning. An Advocacy Coalition Approach*, Colorado, Westview Press

Sacchi, S., Bastagli, F. and Ferrera, M. (2002) *Fighting Poverty and Social Exclu-*

sion in Southern Europe: the Case of Italy (Report commissioned by the European Commission), Milan, Poleis, Bocconi University (http://www.unibocconi.it/index.php?frcnav=@11%2C4210)

Salvati, M. (1981), *Alle origini dell'inflazione italiana*, Bologna, Il Mulino

Salvati, M. (1984), *Economia e politica in Italia dal dopoguerra ad oggi*, Milan, Garzanti

Salvati, M. (1995), *Crisi politica, risanamento finanziario e ruolo della concertazione*, in: 'Il Mulino', 3: 431-436

Salvati, M. (1997), *Moneta unica, rivoluzione copernicana*, in: 'Il Mulino', 1: 5-23

Salvati, M. (2000), *Breve storia della concertazione italiana*, in: 'Stato e mercato', 60: 447-476

Sani, G. (1980), *The Political Culture of Italy:Continuity and Change*, in: G.A. Almond and S. Verba, *The Civic Culture Revisited*, Boston, Little Brown, 273-324

Sani, G. and Segatti, P. (2001), *Anti-party Politics and the Restructuring of the Italian Party System*, in: N. Diamandouros and R. Gunther (Eds.), *Parties, Policy and Democracy in the New Southern Europe*, Baltimore, John Hopkins University Press, 153-182

Sartori, G. (1976), *Parties and Party Systems*, Cambridge, Cambridge University Press

Sartori, G. (1982), *Teoria dei partiti e caso italiano*, Milan, Sugarco

Sbragia, A. (2001), *Italy Pays for Europe: Political Leadership, Political Choice and Institutional Adaptation*, in: M.G. Cowles, J. Caporaso and T. Risse, (Eds.), *Transforming Europe*, Ithaca, Cornell University Press, 79-96

Scharpf, F.W. (1997), *Games Real Actors Play. Actor-Centered Institutionalism in Policy Research*, Boulder Colo., Westview

Schmidt, V. (2000), *Values and Discourse in the Politics of Adjustment*, in: F.Sharpf and V. Schmidt (Eds.), *Welfare and Work in the Open Economies*, Oxford, Oxford University Press, vol. 1, 229-309.

Schmidt, V. (2001a), *The Politics of Adjustment in France and Britain: When Does Discourse Matter?* in: 'Journal of European Public Policy', vol. 8, no. 2: 247-264

Schmidt, V. (2001b), *Europeanization and the Mechanics of Economic Policy Adjustment*, in: 'Eiop papers', vol. 5, no. 6 (http://eiop.or.at/eiop/texte/2001-006.htm)

Schmitter, P. (1974), *Still the Century of Corporatism?*, in: 'Review of Politics', 36: 85-131

Schmitter, P. and Grote, J.R. (1997), *Sisifo corporatista: passato, presente e futuro*, in: 'Stato e mercato', 50: 183-215

Sestito, P. (2002), *Il mercato del lavoro in Italia. Com'è. Come sta cambiando*, Bari, Laterza

Signorini, L.F. and Visco, I. (1997), *L'economia italiana*, Bologna, Il Mulino

Skinner, B. (1937), *The Behaviour of Organisms*, New York, Appleton

Somaini, E. (1989), *Politica salariale e politica economica*, in: G.P. Cella and T. Treu (Eds.), *Relazioni industriali*, Bologna, Il Mulino, 307-344

Spaventa, L. and Chiorazzo, V. (2000), *Astuzia o virtù? Come accadde che l'Italia fu ammessa all'Unione monetaria*, Rome, Donzelli

Streeck, W. and Schmitter, P.C. (1985), *Comunità, mercato, stato e associazioni?*, in: 'Stato e Mercato', 13: 47-85

Surel, Y. (2000), *The Role of Cognitive and Normative Frames in Policy-Making*, in: 'Journal of European Public Policy', vol. 7, no. 4:495-512

Tartaglione, C. (2001), *Riallineamento e sommerso nel Mezzogiorno*, Rome, Ires-Cgil

Tilly, C. (Ed.) (1975), *The Formation of National States in Western Europe*, Princeton, Princeton University Press

Treu, T. (2001), *Politiche del lavoro. Insegnamenti di un decennio*, Bologna, Il Mulino

Trigilia, C. (1992), *Sviluppo senza autonomia. Effetti perversi delle politiche nel Mezzogiorno*, Bologna, Il Mulino

Trubeck, D. and Mosher, J.S. (2003), *New Governance. EU Employment Policy and the European Social Model*, in: J. Zeitlin and D. Trubeck (Eds.), *Governing Work and Welfare in the New Economy: European and American Experiments*, Oxford, Oxford University Press, 33-58

Turone, S. (1988), *Storia del sindacato in Italia dal 1943 ad oggi*, Bari, Laterza

Van Kersbergen, K. (1995), *Social Capitalism: a Study of Christian Democracy and the Welfare State*, London, Routledge

Varesi, P.A. (1998), *Regioni ed enti locali di fronte ai nuovi poteri in materia di politica del lavoro*, in: 'Le istituzioni del federalismo', vol. 2, no. 3: 237-257

Vassallo, S. (1994), *Il governo di partito in Italia*, Bologna, Il Mulino

Vassallo, S. (2000), *La politica del bilancio. Le condizioni e gli effetti istituzionali della convergenza*, in: G. Di Palma, S. Fabbrini and G. Freddi (Eds.), *Condannata al successo? L'Italia nell'Europa integrata degli anni Novanta*, Bologna, Il Mulino, 287-323

Vassallo, S. (2001), *Le leggi del governo. Come gli esecutivi della transizione hanno superato i veti incrociati*, in: G. Capano and M. Giuliani (2001), (Eds.), *Parlamento e processo legislativo in Italia*, Bologna, Il Mulino, 85-126

Vassallo, S. and Verzichelli, L. (2003), *Il processo di bilancio nel sistema politico italiano*, in: G. Freddi (Ed.), *Pubblica amministrazione e politiche pubbliche*, Rome, Carocci, Forthcoming

Verzichelli, L. (1999), *La politica di bilancio*, Bologna, Il Mulino

Verzichelli, L. and Cotta, M. (2003), *Il governo Berlusconi II alla prova: un anno di complicazioni*, in: J. Blondel e P. Segatti (Eds.), *Politica in Italia*, Bologna, Il Mulino, 49-71

Viesti, G. (2003), *Abolire il Mezzogiorno*, Bari, Laterza

Visser, J. and Hemerijck, A. (1997), *The Dutch Miracle*, Amsterdam, Amsterdam University Press

Visser, J. and Hemerijck, A. (2001), *Learning and Mimicking: How European Welfare States Reform*, typescript

Walsh, J. (2000), *European Monetary Integration and Domestic Politics*, Boulder, Lynne Rienner Publisher

Weick, K.E. (1976), *Educational Organisations as Loosely Coupled Systems*, in: 'Administrative Science Quarterly', 21:1-19

Wiarda, H.J. (1997), *Corporatism and Comparative Politics. The Other Great 'Ism'*, New York/London, M.E. Sharpe Inc.

List of Abbreviations

AN   Alleanza Nazionale (National Alliance)
ASL   Azienda Sanitaria Locale (Local Health Agency)
CNEL   Comitato Nazionale per l'Economia e il Lavoro
DPEF   Documento di Programmazione economica e finanziaria
DS   Democratici di Sinistra (Democrats of the Left)
EES   European Employment Strategy
EMS   European Monetary System
EMU   Economic and Monetary Union
FI   Forza Italia
INPS   Istituto Nazionale di Previdenza Sociale
ISE   Indicatore della situazione economica (Indicator of the Economic Situation)
ISFOL   Istituto per lo sviluppo della formazione dei lavoratori
ISTAT   Istituto Nazionale di Statistica
LN   Lega Nord
NAPS   National Action Plans
PDS   Partito Democratico della Sinistra (Democratic Party of the Left)
RC   Rifondazione Comunista
RMI   Reddito minimo di inserimento (Minimum Insertion Income)
SSN   Servizio Sanitario Nazionale (National Health Service)
TFR   Trattamento di fine rapporto (End-of-contract-payment)
UDEUR   Unione Democratici per l'Europa
USL   Unità Sanitarie Locali (Local Health Units)

Index of Names

Index of Subjects